Discovering Country Music

Don Cusic

Westport, Connecticut
London

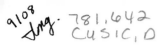
Library of Congress Cataloging-in-Publication Data

Cusic, Don.
  Discovering country music / Don Cusic.
    p. cm.
  Includes bibliographical references and index.
  ISBN 978-0-313-35245-4 (alk. paper)
1. Country music—History and criticism. I. Title
ML3524.C87 2008
781.642—dc22   2008013668

British Library Cataloguing in Publication Data is available.

Library of Congress Catalog Card Number: 2008013668
ISBN: 978–0–313–35245–4

First published in 2008

Praeger Publishers, 88 Post Road West, Westport, CT 06881
An imprint of Greenwood Publishing Group, Inc.
www.praeger.com

Printed in the United States of America

The paper used in this book complies with the
Permanent Paper Standard issued by the National
Information Standards Organization (Z39.48–1984).

10 9 8 7 6 5 4 3 2 1

Contents

Acknowledgments

This book is a culmination of writing, researching, and teaching country music for over 35 years. In 1973 I joined the Country Music Association as a staff writer; the following year I became country editor of *Record World*, a trade magazine. I joined Monument Records in 1977 as head of artist development and publicity and then started a management firm with Dan Beck; among the artists we managed were Dickey Lee and Riders In The Sky. After that I served as country and gospel editor of *CashBox*, another trade. Along the way I've written for a number of publications, including *Billboard, Country Song Round-Up, Country Music,* and several academic publications.

In 1982 I began teaching at Middle Tennessee State University and from 1987 or so I taught a "History of the Recording Industry" course.

In 1994 I joined Belmont University where I am Professor of Music Business and hold a professorship, Music City Professor of Music Industry History, endowed by Mike Curb and the Curb Family Foundation. I teach the "History of the Recording Industry" course here and speak to numerous groups on the history of country music. I have written 16 books, mostly on country music. The research I did for the biography of Eddy Arnold was especially helpful for this book.

All of that is to say that through the years I have worked in the Nashville music industry, interviewed a number of those in the country music industry, written and studied country music to the point that it is hard to acknowledge all of the people and events that have contributed to this work. However, I would especially like to thank Mike Curb and the Curb Family Foundation for their support, Belmont University for its support, and, specifically for this book the friendships of Mike Curb, Joe Galante, Lon Helton, Jeff Walker, David Ross, Mark Hagen, Dave Barnes, Paul Fenn, and Harold Bradley as I pulled this work together. I must also thank my assistant Allecia Morrone, who spent numerous hours transcribing tapes of interviews. At Praeger I would like to thank Dan Harmon, who thought this book was a good idea and Kristi Ward at Greenwood Press who led me to Dan and Praeger.

As always, I must thank my wife Jackie, who supports my endeavors and my children, Jesse, Eli, Alex, and Delaney, for putting up with their father's interests, which do not always coincide with their own.

It is obligatory to accept full responsibility for all errors and shortcomings in a book; I have never liked doing that but must bow to the inevitable.

I have loved country music since I was a small boy; I hope that love comes through and that you share that love of country music as you read this book.

1

Country Music: What Is It?

DEFINING COUNTRY MUSIC

Country music ain't what it used to be but, then again, neither are country people and neither is America. People who wish for the good old days never had to live in those days when folks were poor but proud, hungry but helpful. Anybody who grows up poor wants to end up rich, or at least end up doing a whole lot better than how they started out. Those who say that money can't buy happiness were never miserably broke. That's the story of country music, a story of the poor country boy or girl who goes out into the world and, against all odds finds success. Actually, it is one of the stories of country music because country is not a music with just one story; there are thousands and thousands of stories. Each singer, each musician, each fan has a story. You can look at country music from a star's point of view or from a fan's; the story can be told from the point of view of musicians or businessmen, of scholars and historians with analysis and footnotes, or the working man or woman who found in country music a soundtrack for their life but can't really explain how or why that happened.

Country music is the story of America set in song; it is America's music because it tells the story of those who are the backbone of America, the hard-working men and women who are patriotic, God-fearing, and unpretentious, who struggle through life with neither great riches or fame and yet carve a meaning out of life through family, friends, work, and good times. These are the people whose talents and abilities are always needed but seldom appreciated, who look to the afterlife for their greatest reward and who have been called "the silent majority" and "the average American." These are a proud people who never find their names in headlines and never appear on television until one of their own finds his or her way to a record deal in Nashville and finds a song to sing. This song and others that follow can open doors to a wider world, a world where a singer who was born a "nobody" can almost overnight become a hot in-demand ticket to sing before huge crowds and even presidents and prime ministers. The singer then becomes a treasured member of thousands of families they've never met, welcome to visit at any time because what they sing and the way they sing it has raised spirits, touched hearts, and moved souls for those who listen to country music.

Country music articulates the thoughts, feelings, lifestyles, concerns, and topical issues of the southern white working middle class in America. That definition has changed slightly over the years from the working class to include the working middle class in America because the increase in incomes and shift in American work from an agricultural to an industrial and now an information-based economy means the nature of work and incomes has changed. The "working class" no longer consists of farmers and manual laborers; today's working middle class still includes those who work with their hands, but their hands are probably on a computer keyboard. Men still wear blue collars, but they may be button-down and come with a tie.

In short, what used to be called the American working class is today the American working *middle* class who work for a salary or wages and who are best described as ordinary, everyday people, although a sociologist or economist would have a fit with that vague description. Still, these country music fans feel they have the touch of "the common man" or "everyday American" and the lyrics of country music reflect that.

That definition does not mean that only the white working middle class listens to country music. The genre has an appeal to a wide variety of fans, from the rich to the poor, from well educated to uneducated, and from east to west and north to south. It is, in many ways, America's music, especially the "fly-over people," those in middle America that the L.A. and New York jet-setters fly over as they go from one coast to another. The three groups that country music has trouble appealing to are (1) the young, who prefer rock; (2) the cultural elite, who prefer classical and jazz; and (3) African-Americans, who often feel the music doesn't speak to them. Some African-Americans feel the music is racist, many in the cultural elite feel the music is vulgar and smells of the riff raff, while young people in general want to be accepted by their peers, who tend to like the high energy of rock or the pop music of the day.

Musically, country music is descended from the British ballads, brought over by the early settlers. There are two major sources for country music: folk tunes of no known authorship—often fiddle tunes—which were passed from musician to musician as each musician or singer added something different to the melody or lyrics. And, songs written for the stage to be performed before an audience.

Although academic scholars, journalists, and others may argue about the definition of country music using musical ancestors, recordings, and other factors, in reality country music is defined by its audience: If the fans of country music think a recording is "country," then it is. If the audience accepts an artist as "country," then he or she is. When a group judges an individual they basically ask, "Is he/she one of us?" In other words, can I relate to this person, feel comfortable with them, and feel a kinship with them? This is the litmus test for country artists and country recordings; the audience asks "Are they part of who I am?" The answer defines country music.

In addition to the audience for country music, the media and marketing structure also defines what is country. Major record companies have a country division and independent labels define themselves as country. Radio stations who define themselves as country play country records; if they accept an artist and/or a recording and play them on their station, then that artist and/or recording is labeled country. However, the final factor in determining whether an artist or recording is authentically country rests with the audience, or fans.

This acceptance of an artist by the country music community may depend upon (1) an artist's biography (a rural background or background with country music—e.g. growing up listening to the Grand Ole Opry and/or loving artists such as Merle Haggard, George Jones, and so on); (2) an artist's previous hits (if the hits sound country then an artist may be given some leeway when they record a pop-type song); (3) if an artist embraces the genre of country and identifies with country as his or her music; (4) if an artist is embraced by country-oriented media like country music publications and television shows; and (5) if the artist is signed to the country division of a major label or signed to an independent label that defines itself as country. This usually means the label is connected to Nashville.

Having said that, there are some defining characteristics of country music recordings. It is generally sung by nontrained singers in a southern or quasi-southern accent. The accompaniment includes a rhythm section that usually features a prominent acoustic rhythm guitar. Country music tends to be partial to "open" chords (as opposed to closed or bar chords) on the rhythm guitar and other common instruments are the fiddle (as opposed to the violin), steel guitar, electric lead guitar, piano, and drums played in either 2/4 or 4/4 rhythm. However, as noted before, the audience ultimately either accepts or rejects a recording or an artist as country or not.

Country music is a music that has evolved but its string band ancestor is still recognized; listen to a recording of an early string band and you will immediately recognize this as country music. However, country music has absorbed pop and rock music through the years, integrating those sounds into its music. This causes endless arguments amongst those who debate what "real" country music is, with the argument often concluding amongst older listeners that today's country recordings "ain't real country."

The problem is a human one. Americans generally connect with a music when they are around 15 years old; for the rest of their lives, they will compare contemporary music with the music they became attached to at that time. Often, people over 40 will complain the music of today is all "noise" that it "all sounds alike." They'll usually refer to what music should sound like by naming some artists and/or recordings. If you do the math, then you'll find the music they love came when they were around 15 years old.

The country fan is generally an older fan; although there are some young fans, the primary audience is over 30. So when a fan reaches 30 and "converts" to country music (because country music relates to his or her life and because he or she can no longer relate to the pop music of the day) they want the country music they embrace to sound similar to the music they loved when they were 15. If you listen to the "Nashville Sound" era music of the 1960s you'll find it sounds similar to the pop music after World War II and into the early 1950s, before rock 'n' roll hit. The Nashville Sound was an echo of pop singers such as Perry Como, Jo Stafford, and Bing Crosby. The "outlaw" movement of the mid-to-late 1970s brought a heavier beat into country music, reminiscent of the heavier beat in rock music 15 years before. The slickly produced country music of 2000 sounds similar to the synthesizer-laden pop music of the mid-1980s.

A 2007 survey by Edison Media Research that profiled country radio listeners showed that women accounted for 56 percent of listeners and men 44 percent; 65 percent of listeners were over 35 years old, 6 percent were 12 to 17, and 13 percent were 18 to 24. The audience was 93 percent white and 56 percent were married. The survey showed that 29 percent had a high school or less educational background while 42 percent had one to three years of college. Only 17 percent had a bachelor's degree and 6 percent had an advanced degree. In terms of income, 7 percent made less that $25,000 a year, 13 percent made between $25,000 and $40,000; 18 percent made between $40,000 and $60,000; 14 percent made between $75,000 and $100,000; and 13 percent of country radio listeners made over $100,000 a year.

When asked how long they had listened to country music 59 percent said they "have always" listened; if they did not listen to country music they liked oldies, classic rock, soft rock, and Top 40. There were changes in listening habits as country fans listened to the radio less; 90 percent listened in their car, down from 95 percent a year before, and 81 percent listened in the morning, down from 84 percent the year before. Instead of listening to their radio, 40 percent listened on the Internet, an increase from 33 percent the year before. There was also an increase in country fans listening on their iPod or portable MP3 player listening device from 16 percent in 2006 to 26 percent in 2007. Ownership of iPods and MP3 listening devices increased from 15 percent of country listeners in 2005 to 28 percent in 2006 and 42 percent in 2007. By 2007 45 percent of male country radio listeners and 41 percent of women country radio listeners owned an iPod or portable MP3 player.

In 2007 81 percent of country radio listeners watched the CMA Awards show, up from 76 percent the previous year.

Although country fans like to hear their acts on radio or listening devices and watch them on television, less were purchasing albums by these acts. Of those who bought country CDs, 57 percent purchased them at a discount store (Wal-Mart or Target) while 13 percent purchased them from an electronics store (Circuit City or Best Buy). That means that 70 percent of country albums are sold in these outlets.

Radio is still important in country music; 91 percent of country fans said they learned about new music and new artists from the radio.

Favorite artists of country radio listeners in 2007 were Toby Keith (64 percent liked him), George Strait (62 percent), Brad Paisley (60 percent), Tim McGraw (59 percent), Rascal Flatts (58 percent), Kenny Chesney (57 percent), Carrie Underwood (56 percent), Alan Jackson (56 percent), then Keith Urban, Martina McBride, Garth Brooks (at 50 percent), Sugarland, Reba McEntire, Montgomery Gentry, and Dierks Bentley.

In terms of "all time favorite" country artists, country radio listeners in 2007 named George Strait first followed by Kenny Chesney, Garth Brooks, Toby Keith, Rascal Flatts, Tim McGraw, Alan Jackson, Alabama, Brooks & Dunn, and Reba McEntire.

Because mainstream commercial country music continues to adapt to the market, it continues to attract new audiences who did not grow up on country music. The music itself does not grow stale and remain locked in place, although some fans would prefer that it remain locked into their favorite era. Still, country music retains enough of its core identity so that a listener always knows his or her "country," even though the long-time die-hard country fans may complain that it doesn't sound country enough.

Although contemporary country music still recognizes its string band ancestors, it has absorbed the sounds of pop and rock music to the point where the string band ancestor might not fully recognize current country music as a close relative. This differs from other forms of country, like bluegrass, western, or southern gospel music. Those music genres have stayed true to their original musical sound while commercial country music has remained true to the market.

2

Early Country Music

THE BEGINNING OF COUNTRY MUSIC ON RECORDS

The commercial country music recording industry began in the early 1920s after World War I and after the blues had been recorded. The first recordings by what was later labeled a "country artist" came in 1922 when Uncle Eck Robertson and Henry Gilliland went to New York after a Confederate Civil War reunion and made several recordings for Victor Records. Robertson and Gilliland recorded four tunes: "Arkansas Traveler," "Turkey in the Straw," "Forked Deer," and "Apple Blossom." The next day Robertson returned alone and recorded six more tunes, including "Sallie Gooden," which was released, along with one of their duet tunes, on September 1. Another fiddler, Kentucky native William B. Houchens, first recorded some fiddle tunes on September 18, 1922, for the Gennett label, owned by the Starr Piano Company in Richmond, Indiana. However, none of these recordings received wide circulation or commercial success.

The first commercially successful recording of what became known as country music—and hence the true beginning of what was then known as "the hillbilly business"—came on June 23, 1923, when Fiddlin' John Carson recorded "Old Hen Cackled and the Roosters Gonna Crow" backed with (b/w) "Little Old Log Cabin in the Lane" for OKeh Records. (These early records were 78 rpm discs with one side considered the "A" side and the other the "B" side.) The recordings were made in Atlanta and taken back to New York, where they were pressed and sent back to Atlanta.

The record is an interesting example of the roots of country music. "Old Hen Cackled and the Rooster's Gonna Crow" is an old fiddle tune, handed down from fiddler to fiddler. Each fiddler had altered it a bit and nobody knows who composed the original tune. The only thing certain is that countless fiddlers played that tune through the years as people danced, partied, or enjoyed themselves. The other song, "Little Old Log Cabin in the Lane" was written for the minstrel stage by Will Shakespeare Hays, a songwriter who lived in Cincinnati. This song has a definite, known author and was written for the express purpose of being performed in a minstrel show before a paying audience. Here are the two tap roots of country music: a folk tune of no known origin and a song written for a commercial stage production.

Fiddlin' John Carson was well known in the Atlanta area. He had won fiddling contests and performed on Atlanta's radio station, WSB. The recording came about because Polk Brockman, who was in charge of purchasing records for his grandfather's furniture store in Atlanta, saw a newsreel of a fiddling contest at a theater in New York while he was there on a business trip. Brockman persuaded the people running OKeh Records to come to Atlanta to record Fiddlin' John and some other acts. A group led by Ralph Peer came to Atlanta and recorded Fiddlin' John as well as the Morehouse College Quartet and other acts.

When Ralph Peer took Fiddlin' John's recording back to New York to play for the OKeh executives, the group pronounced it "pluperfect awful" but pressed 500 copies to send to Brockman in Atlanta. They were so convinced the record was a dud that they didn't even put a number on it. By the time copies of the recording reached Atlanta, Brockman had arranged a fiddlers' contest in conjunction with an Elk's convention. On stage, Fiddlin' John played his record and then sold them across the footlights. OKeh Records soon received an order for 15,000 more.

When the new order came in, the music sounded a lot better to the New York executives, who put a number on this release and shipped off an additional amount to their other distributors. After sales of the record reached 500,000, the OKeh executives had to admit they'd been wrong and called Fiddlin' John up to New York, where they recorded him doing more songs.

The success of Fiddlin' John set off a demand for hillbilly music and showed New York record executives there was a market of rural Southerners who would purchase this music. At first, a number of fiddlers were recorded because they were the "true" musicians; they played the melody, breakdowns, began the tune, and were the lead instrumentalists in a string band. Throughout the nineteenth century the major accompanist was the banjo but in the early twentieth century the guitar became more popular. Still, the banjo and guitar players played supporting roles, keeping a rhythm for the fiddle or singer.

Rural fiddlers had to endure those more cultured souls who preferred the violin to the fiddle. Most old time fiddlers were proud of the fact that they played by ear—a more "natural" talent—and could not read music. Wayne Daniel in his book *Pickin' On Peachtree: A History of Country Music in Atlanta, Georgia* quotes a fiddler who states, "Fiddlers are never taught; they do their own learning. We figure that music comes from a person's soul. If you have it in you, you can play; and if you haven't there is no use trying to learn. If a person taught you how to play a tune, you would simply be playing his music, and not your own."[1]

The first recordings of country music were by fiddlers and small record companies were among the most adventurous. But early country music was not just fiddle music; there were singers and songs too.

ROBERT BURNS

Although what is now known as country music was first recorded during the 1920s, there was already a foundation laid which brought this music into the American mainstream. Robert Burns, the Scottish poet and songwriter who lived in the eighteenth century, should be considered the grandfather of country music songwriters because his writing and collecting folk songs is reminiscent of many early country songwriters. He was born on January 25, 1759, in the Scottish lowlands in south Scotland. His father and mother knew a number of old folk songs and sang them at home.

Like his father, Robert Burns was a farmer and, also like his father, never did well farming; however, he possessed a lively, fertile imagination, which became apparent in his poetry and songs. The first collection of Burns's poetry, *Poems, Chiefly in the Scottish Dialect,* was published in 1786 and paid for by Burns. The book came to the attention of literary critic Thomas Blacklock in Edinburgh, who praised it and soon the 27-year-old poet was well known in southern Scotland. In 1789 the second edition of this work was published by William Creech, and this edition was also published in London and the United States. The second edition contained a number of Burns's songs, which established him as a songwriter as well as a poet.

Burns heard folk songs from his mother when he was a child; as he grew older he heard them when he traveled. In Edinburgh, James Johnson collected folk songs and published them in his book, *Scots Musical Museum.* Burns collected songs for this work and Johnson's book soon contained a number of Burns's songs. Generally, Burns heard an old folk song and either put new lyrics to it or rewrote the old lyrics. This would be similar to the method used by the Carter Family when they began recording country music for Victor in 1927; A.P. Carter collected old folk songs and rewrote them or added lyrics, making them "commercial." Thus a number of old folk songs such as "Wildwood Flower," originally titled "I'll Twine 'Mid the Ringlets," came into country music.

Robert Burns fit the image of the careless, carefree songwriter, fathering several children before marrying; after he married, his wife and mistress gave birth to children within days of each other. He failed as a farmer and finally earned his living as a tax collector in several cities. Burns described himself as "a man who had little art in making money, and still less in keeping it."[2] His most famous song, "Auld Lang Syne," written in 1789, is still sung each New Year's Eve.

Robert Burns, like Hank Williams, died an early, tragic death; Burns was 37 when he died. Robert Burns left a legacy of songs that show the roots of country music. Many of his songs found their way to America, which became the United States during Burns's lifetime, and became part of the catalog of country songs when that music was first recorded in the 1920s.

The history of country music begins with the early folk songs from Scotland, Ireland, and England, like those of Robert Burns, but the roots are not "pure" folk music, songs anonymously composed and handed down through oral tradition. Rather, from the beginning, country music was a mixture of songs from anonymous sources as well as songs composed by songwriters.

MINSTREL SHOWS

The development of minstrel shows—whites in blackface imitating blacks—became quite popular before the Civil War. Minstrel songs achieved their effect primarily through their lyrics, which were in dialect; musically, the songs were an extension of theatre songs and British folk melodies. The first minstrel songs reinforced stereotypes of blacks: they were lazy, loved to eat watermelon, could not speak proper English, and were inferior creatures, but they had a knack for singing and dancing and entertainment. And, of course, they were very entertaining for white folks.

The first full-time minstrel group was the Virginia Minstrels, formed in early 1843 in New York. This "Ethiopian band" consisted of banjo, fiddle, bone castanets, and tambourine. It was led by Daniel Decatur Emmett, who is credited with writing "Dixie." The Virginia Minstrels performed mainly between acts in plays or circuses and performed a number of songs throughout an evening, but never as a whole show.

E.P. Christy's Minstrels consisted of E.P. on banjo and singing; George Christy, dancing; actor and bones player, Tom Vaughn; and "jig dancer," Lansing Durant. The company eventually totaled seven members and provided a whole evening's entertainment, generally in three parts. The full band performed songs, skits, dances, and singing, performing a dozen or more songs. In addition to being the first minstrel group to present a full evening's program, they introduced the songs of Stephen Foster to the American public.

STEPHEN FOSTER

Stephen Foster was born near Pittsburgh, Pennsylvania, on July 4, 1826, the same day that two of the nation's founders, Thomas Jefferson and John Adams, died. At the age of 14 Foster wrote his first song, "The Tioga Waltz" and, in 1844, at the age of 18, he copyrighted his first song, "Open Thy Lattice Love." These were essentially parlor ballads. When he was 20, Foster moved to Cincinnati and became a bookkeeper for his brother; in August 1847, the Eagle Ice Cream Saloon advertised a "Musical Entertainment Extraordinary" and Stephen's brother, Morrison Foster, obtained a copy of

Stephen's song, "Away Down Souf" and submitted it; it was an immediate success. An even bigger success originated from the performance of "Oh! Susanna!" which was soon performed from New York concert stages as well as in California gold mining camps, where it became an unofficial theme song.

No American had ever made a living as a songwriter before Stephen Foster; there were no performance rights organizations to collect money for songwriters and publishers regularly bought the rights to a song outright to avoid paying royalties on sheet music sales. Not that there was a wealth in royalties from sheet music; most "hits" sold less than 50,000 copies and publishers were lucky to break even on most of the songs they published.

In 1850 Foster moved back to Pittsburgh from Cincinnati and rented an office where he set up business as a full-time songwriter. He made a living that way until his death 14 years later. In those 15 years as America's first professional songwriter—or at least the first to make a living solely from songwriting—Foster's songs were heard all over the United States but he could not become wealthy because the business structures were not in place to allow a songwriter to become rich.

Foster achieved most of his fame and made most of his money from his early minstrel songs like "Oh! Susanna," "Old Uncle Ned," and "The Lou'siana Belle." Later he wrote "Old Folks at Home," "Nelly Was a Lady," and "My Old Kentucky Home."

Foster died on January 13, 1864. At the time of his death he had no debts and his rent was paid; his possessions were "a worn brown leather purse containing a piece of paper where he had written the words 'dear friends and gentle hearts'" and 38 cents in pennies.[3] When Foster died, the Civil War still raged; it was over a year before the surrender at Appomattox in April 1865.

THE MUSIC BUSINESS DURING THE CIVIL WAR

The American Civil War has been called "The Singin'est War ever." Twenty-two years after the war ended, in 1887, a 640-page collection called *Our War Songs, North and South* was published. It contained 438 songs sung by troops but this was only a portion of the songs written during the Civil War; over 10,000 were published during the conflict, mostly in the North where there was unrestricted access to paper, ink, type, and plates as well as other materials and goods distribution. In the South, songs were published under the control of the Board of Music Trade, which existed until the end of the nineteenth century.

When the Civil War ended, the music publishing industry continued to thrive and sheet music was printed with the hopes that each newly composed song would become a hit and sell thousands of copies. But there was a shift in the tastes of the public. Minstrel shows became less popular in New York and so a number of traveling minstrel shows developed; blackface and minstrelsy was an important and integral part of stage shows although audiences wanted it as part of a variety of entertainment, rather than just an entire evening of minstrelsy.

Variety shows included a number of minstrel numbers as well as comics, acrobats, jugglers, dancers, skits, tragicomic plays, animals, freaks, singers, and anyone else who could entertain a crowd. In the "varieties" during the latter 1800s, a banjo was always an important instrument, accompanying dances of jigs, clogs, and solo numbers as well as serving as a prop for comics and to fill in any gaps during the show. In the better theatres in the larger towns there was often an orchestra, usually consisting of three pieces—piano, cornet, and drums—for the show. A drum was important because percussive sounds—drum rolls, cymbal crashes, and rim shots—accompanied falls of comics, the flight of an aerialist, and jumps through rings of fire.

The music performed during "varieties" was generally minstrel show numbers and comedy songs. The comedy of the varieties depended heavily on stereotypes, with the Irish being lampooned the most, followed closely by blacks. During the latter part of the nineteenth century the term "vaudeville" was increasingly used to describe "varieties."

HILLBILLIES AND THE ROOTS OF COUNTRY MUSIC

The term "hill billie" was defined by the *New York Journal* in 1900 as "a free and untrammelled white citizen of Alabama, who lives in the hills, has no means to speak of, dresses as he can, talks as he pleases, drinks whiskey when he gets it, and fires off his revolver as the fancy takes him."[4] The first movie version of a "hillbilly" came in 1904 with *The Moonshiner* and between 1910 and 1916 about 300 movies about moonshining and feuding were produced, including the movie *Billie—The Hill Billy,* which appeared in 1915. In 1913 the vaudeville group Cicero and Elviry with Abner (later known as the Weaver Brothers and Elviry) performed as hillbillies on the Vaudeville circuit playing mandolin, guitar, fiddle, banjo, and musical handsaw.

The fact that early country music was called hillbilly and the performers hillbillies indicates that most Americans looked down their noses at them. The fight for respect country musicians and country audiences fought for their music then has continued to be an ongoing battle throughout most of the twentieth and twenty-first centuries.

INSTRUMENTS

Country music before World War I was fiddling contests, home entertainment, and local dances in rural areas. The basic instruments had been developed: the violin was refined in the 1600s and the first known fiddling contest was held in 1736 near Richmond, Virginia. Famous early "fiddlers" include Thomas Jefferson and Davy Crockett, who played his fiddle at the Alamo in 1836 before it was overrun by Santa Anna's troops. The banjo was developed in West Africa and brought to the United States by slaves; these early instruments were refined and popularized during minstrel shows.

By 1800 the guitar had evolved in Europe from lute-like instruments with paired strings into a six-stringed instrument. In 1850 C.F. Martin of Nazareth, Pennsylvania, perfected a flat-top guitar, and in the 1890s Orville Gibson of Kalamazzo, Michigan, perfected the arch-top guitar. By the 1890s guitars and mandolins came into wider use after inexpensive models were offered in the Sears, Roebuck, and Montgomery Ward mail order catalogs.

Hawaiian music first became popular in the United States in 1909 when Joseph Kekuku played a slide guitar in exotic dancer Toots Paka's troupe in New York. In 1912 Walter Kolomoku with the Hawaiian Quintette performed at New York's Winter Garden, and in April 1913 they recorded Hawaiian music for Victor and these recordings popularized the genre; this "sound" from Kolomoku playing a slide on a guitar evolved to the sound of the steel guitar in country music.

A German, Christian Buschmann, patented an instrument called the "aura" with steel reeds in small channels in 1821; in 1825 a mouth organ was developed and this became the basis of the harmonica. Later, a German, Matthias Hohner, applied mass production technology to harmonicas which were imported into the United States. The accordion was perfected by Charles Wheatstone in England in 1844.

By the end of the nineteenth century, the most popular country instruments were the fiddle and banjo; the guitar and harmonica were popularized during the 1930s in the singing cowboy movies from Hollywood.

During the 1820s Americans began manufacturing pianos; previously, they were imported from Europe. The sales of pianos created a demand for sheet music, which led to the development of the business of music publishing. As publishing companies began to centralize in New York, beginning with T.B. Harms' move there in 1878, they congregated in the theater and variety house district around Union Square at East 14th Street. This area became known as "Tin Pan Alley," a term originally coined by journalist Monroe H. Rosefeld (who was also a part-time songwriter) when he noted the cacophony of sounds coming from the open windows of the publishing companies with their tinny upright pianos sounding like tin pans being banged on. The term caught on in the 1903–1910 period and came to mean manufactured songs.

The growth in sheet music and music book sales indicated a heavy demand for new songs, spurred by the popularity of the piano in the home. Also, the importance of vaudeville and musical theater meant songs were constantly needed for the stage.

COPYRIGHT LAW

In 1909 President Teddy Roosevelt signed into law the Copyright Act which, for the first time, gave legal protection to songs. The 1909 Revised

Copyright Act reflected the "progressive" movement of the late nineteenth and early twentieth centuries. A publisher's trust controlled most of the popular sheet music sales which led President Theodore Roosevelt to sign the 1909 Copyright Act. This act fixed a fee of two cents per "reproduction," the first time "musical reproductions" had been addressed in a copyright law. However, the "reproduction" of music was created by piano rolls in player pianos. Later, these fees were collected from the sale of recordings.

In January 1914, the American Society of Composers, Authors, and Publishers (ASCAP), the first performing rights organization, was formed to collect monies for publishers and songwriters from public performances of their works. Radio was first developed in the 1890s and by the end of World War I the radio industry was prepared to move forward as a vibrant business, broadcasting music, news, and shows.

THE PHONOGRAPH

Thomas Edison invented the phonograph in 1877 and the following year formed The Edison Speaking Phonograph Company; however, for the next eight years Edison primarily worked on the electric light. During that period Chichester Bell and Charles Tainter invented the "graphophone," which was similar to the phonograph (both recorded on cylinders). In June 1887, Bell and Tainter formed The American Graphophone Company in Washington, DC. This company evolved into the Columbia Phonograph Company.

In 1888 Emile Berliner received a patent for a "gramophone," which used discs instead of cylinders. The United States Gramophone Company was formed in Washington, DC, in the fall of 1893 by Berliner and this company evolved into Victor Records, founded by Eldridge Johnson in 1901.

A union for musicians was established in the late nineteenth and early twentieth centuries. On November 11, 1896, the American Federation of Musicians (AFM) was established in New York City with Owen Miller as president; on March 15, 1897, a local AFM was chartered in Los Angeles and a Chicago local was formed on September 17, 1901. In 1902 the Nashville AFM, local 257, was established.

Thus, by the time country music was first recorded in the early 1920s, the business structure was in place to make country music a business as well as an entertainment.

FOLK MUSIC

The term "folk music" may be defined as music of the "common" folk—black and white—who later became known as the working class. It is a music from those who are generally musically illiterate, but who have musical talent and are musically accomplished. This music is developed outside the circles of the musical elite and represents the basis of popular culture where music comes from the grass roots, bottom up to the mainstream. This "folk" music was usually played on stringed instruments and the musicians were, by and large, self-taught while the songs were passed along through the oral tradition.

In 1888 the American Folklore Society was formed and by the beginning of World War I, a number of folk song collectors were busy writing down songs they found. In 1898 a Harvard professor, Francis James Child, published the last of his five-volume work, *The English and Scottish Popular Ballads,* a collection of 305 ballads found in England and Scotland, and this inspired American collectors to look for and find these ballads, or variations, in rural areas of the United States. A "ballad" was a British narrative song that told a story; immigrants from England, Scotland, Ireland, and Wales brought them over and some, like "Barbara Allen," were sung by early country recording artists.

Hubert G. Shearin, a professor at Transylvania University in Lexington, Kentucky, and his pupil, Josiah H. Combs, collected songs for their book, *A Syllabus of Kentucky Folksongs,* published in 1911. In 1916 British folk song collector Cecil Sharp collected ballads in the Appalachian Mountains of Kentucky; he was interested in British balladry and also collected some American originals but ignored gospel music. During the 1916–1918 period he spent 46 weeks in the mountains and published *English Folk Songs from the Southern Appalachians.*

Americans often used European songs and "Americanized" them by changing the lyrics. The early cowboy song "Old Chisholm Trail," was derived from "A Dainty Duck," an English folk song that dates back to 1640 while "Streets of Laredo," also known as "The Cowboy's Lament," was derived from a British song, "The Unfortunate Rake," which dates back to 1790. Other songs came from poems; "Bury Me Not on the Lone Prairie" was originally a poem, "The Ocean-Buried," by Edwin Hubbell Chapin, written in 1839.

In 1889 cowboy N. Howard "Jack" Thorp collected songs as he traveled in the West. In 1908 Thorp paid a New Mexico print shop to publish his book, *Songs of the Cowboys.* In this book was a song he wrote, "Little Joe, the Wrangler." In 1910 John Lomax's seminal work, *Cowboy Songs and Other Frontier Ballads,* was published.

A number of songs that became part of early country music repertoire were written in the nineteenth century, including the fiddle tune "Zip Coon," which later became known as "Turkey in the Straw." Although Stephen Foster died in 1864, his songs "Camptown Races," "Old Folks at Home," "Oh, Susannah!" and others remained popular throughout the nineteenth and early twentieth centuries. Another popular songwriter was Will Shakespeare Hays, born in 1837 in Louisville, who worked as a riverboat captain, then as a newspaperman in that city and wrote songs in his spare time. By the time he died in 1907, Hays had written "Write Me a Letter from Home,"

"Nobody's Darling," "Mollie Darling" (later popularized by Eddy Arnold), "Jimmy Brown the Newsboy" (later popularized by the Carter Family and Flatt and Scruggs) and "The Little Old Log Cabin in the Lane," which was recorded by Fiddlin' John Carson in 1923.

CLOTHING

The clothing most associated with country music was developed in the nineteenth century. Pants which became known as "jeans" were first made by Levi Strauss, a New York tailor who went to San Francisco during the Gold Rush of 1849 with some bolts of canvas he planned to sell for tents. He soon discovered that miners needed trousers and so he made them from the canvas material; by 1860 he had developed the sturdy indigo dyed "blue jeans" with copper rivets that became popular with miners and cowboys. During the 1860s "cowboy boots" were derived from British cavalry boots and became popular. In 1865 John B. Stetson, a Philadelphia hat maker, went to Colorado during their gold rush and made a broad-brimmed, high crowned hat from beaver and rabbit hide that he boiled and turned into felt. This waterproof hat was derived from the Mexican sombreros the vaqueros wore. After Stetson returned to Philadelphia he began producing his "Boss of the Plains" hat and called it a "ten-gallon" hat because of its high crown. This "cowboy hat" was popularized by Buffalo Bill Cody in his *Wild West* show.

EARLY COUNTRY RECORDINGS

During the early 1920s, the United States was in a recession, a direct result of the problem of returning World War I veterans trying to find work and the reduction in government spending for the war effort. Additionally, radio was becoming popular and the recording industry blamed it for a decline in sales; why would people buy records if they could hear music on the radio *free?*

The record companies had nearly exhausted their initial markets and looked for ways to broaden their consumer base. They recorded a number of "ethnic" acts and songs to appeal to the large number of immigrants, particularly in New York. This search for new markets ultimately led them to record blues and country music (or "race" and "hillbilly" as it was generally known then) as they reached toward new fields to obtain profits.

Fiddlin' John Carson's recordings in 1923 mark the beginning of the commercial country music industry, but it was because Vernon Dalhart sold over a million copies of "The Prisoner's Song" b/w "Wreck of the Old '97," a "hillbilly" recording he made in 1924, that the interests of recording labels became focused on this music.

Parlor songs, popular songs, and old minstrel numbers as well as folk songs were part of the repertoire of early country performers and were labeled folk, old time, and old familiar tunes when record label executives first discovered them. Since there was a market for these old songs, proven by the early hillbilly record sales, executives hired New York singers to record these songs. The use of singers in New York meant there were singers readily available for recording sessions who sang in a more pure, clear voice than the nasal, tight-throated style of rural singers. People who dislike country music often complain that singers are too "whiney" and the music is too "twangy" to be enjoyable. Record label executives generally felt this "pure" singing style made the recordings more palatable and appealing to a mass audience.

VERNON DALHART

Born in 1883 in Jefferson, Texas, Marion Slaughter was a member of the Century Opera Company in New York. The tenor had moved to New York to pursue a career in light opera and began making records in 1916. Slaughter recorded under approximately 150 different pseudonyms; the one he used for his most successful hillbilly recording was Vernon Dalhart. He heard Henry Whitter sing "The Wreck of the Old '97" and copied Whitter's version. On the other side of the record he sang "The Prisoner's Song" for Victor in 1924. This record became a huge success—country music's first million seller—outselling recordings of pop and jazz artists. This, of course, created a demand for more hillbilly recordings by the labels, who by this point (the mid-1920s) had saturated their original market of opera, vaudeville, and pop songs so they needed new audiences. The rural southern audience was a good target. The development of the electrical recording process made it possible to have portable recording equipment and thus recording engineers began to travel to various cities doing "field" recordings. This led to the period 1926–1929 becoming the heyday for hillbilly and rural blues field recordings as record company talent scouts toured the South and recorded hillbilly and blues performers. The most popular cities for recording were Atlanta and Dallas, followed by Charlotte, North Carolina, New Orleans, and Cincinnati.

During the 1920s Atlanta was the most visited site for early field recordings and the acts recorded there; Fiddlin' John Carson, Gid Tanner, and the Skillet Lickers with Riley Puckett and Clayton McMichen are among the most important of the early country artists. In 1925 "the band that named the music" first recorded. After a session by a group led by Al Hopkins, record producer Ralph Peer asked the quartet for their name and Hopkins replied, "We're nothing but a bunch of hillbillies from North Carolina and Virginia. Call us anything."[5] Peer called them "the Hill Billies" and named the music "hillbilly" music—a name it continued to have in the music business until the 1940s.

RALPH PEER

Victor dominated the recording industry throughout the 19-teens and early 1920s with their recordings of pop, classical, and opera music. In 1926 Ralph Peer joined Victor to help them enter the hillbilly recording business.

Ralph Peer was born in Kansas City, Missouri, the son of a store owner whose merchandise included records and gramophones. Peer began working for the Columbia Phonograph Company around 1910 and then joined OKeh Records in 1919, assisting production director Fred Hagar in New York. At OKeh, Peer assisted in recording the first commercially successful blues record, "Crazy Blues" by Mamie Smith. In 1925 Peer left OKeh and joined Victor Records the following year.

Peer agreed to work for Victor for no salary; instead, he received the publishing on the songs he recorded. He pioneered a royalty contract whereby the artist assigned the copyright of the song to a publishing company then, a royalty of 25 percent of two cents or a half a cent a record ($0.005) was paid to the songwriter for each record sold. This figure came from the "standard" composer royalties during the 1920s and 30s, known as "mechanicals" because the two cents figure was set by the 1909 Copyright Law and was originally written for the player piano rolls.

By drawing up contracts with artists and paying a royalty on each record sold instead of just paying a flat performance fee and then collecting all the composer royalties, Peer set up a legal, binding contract that established a precedent for publishers and songwriters in the music business. In the music business, the publisher—not the songwriter—controls the copyright for a song. The record company generally holds the copyright for the recording.

To do field recordings a label talent scout traveled to various cities or towns to scout local talent, aided by recommendations from native citizens, usually the owner or manager of a store which sold records. In the 1920s this was usually a furniture store that sold Victrolas as part of furniture, thereby creating a demand for records to play on their Victrolas. Peer auditioned talent to determine who had commercial potential. He looked for songs that had not been recorded or copyrighted as well as good singers. Because he was interested in copyrighting a song, he wanted one with lyrics so other singers might record it as well, increasing his income as a publisher.

THE BRISTOL SESSIONS

Victor budgeted $60,000 for Peer's southern recording trip in 1927, which included sessions in Bristol, Tennessee; Charlotte, North Carolina;

and Savannah, Georgia. The Bristol sessions were the first held by any company in the Appalachian region except for a session Peer did for another label in Asheville, North Carolina, during the summer of 1925. Bristol, located on the Tennessee-Virginia border (the main street is the state line) is part of "the Tri-Cities" consisting of that city, Kingsport, and Johnson City and this area had a population of 32,000 in the 1920s—the largest city in Appalachia. Additionally, it was within driving distance of Kentucky, North Carolina, and West Virginia, allowing Peer to draw talent from five different states.

Ralph Peer arrived in Bristol on Friday, July 22, 1927, accompanied by his wife and two engineers who ran the new electrical recording equipment. This was Peer's first field session using microphones; previously he recorded using the acoustic process which did not give a clean, clear sound like the electric microphone or allow him to "balance" the vocal with the musical accompaniment.

Bristol was a fertile area for recording artists and a number of the acts in the area had recorded previously. Peer contacted the Victor dealer there, Cecil McLister, and asked him to help find talent; Peer also contacted Ernest Stoneman to help set up auditions for talent.

Peer recorded 19 different groups performing 76 songs in Bristol; seven were instrumentals and 31 were gospel songs. Before the session Peer had the artists sign three different contracts; the first was a recording contract with Victor which guaranteed $50 per side and a royalty; a publishing contract with his firm, Southern Music; and a personal management contract with Peer. Peer did not manage the artists in terms of career development but instead used the contract to keep the artist tied to him and Victor.

On Monday, July 25, Peer spent the entire day with Ernest Stoneman, recording 10 songs. The next day Peer recorded Ernest Phipps and His Holiness Quartet doing six songs. On Wednesday, July 27, Peer invited the editor of the *Bristol News-Bulletin* to the morning session, which featured Uncle Eck Dunford and Ernest Stoneman (and resulted in the first recording of the song "Skip To Ma Lou, My Darling") and gave an interview. The story appeared in the afternoon paper and concluded with the paragraph that the session allowed Stoneman to receive $100 and "each of his assistants $25" and that Stoneman had earned "$3,600 last year as his share of the proceeds on his records."[6] After this story, a number of acts telephoned Peer, requesting auditions.

THE CARTER FAMILY

On Monday, August 1, 1927, the Carter Family, consisting of A. P. Carter, his wife Sara, and Sara's cousin and A. P.'s sister-in-law, Maybelle, drove to Bristol from Maces Springs, Virginia, auditioned for Peer, and recorded four songs that evening: "Bury Me under the Weeping Willow," "Little Log

Cabin by the Sea," "The Poor Orphan Child," and "The Storms Are on the Ocean." The next morning Sara and Maybelle recorded "Single Girl, Married Girl," and "The Wandering Boy."

Alvin Pleasant Delaney (A.P.) Carter was born on December 15, 1891, in Maces Spring , Virginia; Sara Dougherty was born on July 21, 1899, in nearby Flat Woods, Virginia; they were married on June 18, 1915. A.P. was the son of a banjo playing father and mother who sang old folk songs; he learned shape note singing from churches and played the fiddle; Sara played autoharp. The couple performed, often at churches, in the area and in early 1927 auditioned for the Brunswick Record Company but had not recorded. Maybelle Addington, born May 10, 1909, in Nickelsville, Virginia, learned to play the guitar and developed a method of plucking the melody with her thumb on the bass string while brushing the chord with her fingers which became known as the "Carter lick." Her guitar technique became influential for country pickers in the years ahead. She married Ezra Carter, A.P.'s brother, in March 1926, and soon joined Sara and A.P. when they performed locally.

Sara was the lead singer in the group, often joined by Maybelle with A.P. occasionally singing harmony. A.P. was the one who found songs. He collected them from old songbooks, other folk singers, or remembered them from his childhood. Ralph Peer listed the songs that had not been copyrighted in A.P.'s name.

This rich repertoire of songs, as well as Maybelle's unique guitar playing, established the Carters as one of the most influential groups in country music. Among the more than 300 songs they recorded for Victor were "Keep on the Sunny Side," "Wildwood Flower," "I'm Thinking Tonight of My Blue Eyes," "Wabash Cannonball," "Worried Man Blues," "Anchored in Love," "John Hardy Was a Desperate Little Man," "You Are My Flower," and "Hello, Stranger."

JIMMIE RODGERS

On Thursday, August 4, 1927, Ralph Peer recorded two songs by Jimmie Rodgers, "The Soldier's Sweetheart" and "Sleep, Baby, Sleep." Rodgers arrived in Bristol with his group, the Jimmie Rodgers Entertainers, consisting of himself, Jack Pierce, and the Grant Brothers on the previous evening and auditioned for Peer, who was not impressed with their dance songs. However, Rodgers assured him they would rehearse that night and Peer agreed to record them the next day. During the rehearsal the group quarreled and broke up so Pierce and the Grants recorded Thursday morning as The Tenneva Ramblers while Rodgers recorded solo that evening.

Jimmie Rodgers is considered the father of contemporary country music and was the most influential early country recording artist. Rodgers's "blue yodels," a series of songs that featured him breaking into a falsetto yodel, inspired almost every country artist before World War II. Gene Autry, Ernest Tubb, Roy Rogers, Eddy Arnold, and numerous others all looked to Rodgers as their first inspiration from the country field; they sang his songs, and their early works reflected the influence of Rodgers.

Rodgers was born September 8, 1897, in Meridian, Mississippi. The son of a railroad foreman, he wanted to be an entertainer but worked for the railroad for a number of years. In 1924 he developed tuberculosis and turned to music full time. In the summer of 1927 he performed on WWNC in Asheville, North Carolina, with the Tenneva Ramblers at a resort in the Blue Ridge Mountains. His first Victor recording was released in October 1927 and achieved modest success; the ambitious Rodgers traveled to New York, met with Peer, and persuaded him to record some more selections.

In the following years Rodgers had a string of hits, including "T for Texas," "Waiting for a Train," "Daddy and Home," "In the Jailhouse Now," "Miss the Mississippi and You," "Mother the Queen of My Heart," and "Peach Pickin' Time in Georgia." Many of these he co-wrote with his sister-in-law, Elsie McWilliams. In all, he recorded 110 songs for Victor.

Jimmie Rodgers was considered a hillbilly or folk artist because he came from the South and his recordings sold to rural audiences. But Rodgers was no hillbilly; he dressed like a dandy and his most famous recording, "Waitin' for a Train" was recorded with a Dixieland jazz band. Jimmie Rodgers was a southern country artist who sang pop-influenced music, and this combination of a rural Southerner reaching beyond his origin and roots into the pop world is the story of country music's first major success.

The financial success of Jimmie Rodgers for a major recording label did not go unnoticed in the label's northern headquarters, and Rodgers's ability to be worldly and yet relate to country audiences opened the door for other country artists. After Jimmie Rodgers, country artists found employment on radio stations, northern publishers and record men saw the commercial potential of country music, booking agents booked country talent into major theaters and other venues in major cities, and young southern boys bought guitars as early country music changed from a music dominated by the fiddle to one dominated by the sound of a guitar.

Jimmie Rodgers was smooth vocally, his voice akin to popular crooners Gene Austin, Bing Crosby, or any other crooner during the 1930s. The major difference between artists like Jimmie Rodgers and his counterparts in the popular music field was the accident of birth and the early musical influences; if you were born in a northern city and raised on vaudeville and Tin Pan Alley songs, you were a pop performer, but if you were born in the South (particularly the rural South) and grew up with folk or hillbilly music, then you were a hillbilly performer.

Jimmie Rodgers had a foot in both worlds and his success came as a result of that fact. Further, because he had a foot in both worlds, he advanced country music, which saw increased acceptance from those in popular music.

This was a lesson the record business—and country music establishment—learned again and again. Find a country person with a "pop" type voice and you've got a million dollars. It doesn't work if you have a "pop" person who tries to be country—that's fake, phoney, and insincere, and if there's one thing the country music audience won't abide it is insincerity. But take a boy from the country and you'll never take all the country out of him—even though he tries to go pop.

The Bristol recording sessions are considered the beginning of the commercial country music industry because Jimmie Rodgers and the Carter Family were both rooted in the southern folk tradition and sold huge numbers of records that made Victor profitable and dominant in the hillbilly field.

OTHER COUNTRY RECORDINGS

The early hillbilly acts who recorded from 1923 to 1926 were mostly folk musicians who learned their songs orally, and a number of songs from the nineteenth century were recorded. Examples include "Barbara Allen" by Vernon Dalhart, "Pretty Polly" by Dock Boggs, "When the Work's All Done This Fall" by Carl Sprague, "Knoxville Girl" by Mac and Bob, and fiddle tunes such as "Devil's Dream," "Leather Breeches," and "Soldier's Joy." At this time the term "old" had positive connotations, indicating a time more simple and wholesome than the loose morals embodied in the "modern" sounds of jazz. The Skillet Lickers were the best of the string bands which are the basis for what later became known as bluegrass while the harmony singing of the Carter Family pioneered that vocal sound. The brother duet of the Delmore Brothers was an influential sound that echoed through later recordings of the Louvin Brothers, Everly Brothers, and even the Beatles. Solo artists such as Uncle Dave Macon, Bradley Kincaid, and Jimmie Rodgers pointed the way to the future when country music was dominated by vocalists, and the sound of Jimmie Rodgers's blue yodels and his use of white blues influenced later artists such as Gene Autry, Ernest Tubb, Lefty Frizzell, and Eddy Arnold. Rodgers and Vernon Dalhart transcended country music, pulling it towards the pop market, and this too was a harbinger of things to come.

In November 1927, one of the most influential country recordings was made when Tom Darby and Jimmy Tarlton did "Columbus Stockade Blues" and "Birmingham Jail" with a slide guitar in Atlanta for Columbia. This sound would be the basis of the dobro and steel guitar sound in the years ahead.

On May 26, 1933, Jimmie Rodgers died in New York after finishing his last recording session. Rodgers had tuberculosis and during his last sessions had to rest between takes. He died of a massive hemorrhage a few hours after collapsing on the street; he was 36 years old.

GUITAR AND THE DOBRO

During the 1920s the guitar, formerly a parlor instrument, became more important because of its versatility: one could play chords to accompany a singer or fiddler or play a finger picking style. Part of the reason for the guitar emerging as a dominant instrument was because the 1920s saw the end of the era when tunes were more important than singers; by the middle of the decade, record companies stopped looking for fiddlers and string bands and sought out singers, reflecting consumer demand. Most early country recordings were considered successful if they sold 5,000–10,000 units; "hits" did not usually sell more than 100,000 copies. This, too, established a fundamental fact for country music: individual records may seldom sell as much as a pop record, but the genre as a whole sold well and steady. Labels soon realized this and made country recordings an important part of their repertoire.

A new instrument was added to country music during the 1920s: the dobro. It was developed by the Dopyera brothers, John and Rudy, who added resophonic devices in order to mechanically amplify guitars. In 1927 the Dopyera brothers, with three partners, formed the National Guitar Company and named their creation the "dobro."

3

On Radio and in the Movies

COUNTRY MUSIC ON RADIO

Country music in the 1920s was the era of early recordings, beginning with fiddle tunes, then to songs sung by New York singers, and then to field recordings, most significantly the 1927 sessions in Bristol, Tennessee. But country music during the 1930s was defined by radio, primarily through "barn dances" or radio shows that featured a rural-oriented variety show. There were about 5,000 programs featuring hillbilly music in the United States by 1935, generating about $25 million a year in advertising revenue.

The Depression cut deeply into the record business; in 1928 there were 34 million records sold but in 1931 only 10 million were sold. If families had to choose between buying a phonograph or buying a radio, they bought a radio. There were 14 million radio sets in the country by 1930—seven times as many as there had been in 1925—and over 600 stations.[1]

Radio had developed "programs" which appeared regularly at scheduled times; a popular time for country music programs on radio was early in the morning because the rural audience listened to radio before going off to work. On weekdays, noon was also important because farmers usually came in from the fields for their noon meal and listened to the radio before going back to work. Saturday night had once been radio's "dead" night but country music found a home here, playing to rural listeners after they'd finished their week's work. Most of the barn dances were on Saturday nights.

Radio soon became a way of life for Americans; it was almost a member of the family, coming into living rooms with live programming. Performers not only sang to their audience, they talked to them as well and listeners were encouraged to write to the performers who often read their names on the air. Radio provided entertainment—comedy, drama, and musical shows—as well as news and weather forecasts. It helped make the Great Depression a little more bearable.

Radio exposure created a demand for live performances and artists often played on a radio program for free in order to obtain bookings within a listening area. The most popular performers found sponsors who wanted to reach an audience. Sometimes a sponsor paid the performer, but usually paid the radio station so the performer had time on the air. Sponsors also worked on the "PI" (per inquiry) plan whereby a performer advertised a product on the air, then received a commission on those sold via mail order from the performer's shows.

For performers, radio also had a profound impact; no longer were amateurs who played music on the side part of the game. Professional entertainers emerged and, as country music became more commercial, country performers had careers instead of an avocation. Also, because radio demanded a huge repertoire, no longer could a musician or group get by with a few tunes. Audiences no longer accepted the tunes they had been hearing for years; performers either had to compose new songs or find songs from professional songwriters.

The new carbon microphones demanded a different type of singing; gone was the belt-em-out style and in was the crooning sound where singers sang softly with emotion. The most popular singers, like Jimmie Rodgers and Gene Autry, developed an easygoing, conversational vocal style that appealed to listeners who felt it was accessible and sincere.

Tape technology was not available during the 1930s, but performers did record transcriptions. These large discs were recorded by the performers and then shipped out to radio stations. Popular shows and performers were then heard without the performer being in the studio. At this point, records by country artists were almost never played on the air.

THE NATIONAL BARN DANCE

On Saturday night, April 12, 1924, WLS (World's Largest Store) debuted from the Sherman Hotel at Randolph and Clark Streets in downtown Chicago. The station was owned by Sears, Roebuck and Company, the giant mail order firm headquartered in Chicago. The following Saturday night, April 19, *The National Barn Dance* debuted. This barn dance was a variety show aimed at the rural audience and although a variety of talent—and songs—were featured, the core group of songs and entertainers were country. The barn dance on WLS was the first major show to regularly feature country music on radio, although a barn dance debuted on WBAP in Fort Worth, Texas, in January 1923, and Fiddlin' John Carson performed on WSB in Atlanta in September 1922. WSB had featured country performers on their station since 1922 but it was WLS in Chicago that created the first regularly scheduled major country music show on radio.

The weekend of April 26th saw George D. Hay as guest emcee at *The National Barn Dance*. Hay was a newspaper writer for the *Memphis*

Commercial Appeal and an announcer on the Memphis station WMC. Ed Bill, head of WLS, offered Hay a job with WLS and Hay accepted; he became a key figure during the first 15–16 months of *The National Barn Dance* before he left for Nashville and WSM, where he began another barn dance which became known as *The Grand Ole Opry.*

George Dewey Hay is one of those colorful, charismatic characters on which the history of country music is built. Known by the sobriquet "The Solemn Ole Judge," Hay was born in Attica, Indiana, on November 9, 1895, and was first exposed to country music during World War I while he was a newspaperman working for the *Commercial Appeal* in Memphis. Hay went to Mammoth Spring, Arkansas, to cover the funeral of a soldier who died in the war; after the funeral he attended a "hoedown" or "house dance" at a small cabin where he witnessed people dancing to a country fiddler. It was an experience he never forgot.

The *Commercial Appeal* in Memphis owned a new radio station, WMC, and Hay switched from being a newspaper reporter to a radio announcer. With a natural flair for show biz, Hay began to blow on a steam whistle, which he named "Hushpuckena," and called himself "The Solemn Old Judge," which was the name of the newspaper column he wrote in Memphis until 1924 when he moved to Chicago.

Some of the early performers on the *The National Barn Dance* included old time fiddler Tommy Dandurand; square dance caller Tom Owen; Walter Peterson, The Kentucky Wonder Bean with his double barrel shot gun (harmonica and guitar); Pie Plant Pete, Chubby Parker with his banjo singing "Nickety Nackety Now Now Now"; the Ford and Glenn singing team; Grace Wilson, whose signature song was "Bringing Home the Bacon"; the Hawaiian guitar team of Cecil and Esther Ward; organist Ralph Waldo Emerson; and Tom Corwine, a barnyard animal imitator.

The show presented old familiar tunes or folk songs, as they were called at the time. On those early programs a listener might hear "Down by the Old Mill Stream," "When You Wore a Tulip," "Till We Meet Again," "Whispering," "Memories," "Love's Old Sweet Song," and "When You and I Were Young, Maggie."

The person who blazed the musical path for *The National Barn Dance* was Bradley Kincaid, who joined the *Barn Dance* in 1927 and sang old folk songs like "Barbara Allen" that came down from the British ballads. Bradley was the first "star" on the *Barn Dance,* selling thousands of songbooks, and was a favorite with listeners until he left the station in January 1931 for WLW in Cincinnati.

On November 1, 1925, WLS moved to the sixth floor of the Sherman Hotel where a theater seating 100 allowed an audience to watch performers on their radio show. At that time, the wattage increased from 500 to 5,000. On October 1, 1928, Sears sold the station to the *Prairie Farmer* magazine, owned by Burridge D. Butler. The headquarters for WLS became the *Prairie*

Farmer's new office building at 1230 Washington Boulevard. Sears agreed to remain a major advertiser on the station but did not want to deal with any issues of conflict of interest with the station. Butler was 65 at the time of the sale and did not manage the day-to-day affairs of the station; however, "Butler conceived of the *National Barn Dance* as a big, wholesome country party...[this] fit Butler's view of life in the country, a view which most owners of stations rejected as out of date."[2] Butler insisted on a moral, uplifting program, and would not allow songs about drinking or marital infidelity.

The *Barn Dance* was a magnet, drawing audiences to its performances. On October 25, 1930, about 20,000 fans from Chicago and a dozen states came to see a broadcast of the *Barn Dance* from the International Amphitheater; 10,000 others were turned away.

On March 19, 1932, *The National Barn Dance* moved to Chicago's Eighth Street Theater and in May NBC began broadcasting the last half hour of the program. On September 30, 1933, the program became a regular feature on the NBC Blue network, sponsored by Miles Laboratories, makers of Alka Seltzer. During the 1930s WLS had the top lineup of country talent. Among the performers on *The National Barn Dance* were the Cumberland Ridge Runners, Red Foley, Gene Autry, Pat Buttram, Lula Belle and Scotty, Arkie the Arkansas Woodchopper, the Maple City Four, the Hoosier Hot Shots, George Goebel, Patsy Montana and the Prairie Ramblers, Max Terhune, and Louise Massey and the Westerners.

THE GRAND OLE OPRY

WSM in Nashville went on the air on October 5, 1925. WLS announcer George D. Hay, who won the *Radio Digest* announcer's trophy, was invited to the grand opening and was then offered a job as announcer and manager of the station, which he accepted and began on November 9. The National Life and Accident Insurance Company owned WSM, whose call letters stood for "We Shield Millions" and the station broadcast from the National Life headquarters at Seventh Avenue North and Union Street. On Saturday, November 28, Hay invited fiddler Uncle Jimmy Thompson to play fiddle tunes on the station that evening; this marks the beginning of *The WSM Barn Dance,* which expanded to other performers and then, in 1927, changed its name to *The Grand Ole Opry.*

In 1931 the Vagabonds, a pop-type trio, became *Opry* members, the first full-time professional group to appear on the show; they also became the first group in Nashville to publish their own songbook, *Old Cabin Songs of the Fiddle and Bow,* and establish a record company. Their big hit was "When It's Lamp-Lighting Time in the Valley." Also on the *Opry* in 1931 was the Pickard Family. Because of the popularity of Amos 'n' Andy on network radio, the *Opry* hired Lasses White to start a Friday night minstrel show;

he came to Nashville with his partner, Lee Davis "Honey" Wilds (Lasses and Honey). The duo did song parodies and Amos 'n' Andy type routines.

In 1933 the Delmore Brothers joined the *Opry* and Fred Rose moved to Nashville from Chicago and began *The Freddie Rose Song Shop,* a 15-minute daily program on WSM that featured pop songs. That same year WSM's Artist Service Bureau was created to book *Opry* acts. The next year Crazy Water Crystals began advertising on the *Opry* and the show was divided into 15-minute segments and sold to sponsors.

In 1934 WSM was awarded "clear channel" status, which meant that no other AM station in the country operated on the 650 slot on the radio dial. That same year, in February, the *Opry* moved to Studio C at WSM, where it played before a live audience but the demand for seating was so great that in October the show moved to the Hillsboro Theater.

In June 1936, the *Opry* moved to the Dixie Tabernacle on Fatherland Street in East Nashville. By this time the Delmore Brothers were the most popular act on the *Opry;* other acts included Uncle Dave Macon and Curly Fox and Texas Ruby. On June 1, 1937, Pee Wee King and the Golden West Cowboys, managed by J.L. Frank, joined the *Opry* and introduced the trumpet, drums, and electric guitar to the show. Their spiffy western outfits and well-organized touring were reminiscent of the Big Band organizations. In King's group were Redd Stewart and Milton Estes.

OTHER BARN DANCES

By the 1930s, Atlanta was the second largest city in the South (behind New Orleans) with a population of over 350,000 which made it the 22nd largest city in the nation. The powerhouse station in Atlanta was WSB, which increased its power to 5,000 watts in 1930, then to 50,000 watts in 1933. On Monday, January 3, 1936, they began the *Cross Roads Follies,* the first program that featured a group of country performers; before this, each act had its own show. The station also established a booking office to book their acts as well as book outside acts into the station. Acts on WSB included the Texas Wranglers (with fiddle player Boudleaux Bryant), Sante Fe Trailers, Curly Fox and the Tennessee Firecrackers, and Ernest Rogers. On WGST in Atlanta were the Bolick Brothers, known as the Blue Sky Boys, and the *Fulton County Jamboree* was on WJTL.

In 1931 George Smith became program director at WWVA in Wheeling, West Virginia, and saw country music's potential to attract an audience. On January 7, 1933, the *WWVA Jamboree* began at the Capitol Theater in downtown Wheeling. The next month the show moved to the Wheeling Market Auditorium, which seated 1,300. Early performers included Cap, Andy, and Flip, Silver Yodelin' Bill Jones, the Tweedy Brothers, Cousin Emmy (Carver), and Grandpa Jones. The station had a Saturday night studio program for several years called the *Jamboree* before inaugurating its live audience shows on April 1. In 1937, Doc Williams and Big Slim and the Lone Star Cowboy (Harry McAuliffe) joined the show.

WHAS in Louisville was an NBC affiliate with 25,000 watts. In 1934 J.L. Frank moved from Chicago to Louisville after deciding not to accompany Gene Autry to Hollywood and he brought along Pee Wee King, who performed in a Polish-English band on the *Badger State Barn Dance* on WJRN in Racine, Wisconsin. At WHAS King joined Frankie More's Log Cabin Boys. Gene Autry also joined Frank in Louisville for several months between leaving WLS and starring in his first movie in 1935. At WHAS in 1935 were Cousin Emmy, the Callahan Brothers, and Clayton McMichen. J.L. Frank was the driving force at WHAS in Louisville and a great concert promoter until he formed the group The Golden West Cowboys, led by Pee Wee King, and moved to Knoxville in 1936 where, in January, announcer Lowell Blanchard formed a noon time show on WNOX, the *Midday Merry-Go-Round,* which featured Homer and Jethro, Archie Campbell, Roy Acuff and His Crazy Tennesseans, and Bill Carlisle. That same year Roy Acuff made his first records for the American Record Company; "The Great Speckled Bird" was the hit Acuff had been singing on WNOX which ARC wanted on record. This launched Acuff's recording career. Also at WNOX were the Dixieland Swingsters, who combined country, swing, and jazz, Charlie Monroe, the Tennessee Ramblers, and plenty of comedy with routines written by Blanchard that featured Archie Campbell and Homer and Jethro.

In Texas the *Crazy Water Crystals* show began from Mineral Wells's Crazy Hotel; the show was broadcast on NBC and featured the Light Crust Doughboys. The Crazy Water Crystals company was owned by Carr P. Collins and named for an alleged cure of two insane ladies in the 1880s. The "Crazy Water Crystals" was actually a laxative and the company promoted it heavily by sponsoring a number of country music programs during the 1930s. In 1936 they sponsored *Saturday Night Stampede* on Fort Worth's WBAP and a live show from Ranger Junior College that featured Jules Verne Allen singing songs such as "Cowboy's Lament" and "Santa Fe Trail."

In 1932 J.E. Mainer was on the *Crazy Water Barn Dance* on WBT in Charlotte, North Carolina, sponsored by Crazy Water Crystals; the following year The Callahan Brothers performed on WWNC in Asheville. In 1935 Bill and Charlie Monroe moved to Charlotte and had a show on WBT while the Blue Sky Boys were also on North Carolina radio. In 1936 Cecil Campbell was on *Briarhopper Time* in Charlotte on WBT.

In New York City, beginning in 1933, Ethel Park Richardson hosted a weekly program on NBC, *Hillbilly Heart-Throbs,* that featured guests such as Tex Ritter, Frank Luther, Zora Layman, Carson Robison, Texas Jim Robertson, and the Vass Family. In 1933 Foy Willing had a radio show sponsored by Crazy Water Crystals, and in 1934 Patsy Montana and The Prairie Ramblers moved to WOR in New York from WLS for a year before returning to Chicago. Also in 1934 Tex Ritter was the featured performer on *The WHN Barn Dance* in New York. The next year Texas Jim Lewis and the Lone Star Cowboys were at the Village Barn in Greenwich Village. This 250-seat club opened in October 1929, and for over 20 years hosted country talent. In 1936 Louise Massey and the Westerners were on NBC's *Log Cabin Dude Ranch* in New York and became a headline act at the Waldorf-Astoria, the Rainbow Room, and other venues.

In Los Angeles, California, the *Hollywood Barn Dance* was established in 1932; that same year Stuart Hamblen began his *Lucky Stars* program on KFWB. Also in 1932 the Beverly Hill Billies were on KMPC before joining KTM. In 1934 the Sons of the Pioneers were on KFWB, and the following year Cliffie Stone joined Hamblen on KFVD's *Covered Wagon Jubilee*. In 1936 the Sons of the Pioneers had shows on KFOX and KRKD before settling in at KHJ on Peter Potter's *Hollywood Barn Dance*. In 1937 Woody Guthrie moved to Los Angeles where he appeared on KFVD in Hollywood with his cousin, Jack Guthrie on the *Oak and Woody Show*. That same year Zeke Clements joined the *Hollywood Barn Dance* and became the voice of "Bashful" for Walt Disney's movie *Snow White and the Seven Dwarfs*. Up in Modesto, California, on KTRB the Maddox Brothers and Rose, under the name the *Alabama Outlaws* with 11-year old Rose as lead singer, had a show.

In 1932 there was the *Iowa Barn Dance Frolic* on WHO in Des Moines and the Kentucky Ramblers were on WOC in Davenport, Iowa, where a young announcer named Ronald Reagan was working. Tex Owens had his own show as *The Texas Ranger* and was also a member of the *Brush Creek Follies* on KMBC in Kansas City, Missouri. In 1933 Texas Jim Lewis was on WJR in Detroit; he formed a band called the Lone Star Rangers, later renamed the Lone Star Cowboys and in Halifax, Nova Scotia, Hank Snow sang on CHNS. In 1934 the Monroe Brothers were on radio in Shenandoah, Iowa, and the Swift Jewel Cowboys were on WMC in Memphis. In 1935 Louis Marshall Jones worked with Bradley Kincaid on WBZ in Boston; Kincaid renamed him "Grandpa Jones." That same year The Newman Brothers were based at WHKC, Columbus, Ohio, and the Shelton Brothers were on WWL in New Orleans. In 1936 Cousin Wilbur Westbrooks was on WTJS in Jackson, Tennessee; in his group were Eddy Arnold and Speedy McNatt. In 1937 Tennessee Ernie Ford was an announcer at Bristol's WOAI and Ernest Tubb began singing on the radio in Texas.

During the 1930s the Dixie Harmonizers, under the name the Pine Ridge Stringband, furnished the music for the *Lum and Abner Show*. This later became a major show on network radio.

WLS Music Director John Lair with Red Foley and Whitey Ford ("The Duke of Paducah") left WLS with the Cumberland Ridge Runners and began *The Renfro Valley Barn Dance* on October 9, 1937. Lair was from Renfro Valley, Kentucky, but the facilities in Renfro Valley were not ready when he started his program so the first broadcasts originated from the Cincinnati

Music Hall over WLW in that city. At the *Renfro Barn Dance,* Lair organized the Coon Creek Girls, the first all-woman string band, around the talents of Lily May Ledford.

In 1935 the Chuck Wagon Gang was on WBAP in Fort Worth. This was the first full-time gospel group not sponsored by a shaped-note publishing house. They introduced a number of Albert Brumley's songs, such as "I'll Fly Away," "I'll Meet You in the Morning," and "If We Never Meet Again."

Just across the Texas border in Mexico country music received a boost from border stations, established there beginning in 1930 when XED began broadcasting from Renosa, Tamaulipas. The station was originally owned by Will Horwitz, a Houston theater owner and philanthropist, and Jimmie Rodgers played there. Then Dr. John R. Brinkley moved in.

Dr. John Romulus Brinkley grew rich and famous in Milford, Kansas, by pioneering the implementation of slivers of billy goat sex glands into humans to rejuvenate their sex drive. In 1930 he ran for governor of Kansas and almost won, but soon after the election was run out of the state by medical authorities. In 1931 he established XER (later XERA), a 100,000 watt station just across the border from Del Rio, Texas, in Villa Acuna, Mexico, then purchased XED and changed its call letters to XEAW.

In 1933 Brinkley gave up the goat gland business and began a controversial prostate treatment. His radio stations and others on the Mexican border such as XEPN in Piedras Negras and XENT in Nuevo Laredo were formed because Mexico had been denied United States' broadcasting licenses; Canada and the United States had divided these up amongst themselves, leaving Mexico out. And so Mexico initially welcomed these outlaw stations, which broadcast from 50,000–500,000 watts, blanketing the United States.

During the 1930s the border stations played country records and transcriptions and were an important source of country music on the airwaves. Listeners heard the Carter Family, Patsy Montana, the Pickard Family, Pappy O'Daniel's Hillbilly Boys, Roy "Lonesome Cowboy" Faulkner, Jesse Rodgers, a distant cousin of Jimmie, and others.

Country music has traditionally been the music for the white working class and many in this audience left the farms and rural areas for big cities during the 1930s. In 1933 the first major exodus of white workers from the South to the North occurred when the automobile companies in Detroit, nervous about their employees joining a union, chartered buses to bring workers from Kentucky, Tennessee, and Alabama to Michigan, where they worked for 50 cents an hour on the assembly lines. By 1934 there were between 15,000 and 30,000 Southerners in Detroit; this exodus led other Southerners to move north to Detroit, Indianapolis, Chicago, Pittsburgh, Cincinnati, and Cleveland to look for jobs in manufacturing plants.

The barn dances also appealed to African-Americans because there were no early blues records on the airwaves since stations had policies against programming shows by African-Americans so blacks listened to the comedy, drama, and musical shows on radio, including the barn dances. R&B legends B.B. King, James Brown, Chuck Berry, and others all grew up listening and loving country music on barn dances because they were on the radio.

CLYDE MCMICHEN

Not all country musicians embraced the country image. Clayton McMichen, an original member of the Skillet Lickers in Atlanta, never cared for string band music. McMichen was a master at old-time fiddling; he won the national fiddling championship 18 times, broadcast over a number of stations, and performed in a number of shows. He toured with Jimmie Rodgers, played on his recordings and wrote his hit, "Peach Pickin' Time in Georgia." But McMichen hated the hillbilly image; he was a serious musician.

This was a major reason he disliked performing with the Skillet Lickers. The band, put together by Columbia A&R man Frank Walker, consisted of Gid Tanner and Riley Puckett in addition to McMichen and perpetuated the image of southern musicians as moonshine drinking, hound dog hugging, uncouth backwoodsmen. In 1931, at the final Skillet Lickers session for Columbia, McMichen came with a new band, The Georgia Wildcats, and played a jazzy swinging fiddle on "Yum Yum Blues" and "When the Bloom Is on the Sage." But these records did not sell as well as the Skillet Lickers string band music.

McMichen wanted hillbilly music to be more refined and so, according to author Charles Wolfe, "McMichen continued his long, lonely battle to take country music uptown, to open the music up to experimentation, to technical expertise, and to professional musicianship. The trouble was, the music didn't want to go uptown just yet."[3] Still, McMichen tried to incorporate jazz and pop music into the Georgia Wildcats. This group included guitarist Slim Bryant, fiddler Carl Cotner, and guitarist Merle Travis, but the "progressive" country never sold; McMichen had to stick to "swamp opera," as he called it, because "there's 500 pairs of overalls sold to every one tuxedo suit."[4] Clayton McMichen stayed frustrated with country music at the same time he made a living at it. He continued to lean towards jazz and pop, but was too far ahead of his time and place, despite the fact that he was one of the most influential musicians and performers of his era.

WESTERN SWING

Down in Texas, the seeds of western swing were planted during the summer of 1930 when fiddler Bob Wills and singer Milton Brown, joined by guitarists Herman Arnspiger and Derwood Brown, performed as the Aladdin Laddies on WBAP in Fort Worth, Texas. Late that year, Burrus Mills sponsored a radio program with this group, who changed their name to the Light Crust Dough Boys after W. Lee "Pappy" O'Daniel, who worked for the Burrus Mill and Elevator Company, recruited them for a radio show sponsored by Light Crust Flour, a product of the Burrus Mill Company. O'Daniel purchased an expensive automobile, painted it with signs and slogans about Light Crust Flour and the Light Crust Doughboys and installed a public address system; he also demanded the musicians spend 40 hours a week at the mill practicing for their broadcasts.

The show was broadcast over the Southwest Quality Network on a number of Texas stations. O'Daniel built a studio at the mill and bought the musicians a phonograph and the latest recordings in order to learn new songs. In 1932 the Light Crust Dough Boys recorded for Victor at a session in Fort Worth.

In September 1932, Milton Brown left the Light Crust Doughboys and formed the Musical Brownies with himself on vocals, brother Derwood on guitar, Jesse Ashlock on fiddle, Wanna Coffman on bass, and Ocie Stockard playing tenor banjo. Soon, jazz pianist Fred "Papa" Calhoun joined, followed by swing fiddler Cecil Brower. The twin fiddle sound of Brower and Ashlock created the western swing sound on those instruments. Another influential "sound" came when Bob Dunn brought his amplified steel guitar to Brown's group in 1934. Dunn was influenced by the Hawaiian music of Sol Hoopii and Sam Koki, who played an amplified steel or "Hawaiian" guitar. In 1932 Brown's group was on a daily radio show on KTAT.

In 1933 Bob Wills was fired by the Light Crust Dough Boys (for drinking) and formed his own group, the Texas Playboys. Singer Tommy Duncan, a classic western crooner, had replaced Brown in the Light Crust Doughboys but left the group to join Wills. Leon Huff replaced Duncan in the Light Crust Dough Boys while Leon McAuliff became the steel guitarist for that group.

BOB WILLS AND HIS TEXAS PLAYBOYS

It was the Jazz Age and Big Bands that influenced country music through western swing. The most important pioneer in the history of western swing was Bob Wills and His Texas Playboys.

Bob Wills was born on March 6, 1905, on a farm in Limestone County, Texas. The son of a Texas fiddler, Wills learned the fiddle when he was young and played for dances at ranch parties. The fiddler was required to play all night for people dancing far away from bright city lights. According to Wills's biographer Charles Townsend, the emphasis on music for dancing was the major reason the country or folk music Wills played was so different from music in the East which also had rural and folk roots; west of the Mississippi the country folk wanted music to dance to while east of the Mississippi the rural musicians performed a show at a school house where people sat and listened.

Wills was influenced by Negro blues (Bessie Smith was his favorite singer) and began playing blues songs on his fiddle. The fiddle itself was going out of style with dance bands and city musicians; it was considered a rural instrument for backward whites or dirt poor blacks.

In 1929 Wills left West Texas for Fort Worth, where he worked as a barber and tried to find work as a musician. An ambitious, aggressive man, Wills obtained an audition at WBAP in Fort Worth and performed there as well as entertaining as a musician and blackface comic on a medicine show. There he developed his showmanship and his wisecracking asides during a performance. His first recording came in the fall of 1929 for Brunswick; on November 1 in Dallas he recorded "Wills Breakdown" and a Bessie Smith song, "Gulf Coast Blues."

In the fall of 1930, Wills performed on a show on WBAP sponsored by the Alladin Lamp Company; the radio station, one of the most powerful in the Southwest, led to bookings at Crystal Springs, a dance club where he added more members to his band. Wills developed his music for dancers; at the same time, he listened to network radio and heard the great dance bands playing and wanted to incorporate their sound and style. But he did this with a West Texas fiddling background so the fiddle was a key part of the band.

After Wills left the Light Crust Doughboys he moved to Waco, Texas, where he formed his own band, The Playboys on WACO. "Pappy" O'Daniel tried to destroy Wills's group so, to escape the clutches of O'Daniel, Wills moved to Oklahoma City, Oklahoma, where he began a show in February 1934. O'Daniel offered the Oklahoma station the possibility of the Light Crust Doughboys if they would fire Wills so Wills moved on to KVOO in Tulsa; O'Daniel did not fulfill his promise. In Tulsa there was an oil boom and Wills and his group were soon playing dances.

In the spring of 1935 Wills hired Leon McAuliff and his amplified steel guitar, adding a new sound to the band. He also began to add brass when announcer Everett Stover joined on trumpet. With this move, the string band started to become a brass band that eventually rivaled the big swing bands. Wills had to play in Tulsa nearly two years before his band members were allowed to join the union because they were informed by the Tulsa local musicians union "that they 'were not musicians' and did not play what could correctly be called 'music.'" Only reading musicians, according to the local, were considered musicians, and only they were allowed to join the union.[5]

In 1935 Milton Brown and his Brownies had a daily radio show on WBAP in Fort Worth and also played local dances. They played a jazz akin to Cab Calloway and did songs such as "Right or Wrong," "Corrine Corrina," and "Sitting on Top of the World." That same year W. Lee O'Daniel was fired from the Burrus Mill Company and began his own flour firm, Hillbilly Flour. He also started a new band after firing the Light Crust Doughboys, who had a hit in 1936, "Ding Dong Daddy" sung by Dick Reinhart, and also appeared in a Gene Autry movie.

On April 13, 1936, Milton Brown was critically injured in an automobile accident that killed his passenger; five days later he died.

By this time the "sound" of western swing was pretty well defined; it was Texas string band music meeting big band jazz head on. Western swing fiddlers like Cecil Brower and Cliff Bruner were influenced by jazz violinists Joe Venuti and Stephane Grappelli and the western groups were influenced by the big band sounds of the Dorsey Brothers, Benny Goodman, Duke Ellington, and Paul Whiteman.

The old time fiddling was fading away; in 1935 the last old-time fiddling contest was held in Atlanta. Fans didn't miss them much because they saw fiddlers on live shows when radio performers toured. Times had changed; in his book *Pickin' On Peachtree,* author Wayne Daniel quotes one of the organizers of the Georgia Fiddling contest in 1935 who said, "Folks used to be satisfied with just straight fiddling...[but] the country folks ain't satisfied with the simple old fiddle tunes no more. They want this jazz band music."[6]

By 1938 Bob Wills recorded with brass and drums, influenced heavily by the big band sound and swing music coming from the networks. That year, recording for Columbia, Wills rearranged his old song "Spanish Two Step" and named it "San Antonio Rose." By this time, the group played on the radio, at Cain's Dancing Academy in Tulsa, and on the road. In 1938 they began to dress in western clothing—cowboy boots and hats—so the image of the band was distinctly western while the music, despite its big band leanings, still embraced Wills's Texas roots. His band was the most popular in the Southwest and he began to develop a musical organization akin to the orchestras on network radio.

"San Antonio Rose" was the biggest hit Wills had; it attracted the attention of Fred Kramer with the Irving Berlin publishing company. Because the song had not been published, Kramer wanted it; however, he insisted lyrics be added. Wills and his band members wrote some lyrics, gave it to Kramer for a $300 advance, and Bing Crosby recorded it. Wills also recorded it with a big band sound and received a Gold Record for this recording in 1940. Crosby's recording, released in January 1939, sold over a million and a half units; this was a turning point in Wills's career.

OTHER WESTERN SWING GROUPS

There were other dance bands in Texas during the 1930s. In 1934 the Blue Ridge Playboys were formed in Houston by Ted Daffan with guitarist Floyd Tillman and fiddler Leon Selph; that same year the Tune Wranglers were formed in San Antonio by fiddler Tom Dicket and guitarist Buster Coward and performed on WOAI. The following year Adolph Hofner and his brother Emil (guitar and steel) joined with fiddler Jimmie Revard, guitarist Curley Williams, and jazz pianist Eddie Whitley to form the Oklahoma Playboys.

JUKEBOXES

The music of blues and hillbilly found a market in the Great Depression on jukeboxes in joints and honky tonks. These juke joints or barrooms became popular when Prohibition was repealed in 1933 after President Franklin Roosevelt took office. The legalization of booze created the business of bars, which often installed a jukebox for their patrons. Hillbilly recordings accounted for about a fourth of record sales during the Great Depression, and a significant number of them were sold to jukeboxes. In fact, jukeboxes essentially saved the recording industry during the 1930s; they were the major purchaser of recorded music during this time. People dropped a nickel in the slot to hear their favorite recording, unable to afford a phonograph or record of their own.

Not only did jukeboxes save the music industry financially, they also provided the major exposure for blues and hillbilly music. Although a number of radio stations increasingly programmed this music (particularly hillbilly), for many people it was the jukebox that allowed them to hear this nonmainstream music.

Still, blues and hillbilly did not thrive during the Depression. The South was the hardest hit of all areas during the Depression, and here is where most hillbilly and many blues buyers lived. Recording companies could not afford to do field recordings, so artists had to travel to company facilities in New York or Chicago to record. Performers in the South, unlike their counterparts in New York or Hollywood, had to perform for audiences who were poor and unable to afford the basics of life, much less entertainment.

THE SINGING COWBOYS

In the mid-1930s country music was heard primarily on live radio shows—especially the Saturday night barn dances on clear channel radio stations—and jukeboxes. There were almost no country records played on radio, which consisted primarily of live entertainment. But country music received a new outlet during this period through the movies, led by Gene Autry but soon followed by Tex Ritter, Roy Rogers, and others.

Throughout 1930 and 1931, Gene Autry lived in the Tulsa area, sang on KVOO, and recorded several sessions in New York doing a number of Jimmie Rodgers songs. In late October 1931, Autry and Jimmy Long, his supervisor at the Frisco Railroad where Autry was a telegrapher, recorded "That Silver-Haired Daddy of Mine." On December 1, Autry debuted on WLS on a morning show, *Conqueror Record Time*, sponsored by Sears to promote their recording label, which coincided with the release of "That Silver-Haired Daddy of Mine." This became Autry's first big hit, selling a reported 30,000 in its first month.

Throughout 1932–1934, Autry sang on shows on WLS, including *The National Barn Dance,* and established himself in the area, performing within a roughly 200-mile radius of Chicago. In mid-1934 Autry and Smiley Burnette, his musical accompanist, drove to Hollywood and appeared in the Ken Maynard western *In Old Santa Fe* where Autry called a square dance and sang "Down in Old Santa Fe" and "Someday in Wyoming" while Smiley sang "Mama Don't 'low No Music in Here." This led to a starring role for Autry in *Phantom Empire*, a 13-chapter serial released in February 1934, where Autry sang "That Silver-Haired Daddy of Mine" and a number of other songs; the reaction was good so Mascot Pictures signed Autry to his first starring role in a western and the singing cowboy was born. In this movie, *Tumbling Tumbleweeds,* Autry did the title song, as well as "That Silver-Haired Daddy of Mine," "Ridin' Down the Canyon," and "Oh, Susanna."

The singing cowboy created the first positive public image for country singers in America as the image of the performers began to shift from mountaineers to cowboys. Because of the singing cowboy movies, the cowboy became the most enduring symbol of country music.

SONS OF THE PIONEERS

When Gene Autry arrived in Hollywood in 1934 there was already a fertile western music scene that had been developed through live programs over the radio as well as a tradition of western songs in country music.

In 1931 Leonard Slye moved to Los Angeles from Ohio; the year before the Slye family first came to Los Angeles to visit Leonard's sister. In mid-1931 he entered an amateur program with his cousin Stanley; this led to an appearance on the "Midnight Frolic" on KMCS where Ebb Bowen invited Slye to join his group, the Rocky Mountaineers, who appeared on KGER. The instrumental group needed a singer; Slye was hired but wanted harmonies so he ran an advertisement in the newspaper and Bob Nolan answered, got the job, and the two began to rehearse. Nolan recommended a friend, Bill "Slumber" Nichols, for a third slot and the trio of Slye, Nolan, and Nichols began singing on KGER in Long Beach in December 1931.

In summer 1932 Nolan left the group; Slye ran another advertisement which was answered by Tim Spencer, who joined the group in mid-August. The trio of Slye, Nichols, and Spencer worked with the Rocky Mountaineers for a few weeks, then joined Benny Nawahi's International Cowboys where they did personal appearances and appeared on KGER and KRKD in Los Angeles. In June, calling themselves the O-Bar-O Cowboys, the trio left for a tour of the Southwest before returning to Los Angeles in September 1933. The trio then broke up and Slye joined Jack and His Texas Outlaws. However, Slye still wanted a trio and persuaded Tim Spencer to give it another shot; these two convinced Bob Nolan to also try again. This trio began rehearsing and within a few weeks, calling themselves The Pioneer Trio, joined Jack and His Texas Outlaws and began working on KFWB on a morning show. On a late afternoon show they performed again as the Gold Star Rangers, then played in the evening with the Jack Joy Orchestra. At the beginning of 1934, the trio of singers added an instrumentalist, fiddler Hugh Farr. Also early in 1934, they were introduced on the radio by announcer Harry Hall as "The Sons of the Pioneers." The group was upset with Hall, who told them the new name was more appropriate because they were all so young they looked more like "sons" than "pioneers." The name stuck and by March 1934, just before their first recording session for Decca, they were officially known as the Sons of the Pioneers. During this session they recorded "There's a Roundup in the Sky" and "Roving Cowboy." They recorded two more sessions that month then, on August 8, recorded "Way Out There" and "Tumbling Tumbleweeds," both written by Bob Nolan, for Decca.

The idea of "singing westerns" was an idea whose time had come and movie studios quickly added them. In mid-1935 the Sons of the Pioneers were featured in their first movie appearance, *The Old Homestead* for Liberty Pictures, released in August 1935, a few weeks before Autry's picture was released. In this picture they were known by a name they continued to use, The Gold Star Rangers. They also appeared in *Slightly Static*, an MGM short, and *Way Up Thar* with Joan Davis, also in late 1935. They then appeared in two pictures for Columbia with cowboy star Charles Starrett.

In addition to *Tumbling Tumbleweeds*, Gene Autry starred in three more movies in 1935: *Melody Trail, Sagebrush Troubadour*, and *Singing Vagabond*. Other singing cowboys soon followed to the silver screen; first there was Dick Foran, then Tex Ritter.

In 1935 the M.M. Cole Company, a songbook publishing company based in Chicago, published Tom Mix's *Western Songs*. In New York, Patsy Montana recorded "I Want to Be a Cowboy's Sweetheart," the first hit record by a female country act. Up in Halifax, Nova Scotia, Hank Snow sang cowboy songs on CHNS, sponsored by Crazy Water Crystals. In 1936 Gene Autry appeared on the silver screen in seven movies, including one appropriately named *The Singing Cowboy*. The Sons of the Pioneers were featured in four movies, and Tex Ritter made his debut as a singing cowboy on the movie screen. In a poll, Gene Autry was voted the number 3 favorite movie cowboy.[7]

In early 1938, Autry walked out on Republic Studios, disgruntled over his contract. The studio at first refused to renegotiate the contract and, instead, held auditions to develop another singing cowboy to replace him. Leonard Slye, founding member of the Sons of the Pioneers, auditioned and won the job; studio executives changed his name to Roy Rogers and cast him in his first starring role in *Under Western Stars* (1938). Although Autry later returned to the studio, Republic continued to use both singers and both proved popular with audiences.

The songs these singing cowboys sang were primarily written by professional songwriters, many of whom had moved from New York and Chicago to write for the movies. The "sound" of western music was defined by the harmonies of the Sons of the Pioneers as well as the vocals of Gene Autry and Roy Rogers, who were inspired by the first country music singing star, Jimmie Rodgers.

NASHVILLE TAKES FIRST STEPS

On January 7, 1939, the Esty Agency, which had the account for R.J. Reynolds, sponsored a portion of the *Grand Ole Opry* promoting their product, Prince Albert tobacco. Prince Albert was a loose tobacco sold in a can; it was smoked in pipes or to "roll-your-own" with cigarette papers. It was an inexpensive brand aimed for the blue collar class. The show was presided over by Judge Hay, who ran each show as talent organizer, master of ceremonies, and power to be reckoned with.

Prior to Hay coming to WSM there were several appearances by country performers; Dr. Humphrey Bate, a physician from nearby Sumner County, appeared with his string band as did Uncle Dave Macon, a lively banjo player and performer who performed on the vaudeville circuit. At this time the station's programming was often a hodgepodge of performers as radio was in its experimental stage, trying to determine who the audience was and what they wanted.

Hay instituted a regular Saturday night program of country music with fiddler Uncle Jimmy Thompson on December 26, 1925, after Thompson spent about a month performing on Saturday nights to enthusiastic listener response. Thompson's first Saturday evening performance was November 28, 1925, so that is the date given as the "birth" of the *Grand Ole Opry,* although the original name of the program that officially began on December 26 was *The WSM Barn Dance.* In 1927, Hay told his audience, who had just heard the Metropolitan Opera, that while they had been listening to "grand opera," now they were going to hear "The Grand Ole Opry." And thus the name was born.

Hay organized groups such as the Fruit Jar Drinkers and the Gully Jumpers, combining or renaming existing groups, and insisted they carry the image of mountaineers, an image of country people perpetuated by vaudeville. The earliest *Opry* performers generally wore suits and ties; the first picture of the *Opry* cast shows them thus attired, but Hay insisted that *Opry* performers wear bib overalls and sit amidst bales of hay in order to present a "country" image so the following photographs taken of *Opry* performers show them dressed as hayseeds as the *Opry* actively promoted the idea that this was a rural-based show comprised of just plain country folks. Even Dr. Humphrey Bate, a physician who graduated from Vanderbilt University, changed the name of his group to The Possum Hunters and traded his suit and tie for the hillbilly look.

The Prince Albert segment of the *Opry,* begun at the beginning of 1939, continued for nine months, during which time the R.J. Reynolds executives, pleased at the success of the *Opry* promoting their tobacco, decided to sponsor a 30-minute show on the NBC "Red" network beginning on October 14.

There were major changes at WSM in 1939, signaled by the *Opry's* connection to a national advertiser and network radio, that led to a decrease in the power of Judge Hay. Hay was described as "too much in the clouds" to be an effective corporate executive, so first Harry Stone, then Jack Stapp, whose personalities made them effective in corporate offices, assumed more and more power. Further, the advertising agency—and sponsor—wanted a "star" to sell their product—not Judge Hay. Although Hay had a prominent role at the beginning of the *Prince Albert* show, Roy Acuff began to emerge as the dominant star. Another casualty was Uncle Dave Macon, a vibrant and colorful performer who was not as comfortable with a microphone.

Jack Stapp was hired by WSM in 1939 when they lured him away from CBS in New York to come down and take over as program manager.

Jack Stapp was successful at CBS in New York and rose through the ranks to become a top executive while his roommate, Bert Parks, became a well-known celebrity on radio. But two things happened which caused Stapp to look south. First, Bert Parks was sent by CBS to Hollywood so Stapp no longer had a roommate. Next, WSM executive Jack Harris came to New York and was given a tour at CBS; when he reached the studio where Stapp was rehearsing a show Stapp stopped the rehearsal and introduced Harris (whom he had never met) to the cast and crew and extolled his station, WSM. Although WSM was affiliated with NBC, Harris noted that Stapp and CBS had given him better treatment when he visited and he never forgot that. So when WSM needed a program manager, Jack Harris called Stapp and offered him the job.

Jack Stapp welcomed the chance to return to Nashville, but before he left he called on Phil Carlin, the production manager of NBC who had been Stapp's friendly competitor. Stapp wanted to stay connected to the networks and since NBC was WSM's network, he told Carlin he'd like to provide the network some programming from WSM in Nashville. Carlin was interested so he and Stapp agreed to stay in touch.

In Nashville Stapp set about building top-notch musical groups but immediately encountered problems with the musicians union, who objected to outside musicians being brought in. Stapp had a problem with the Nashville musicians there at the time: these musicians were pit musicians, basically good musicians who had experience in theaters, but he knew that network exposure demanded a higher quality of musicianship. The problem was solved when he realized a number of musicians had left Nashville because of lack of work; Stapp and others contacted these musicians and invited them back to Nashville, promising there would be opportunities for network exposure. This led to changes in the WSM Orchestra as well as Owen Bradley's Orchestra, Beasley Smith's Orchestra, and Francis Craig's Orchestra in addition to the development of live radio shows like *Sunday Down South, Hospitality Time,*

Mr. Smith Goes to Town, Riverboat Rebels, and the children's program *Wormwood Forest,* which were fed to the network. The *Opry* was only part of the network connection to NBC at the beginning—although it was a network connection that put WSM in prime time on Saturday night.

The *Prince Albert Show* made WSM a major player in country music. Although WSM had a clear channel 50,000 watt station which reached most of the United States (and transcriptions were available for the West Coast) the top barn dance before World War II was *The National Barn Dance* on WLS in Chicago which was a network regular before the *Grand Ole Opry* achieved that distinction.

In the period of the early- to mid-1930s, the dominant star of the *Opry* was Uncle Dave Macon, a colorful character and superb entertainer in the vaudeville tradition. The rest of the *Opry* cast was a mixture of string bands and other "traditional" or "folk" musicians who had regular jobs during the week but played weekends on the *Opry* as well as acts with smooth, pop-type harmonies like the Vagabonds. Although hillbilly entertainers formed the core of the *Opry,* it was essentially a variety show that incorporated musical styles that ranged from mountain music and cornball comedy to pop-type citified acts.

Several important things happened with the *Opry* because of this network connection. First, the *Opry* and WSM became nationally known for a country music show; next, they attracted national advertisers—and advertising agencies—which played a major role in future national exposure. Finally, they began to move away from the original idea of the *Opry* as the major attraction to a star system where one act was promoted over the others. Prior to this time it was the show that was central and the artists were interchangeable; after this, the star was the central figure, although WSM and *Opry* executives continued to try and balance the ideas that the *Grand Ole Opry* itself was essential and that's what people wanted to see and hear versus the idea that people bought tickets in order to see and hear a particular star. This idea of the power of an individual star shifted the balance of power at the *Opry* hierarchy as the *Opry* progressed through the 1940s. One of the first casualties of the change was Judge Hay, who had to give way to Roy Acuff announcing the Prince Albert portion due to the demands of the advertising agency.

Judge Hay also suffered from depression and occasionally left the station for periods of time; these absences, and Hay's inability to blend into the corporate mould in the corridors at National Life and Accident, the insurance company that owned the *Grand Ole Opry,* led to Hay's power being eroded and, finally, stripped away. Although George D. Hay lived until 1968, he moved to Baltimore in 1950 and came back to the *Opry* only for special performances, where he was trotted out and recognized. He was certainly honored by this, and the *Opry* never denied Hay's importance during the early years, but corporate politics made Hay a figure for public consumption, not for the corridors of power.

The connection with a major advertising agency also shifted the balance of power away from the WSM executives in Nashville to New York ad agency executives who approved the talent and wrote the shows. Jack Stapp was in charge of rehearsing the *Prince Albert Show* every Saturday morning for the evening performance, making sure it started and finished on time. Both Stapp and the Esty executives realized there had to be some latitude with the live show—hence the idea that nobody could "control" the *Opry* and that it had to stay loose and unstructured—but the fact remains that while there was some amount of ad libbing and a relaxation of the practice that everything on the network had to be timed to the second, the *Prince Albert Show* was highly structured and controlled by the ad agency, who paid for the network exposure.

THE MUSICIANS UNION

The network connection for the *Grand Ole Opry* was also important to musicians, and this played a major role in establishing Nashville as a major recording center after World War II.

The musicians union was structured so that each local office had control over who was admitted and who was not. Many union offices around the nation did not allow country or blues musicians in their union; some even established a rule that required a musician to be able to read and write music in order to become a union member. Since union officers did not want unemployed musicians in the union, country musicians were regularly discouraged but if an act was employed by a radio station then the union did want them in; the reason was simple: dues were collected from these musicians, which supported the union.

The union had an agreement with the networks that all musicians who appeared on network shows had to be union musicians. This meant that an act employed on the *Grand Ole Opry,* which went out on the network, had to be in the union; therefore, when the major recording labels came to Nashville after World War II to record—and these labels also had agreements that all musicians on record had to be union members—there was no problem finding country musicians who were union members. If the recording labels went to other cities that did not have a country music program like the *Grand Ole Opry* on a network, then chances are the country musicians were not members of the union. Further, the other unions often blocked them from joining—which meant they could not record for major labels. This was an important hurdle to overcome in order for Nashville to become a major recording center for country music, and this hurdle began to be surmounted in 1939 when the *Opry* first went over the network.

Having said that, due credit must also be given to George Cooper, who became president of Nashville's Musicians Union (Local No. 257) in 1937.

Cooper liked the country musicians and welcomed them into the union; he had the vision to see a union not limited to big band musicians. Because of Cooper's open door policy with musicians, and his respect for country music musicians who were talented but musically illiterate, Nashville grew as a recording center for country music.

JIM DENNY

Jim Denny was another executive at WSM who became a major player at the *Grand Ole Opry* beginning in the 1930s. Denny, born February 28, 1911, in Silver Point, Tennessee, about 90 miles east of Nashville, moved to Nashville when he was 11. He obtained a job in the mail room of National Life, the insurance company that owned the *Grand Ole Opry*, in May 1929. Part of his job entailed handling the mail for the *Grand Ole Opry*, which had proven to be more popular than the insurance executives ever imagined. Denny took classes in accounting at the Watkins Institute in Nashville and from IBM, whose machines were used by National Life. Denny moved up to the filing room, the accounting department, and then the machine room of the actuarial department in 1933. An aggressive, ambitious young man, he pushed himself in the company.

When the *Opry* moved to the Dixie Tabernacle, Denny took the job of working at the back door on Saturday nights, where he ushered artists in and kept spectators out. This initial job with the *Opry* led to others. When the *Opry* began selling tickets for their shows at the War Memorial Auditorium in 1939, Denny worked in the ticket booth, as well as an usher, security guard, and ticket taker. Soon he was invaluable and, since he was efficient and effective, gradually became known as the man to see if you wanted something done at the *Opry*.

Denny needed the extra income from his *Opry* activities because National Life traditionally paid small salaries and Denny had a growing family of his own as well as responsibility for his mother (his father had died in October 1929, shortly after Denny was hired) and two brothers. He was also effective and efficient at National Life, where he ran the tabulating division on IBM's machines.

The *Opry* began charging a quarter for admission in 1939 in order to limit the crowds coming to the War Memorial Building each Saturday night. In the new, big building (it seated over 2,000) Denny began a side business of selling souvenirs. Although Denny received permission from National Life to sell souvenirs and keep the profits, it was primarily because National Life saw the *Opry* as a way to sell insurance policies and had no idea there would be such big money in souvenirs. Some of these souvenirs included wooden ash trays with glass bowls, seat cushions, songbooks, fans, wooden dogs, and a hillbilly figure cut out of plywood with "Grand Ole Opry" stamped on it. Soon he began selling concessions, mostly soft drinks and hot dogs, to crowds waiting in line for *Opry* tickets.

When people look at the history of country music some only look at the music and the artists, but for those inside the industry the history is filled with stories of key executive decisions, business developments, and conflicts between key executives. Some of the key executives during the World War II period at WSM (1941–1945) were George D. Hay, Harry Stone, Jack Stapp, Jim Denny, Jack DeWitt, and National Life president Edwin Craig. The decisions and personal conflicts among these six men played a major role in the history of Nashville emerging as the center for country music in the decade after World War II.

COWBOYS AND HILLBILLIES

At the end of the 1930s the singing cowboys were still going strong. In 1938, Gene Autry starred in six movies, Tex Ritter in eight, and Roy Rogers in four. That year the *Motion Picture Herald* named Gene Autry the number 1 movie cowboy; William Boyd (Hopalong Cassidy) was a close second, while Tex Ritter was ninth, Roy Rogers 13, and John Wayne number 18.

The image of country music was divided between hillbillies, or mountaineers, and cowboys. The singing cowboys seemed to be winning, but the movie industry kept putting out "hillbilly" movies as well, reinforcing the stereotype that most country musicians wanted to escape.

During the 1930s movies that featured the hillbilly image of rural people included *Kentucky Kernels* (1934); the animated movies *Hill Billys* (1935), *When I Yoo Hoo* (1936), and *A Feud There Was* (1938); *Musical Mountaineers* (1939), *Naughty Neighbors* (1939), and *Kentucky Moonshine* (1938). Lum and Abner starred in *Dreaming Out Loud, Bashful Bachelor, So This is Washington,* and *Goin' to Town;* the Weaver Brothers and Elviry starred in 13 movies. On the comics of the newspapers were Al Capp's *Li'l Abner* and Billy De Beck's *Snuffy Smith*.

HILLBILLIES

Country performers as a whole disliked being called "hillbillies" and having the mainstream entertainment industry look down their noses at them. In an interview, performer Bob Atcher stated, "We are not hill billies in the sense in which the term is used. We play mountain music as it should be played, without distortion. We inject musicianship into the presentations. And I think that makes a difference."[8]

Author Charles Wolfe quotes John Cohen, who states, "The mountain people are sensitive to and aware of the stereotype applied to them by the national press—and they resent it. At the same time, they are made to feel inadequate before the sophisticated luxuries which bombard them in national advertisements and they are losing pride in their local traditions."[9]

On the other side was the "establishment," who disliked any connections to early country music. Ned Smith, editor of Fairmont (West Virginia) *Times* wrote in an editorial, "Hill billy music is one of the worst nuisances a free people ever were subjected to.... This is the imposition upon our people of the stigma of being the Hill Billy state, and if the name of West Virginia is mentioned, it is immediately associated with hill billy music and a suggestion of a social inferiority which constitutes nothing short of libel upon the name of the state."[10]

Autry and the other movie singing cowboys had enhanced the look of movie cowboys by having custom made outfits done by Nathan Turk in Hollywood. Turk and Nudie Cohen added flash and pizzazz to the cowboy look, enhancing it with elaborate designs and embroidery. This look influenced country performers, who increasingly dressed like the singing cowboy stars during the 1930s. Although the *Grand Ole Opry* in Nashville and the *National Barn Dance* in Chicago initially promoted the "mountaineer" image for country performers, increasingly even performers on these shows adapted cowboy outfits.

RADIO SHOWS

In California in 1938 the Sons of the Pioneers began a syndicated radio show, *Sunshine Ranch,* from KNX that broadcast over the Mutual Broadcasting System. Stuart Hamblen still had his *Lucky Stars* program on KFWB. In Oklahoma, Bob Wills and the Texas Playboys continued to perform on KVOO in Tulsa.

On the border station, XERA, the Carter Family began broadcasting and Maybelle's daughters performed with the group. But Dr. John R. Brinkley's heyday in border radio was coming to a close. In 1939 he sold XEAW to Carr Collins, owner of Crazy Water Crystals; that same year Brinkley sued the American Medical Association over the AMA's complaints about his dubious medical cures. Brinkley lost the suit, patients began to sue him for malpractice, the IRS hit him for back taxes, and the Mexican government confiscated his radio stations. Thus began the fall of the Brinkley empire.

In 1938 the Monroe Brothers recorded "Little Joe" and "A Beautiful Life," then broke up; Charlie formed a band, the Kentucky Pardners, and Bill Monroe formed his own group, The Bluegrass Boys, named after his native state, that played string band music with a hard, driving beat.

On February 5, 1938, Roy Acuff joined the *Grand Ole Opry,* singing his hit, "The Great Speckled Bird." The name of his band was changed from the Crazy Tennesseans to the Smoky Mountain Boys, and Harry and David Stone encouraged him to do "Wabash Cannon Ball." In 1938 the Delmore Brothers left the *Grand Ole Opry* and in 1939 the Binkley Brothers and Dixie

Clodhoppers left the show; the latter group was replaced in October 1939 by Bill Monroe and the Bluegrass Boys.

Red Foley joined the NBC network show, *Avalon Time,* hosted by Red Skelton, in 1939. This made him one of the first country stars to have regular network exposure on his own, rather than as part of a barn dance.

In California, the Maddox Brothers and Rose won a talent contest at the California State Fair and for their prize received a two-year contract to perform on KFBK in Sacramento, performing on the McClatchy Broadcasting network. An Oklahoma City group, The Bell Boys, comprised of Johnny Bond and Jimmy Wakely, moved to Hollywood and appeared in a Roy Rogers movie, *Saga of Death Valley.* They later went to work with Gene Autry, doing personal appearances.

In Texas, Foy Willing joined the western group, Lew Preston and the Men of the Range, at KFJZ in Fort Worth, the flagship station of the Texas State Network. In San Angelo, Ernest Tubb had his tonsils out; this lowered his voice and eliminated the Rodgers yodel he had perfected. From this time on he had to develop his own style instead of copying Rodgers.

The Rouse Brothers, performing at the Village Barn in New York, recorded a song they had written called "South Florida Blues," which was later renamed "Orange Blossom Special." Late in 1939 Woody Guthrie moved to New York City and became active in the social protest song movement; he also recorded for RCA Victor and the Library of Congress. During the 1930s he wrote "Philadelphia Lawyer," "So Long, It's Been Good to Know You," and "This Land Is Your Land."

In Chicago, Louise Massey and the Westerners starred on NBC's *Plantation Party.* On KVOO in Tulsa, *The Saddle Mountain Roundup* began. In 1939 Clayton McMichen left the Georgia Wildcats and moved to Louisville, where he worked on WHAS with a group that combined jazz and pop with country.

Rex Griffin had emerged as a major country recording artist, singing "Everybody's Tryin' to Be My Baby" (later adopted by Carl Perkins), "My Hillbilly Baby," and "The Last Letter." On his last session for Decca, September 25, 1939, he recorded "Lovesick Blues," which Hank Williams later copied nearly note for note.

On September 13, 1939, the first recording of the song "You Are My Sunshine" was done by the Rice Brothers; Paul Rice had written the song in 1937 although Jimmy Davis was later listed as the songwriter and collected the royalties. That same year, Scotty Wiseman recorded "Mountain Dew," a song he co-wrote with Bascom Lamar Lunsford.

The first appearance of the character "Minnie Pearl," created by a young performer and teacher named Sarah Ophelia Colley, was in April 1939 at the Highland Park Hotel in Aiken, South Carolina. In July 1939 the *Grand Ole Opry* moved to the War Memorial Auditorium in downtown Nashville.

In the summer and early fall of 1939, Gene Autry made a triumphant tour of the British Isles; in Dublin he was serenaded by 200,000 people outside his hotel. William Wrigley was there watching it all; he had been looking for a way to promote his chewing gum company and decided to sponsor a program by Autry.

On November 4, 1939, *The Renfro Valley Barn Dance* finally came home to Renfro Valley, Kentucky, 50 miles south of Lexington, after stints in Cincinnati and Dayton, Ohio. The show was broadcast over WHAS in Louisville and fed to the NBC network. The show advertised itself as "clean fun on Saturday night you won't be ashamed of on Sunday." Performers included Red Foley, Whitey Ford (the Duke of Paducah), Homer and Jethro, fiddler Slim Miller, Margaret Lillie (Aunt Idy) and Gene "Honey Gal" Cobb, Lily May Ledford's Coon Creek Girls, the Range Riders, and the Holden Brothers. John Lair continued to distance himself from the trend of country singers wearing western clothes. He renamed the Range Riders the Mountain Rangers and distanced himself from the "hillbilly" image as well, insisting the performers and audience were "home folks."

Guitarist Merle Travis began performing, influenced heavily by Mose Rager and Ike Everly's finger picking style, which they had learned from Kennedy Jones, who in turn had learned from Arnold Schultz in the 1920s. This "Travis-picking" with his thumb and forefinger allowed the guitarist to play the melody, harmony, rhythm, and bass simultaneously. A young man named Chet Atkins heard Travis on the radio and this influenced his style as he learned to play the guitar. However, instead of using just the forefinger, Atkins used all of his fingers (he thought that was how Travis got his sound), which led to the development of the "Chet Atkins style" of guitar playing.

The pedal steel guitar was developed in 1939 by Alvino Rey, pop steel guitarist and leader of a big band, who teamed with machinist John Moore to design a new type of electric steel guitar with pedals and a mechanical system able to alter various string pitches. Prior to this time, there were only "lap" steels. Gibson introduced this as the electaharp.

The Great Depression in the United States took its toll on country music; record sales decreased by 94 percent and phonograph sales by 96 percent. Although sales of country recordings remained respectable throughout the Depression, a number of recordings were unissued. This meant that fewer country recordings were made available to be heard during the 1930s, which curbed the development of country music and stifled its growth. The sound of country music from the South was "frozen" throughout the decade. However, the growth and development of the sound of country music did evolve through the songs from the singing cowboys, mostly written by Tin Pan Alley songwriters, and western swing, developed in Texas and Oklahoma.

4

Country Music in the 1940s

1940–1941

Country music was popular in the movies in 1940; Gene Autry starred in six singing westerns, Roy Rogers in seven, and Tex Ritter in eight. Also in 1940 was the movie *Grand Ole Opry,* starring the Weaver Brothers and Elviry which featured performances by Roy Acuff, Uncle Dave Macon, and Judge George D. Hay.

On January 7, 1940, *The Melody Ranch* program, starring Gene Autry, began airing over CBS on Sunday nights. The half-hour show featured songs by Autry and comedy was supplied by Pat Buttram as Autry's sidekick. There was also a 10-minute adventure story. Autry used "Back in the Saddle Again" as his theme song for the program sponsored by Wrigley's Doublemint gum. Autry was a popular draw in personal appearances that year as well, playing to sold-out rodeos in Madison Square Garden and the Boston Gardens.

In 1941 there were close to 400,000 jukeboxes in operation, and they purchased most of the country music recordings released.

At *The National Barn Dance* in Chicago, the star was Red Foley, billed as "The Sweet Singer of Songs of the Hills and Plains," who had a hit that year with "Old Shep." At KMOX, the 50,000 watt station in St. Louis, was "Cousin Emmy," who became one of the top country radio acts. In 1941 Ernest Tubb's radio program was sponsored by Universal Mills, maker of Gold Chain flour, so he became the Gold Chain Troubadour; that same year he recorded his biggest hit, "I'm Walking the Floor Over You" and joined the *Grand Ole Opry* in Nashville. Minnie Pearl and the Bailes Brothers also joined the Opry that year, but the Opry fired African-American harmonica player DeFord Bailey, who was dubbed "The Harmonica Wizard" and starred on that show.

Jimmy Davis had his biggest hit, "You Are My Sunshine," then Gene Autry and Bing Crosby also released it and it became a hit for them as well. Davis recorded the song on February 4; he and guitarist Charles Mitchell purchased it from Paul Rice, whose group had first recorded the song in 1939.

Country music was popular with live audiences; in 1941 promoter Oscar Davis promoted nine shows featuring Roy Acuff, the Hoosier Hot Shots, and Ernest Tubb and made a reported $100,000. The Grand Ole Opry sponsored tent shows headlined by Jamup and Honey, Roy Acuff, and Bill Monroe.

In 1941 the Carter Family broke up and stopped recording; Sara divorced A.P. in 1932, then later married his cousin and moved to California. A.P. went back to Maces Springs but Maybelle and her daughters continued to perform. That same year the Mexican government confiscated XERA and tried to confiscate XEAW, but owner Carr Collins moved the equipment into Texas before the Mexican authorities arrived.

COUNTRY MUSIC DURING WORLD WAR II

Life changed in the United States on Sunday, December 7, 1941, when the Japanese attacked Pearl Harbor; the next day President Franklin Roosevelt declared war on Japan and by the end of that week war had also been declared on Germany.

Gene Autry enlisted in the Army Air Corps and was inducted on the air during a *Melody Ranch* show in July 1942. He continued to broadcast his *Melody Ranch* show from various bases where he was stationed while training as a pilot until he was sent overseas. With Autry in the service, Republic Studios decided to promote Roy Rogers with a major publicity and promotional campaign. He was crowned "King of the Cowboys" and a movie by that title starring Rogers was released. He began to play a character named "Roy Rogers" and more songs were included in his films, making them more like Autry's. Lavish production numbers were incorporated into the films because studio head Herbert J. Yates had seen the musical *Oklahoma* in New York. In effect, Rogers's pictures during World War II became western musicals instead of cowboy movies with some singing.

The budget for the Roy Rogers movies was increased during the war years, and the movies were marketed to the "A" theaters in major cities, particularly in the South and Midwest, rather than the "B" movie houses that were primarily in small towns and rural areas. Hollywood also continued to turn out "hillbilly" movies, releasing *Joan of Ozark* starring Judy Canova. Two country artists entered the movies in 1942; Ernest Tubb appeared in *Fighting Buckaroo* and *Riding West* while Jimmy Davis was in *Strictly in the Groove*.

A number of war songs were recorded and/or released in 1942: "Get Your Gun and Come Along (We're Fixin' to Kill a Skunk)," "Mussolini's Letter to Hitler," "Hitler's Reply to Mussolini," "It's Just a Matter of Time," and "Plain Talk," all written and recorded by Carson Robison. On March 19, 1942, Elton Britt recorded "There's a Star Spangled Banner Waving

Somewhere" for Bluebird in New York and it became one of the two biggest country recordings during World War II. The other major country hit during World War II was "Pistol Packin' Mama," recorded by Al Dexter a day later on the other side of the country, in Hollywood for Columbia. Both of these songs were covered by pop acts.

Gasoline and tire shortages meant that most musicians could not do personal appearances during World War II; it also stopped crowds from coming to shows. Additionally, a number of musicians were drafted or enlisted, forcing the breakup of bands.

A number of country performers served in World War II: Archie Campbell, Rod Brasfield, Sons of the Pioneers members Lloyd Perryman and Pat Brady (who served with Patton's Third Army in Europe), Jack Anglin, Lawton Williams, the York Brothers, fiddler Tommy Jackson, dobro player Clell Sumney, Redd Stewart, John Sullivan (with Lonzo and Oscar), Slim Whitman, George Gobel, steel guitarist Leon McAuliff, Lightnin' Chance, Bob Wills's singer Tommy Duncan, Ken Curtis, the Delmore Brothers, Homer Haynes and Jethro Burns (Homer and Jethro) all served. Future country artists who joined the armed services included Merle Travis, Marty Robbins, Freddie Hart, fiddler Howdy Forrester, and Jack Shook with the Missouri Mountaineers.

Among the bands that broke up during World War II were the Maddox Brothers and Rose, the Light Crust Doughboys, the Swift Jewel Cowboys, and Bob Skyles and His Skyrockets. Vernon Dalhart worked as a factory night watchman; the career of the singer who had country music's first million selling record in the 1920s had ended by World War II.

Country music was popular on the radio during World War II; the *Grand Ole Opry* was broadcast over the NBC network and attracted about 3,000 fans to each performance; the *Renfro Valley Barn Dance* attracted about 5,000 to its shows each Saturday night. However, the *Wheeling Jamboree* at WWVA moved to a studio and did not perform for a live audience during World War II; by this time WWVA had become a 50,000 watt station. At the *Hollywood Barn Dance,* Foy Willing and the Riders of the Purple Sage and the Jimmy Wakely Trio performed while Stuart Hamblen continued his *Lucky Stars* program on KFWB in Los Angeles. In New York, Esmereldy, "The Streamlined Hillbilly," hosted her own radio show on WNBC and was a regular on NBC's *Mirth and Madness.*

In San Antonio, Dr. John R. Brinkley, former king of border radio, died just before he was scheduled to stand trial for mail fraud.

In addition to "Star Spangled Banner Waving Somewhere" by Elton Britt (which reportedly sold over four million copies) and "Pistol Packin' Mama" by Al Dexter, other big country hits during World War II were "Wreck on the Highway" b/w "Fireball Mail" by Roy Acuff and "Born to Lose" b/w "No Letter Today" by Ted Daffan.

The sound that dominated country music came out of California with the western swing bands led by Bob Wills and Spade Cooley. Wills moved to

California from Tulsa in 1942 and began performing in ballrooms in the Los Angeles area. In Los Angeles a popular nightclub, the Riverside Rancho, was established on Riverside Drive, near Griffith Park. Owned by Kay and Lou DeRhoda, it had a 10,000-square-foot dance floor, three bars, an upstairs dining room, and dressing facilities. It soon became the hottest spot in Los Angeles for country music. Beginning in 1942 promoter Bert "Foreman" Phillips put his two bands, led by Bill "Happy" Perryman and Spade Cooley, in the club. Phillips began swing shift dances at the Venice Pier Ballroom in the summer of 1942 to accommodate defense workers. He also held dances in the Santa Monica Ballroom, the Town Hall Ballroom in Compton, and the Plantation in Culver City; an average of 5,000–7,000 people attended these all night dances. The top act to emerge from these ballroom dances was Spade Cooley, whose western swing group ran head to head in popularity with Bob Wills and His Texas Playboys.

Cooley had been a member of Jimmy Wakely's group before Phillips made him the band leader at the Venice Pier Ballroom. Cooley's group featured vocalists Tex Williams and Deuce Spriggins, steel guitarists Joaquin Murphey and Noel Boggs, and guitarist Smokey Rogers. This group first popularized the term "western swing" and played more like an orchestra than a group based on Texas fiddling. The band dressed in matching outfits and had a lush sound, akin to the best Big Bands of the era, while doing country songs.

FRED ROSE

When Gene Autry enlisted in the Army Air Corps in World War II, Fred Rose was out of a job. He had written a number of songs for Autry and other singing cowboys but decided to move back to Nashville in mid-1942 rather than stay in Hollywood because his wife wanted to return home. Rose was popular at WSM and the *Opry* and quickly landed an afternoon show on the radio station. He was approached by Roy Acuff about starting a publishing company because Acuff wanted to keep the rights to his songs and because the songbook business was extremely profitable, but also a burden—he needed someone to handle that part of his business. Acuff reportedly earned over $200,000 in 1942.

Fred Rose was an ASCAP songwriter with connections in New York, Chicago, and Hollywood. He was also a unique individual who had the talent to compose songs quickly on whatever topic and in whatever mood was needed. He thrived as an editor and talent scout and was an unselfish man who willingly helped other songwriters with their work. He was scrupulously honest, a direct result of his religion, Christian Science, which he practiced. Rose held himself to the highest ethical standards and when he went into business he treated other songwriters fairly and honestly.

The Acuff-Rose Publishing Company was officially incorporated on October 13, 1942, and because of the unique talents of Rose it soon had songs recorded by Opry acts, including Acuff. For startup capital the company had $25,000 from Acuff (which was never touched) and $2,500 from BMI, a new performance rights organization formed by broadcasters which needed new publishing companies to supply songs and catch up with the 25-year head start from ASCAP. BMI practiced an open door policy with writers; any songwriter could join. This meant that for the first time country music had access to the monies derived from airplay on radio and live performances.

Fred Rose was in a unique position. He knew the people at WSM and the Opry, he had learned about the market for country music—and the money involved—through his work with Autry and the singing cowboys in the movies, and he was a pop songwriter who came to Nashville as country music was changing from a folk-based music into a major commercial music. Rose played a major role, introducing the pop song format with country topics to replace the folk song format. This had already been done with western music, most of which was composed by Tin Pan Alley writers who used pop song structures with western themes. Fred Rose took that same process to Nashville and applied it to southern-based country music.

The Camel Caravan was a group of *Opry* performers led by Pee Wee King's group, managed by J.L. Frank, that performed for servicemen. They started a tour in November 1941—before Pearl Harbor was bombed—and by the time the Camel Caravan tour ended at Christmas 1942, the troupe had traveled over 50,000 miles, performed 175 shows in 19 states at 68 army camps, hospitals, air fields, and naval and marine bases. In March 1942 it left the United States and performed in the Panama Canal zone. When it was all over, the Camel Caravan had done as much as anything to spread country music all over the United States to servicemen. It had also done a great deal for Eddy Arnold, who gained a wealth of experience and national exposure as he traveled across the country and performed for a wide variety of audiences. When Arnold returned to Nashville he went into the office of Harry Stone, general manager of WSM, and told him he wanted to go out on his own. Stone agreed to find work for Arnold, put him on the *Opry,* and gave him daily radio shows. Arnold left the Golden West Cowboys and began his solo career in early 1943.

Although groups were limited in touring, those that could tour did well; Bill Monroe toured with Opry tent shows and reportedly grossed $200,000 a year.

Due to the large number of men drafted, female singers achieved popularity during World War II. In California, Bob Wills added his first female vocalist, Laura Lee, daughter of Tex Owens. In New York, Rosalie Allen joined Denver Darling's Swing Billies cowboy troupe.

In Nashville, Ernest Tubb joined the *Grand Ole Opry* in February, after debating whether to move to Hollywood, and on June 5 the *Opry* moved to the Ryman Auditorium after state authorities objected to the chewing gum found under the seats at the Tennessee War Memorial Auditorium. Les Paul moved to Los Angeles where his future wife, Mary Ford, was a western vocalist on KXLA's *Dinner Bell Round-Up Time.*

A major change occurred for the "hillbilly" and "race" record industries in 1944 when *Billboard* and *Cashbox* began listing the top ten records in each genre weekly. The "Folk" (as the country charts were labeled) and "Race" charts provided pop vocalists with new material outside the mainstream.

Billboard was a little murky on exactly what constituted folk, the first number 1 on the charts was "Pistol Packin' Mama" by Bing Crosby and the Andrews Sisters, which held that position for 5 weeks. The next song to reach number 1 was Al Dexter's version of "Pistol Packin' Mama," then rhythm and blues band leader Louis Jordan hit number 1 with "Ration Blues." Other number 1 songs that year were "Rosalita" by Al Dexter, "They Took the Stars Out of Heaven" by Floyd Tillman, "So Long, Pal" and "Too Late to Worry, Too Blue to Cry" by Al Dexter, "Straighten Up and Fly Right" by The King Cole Trio," "Is You Is or Is You Ain't (Ma Baby)" by Louis Jordan, "Soldier's Last Letter" by Ernest Tubb, "Smoke on the Water" by Red Foley," and "I'm Wastin' My Tears on You" by Tex Ritter.

Billboard published a story on folk shows, spotlighting the *Renfro Valley Barn Dance,* stating the show managed to keep two touring shows on the road, averaging about $5,000 in revenue each, despite wartime shortages. At the Chicago Rodeo, Red Foley attracted 210,000 people to Soldier's Field over a two-day period.

Dale Evans first appeared with Roy Rogers in 1944 in *The Cowboy and the Senorita,* the first of 20 films they did together. On November 21, 1944, Roy Rogers began his own network radio program, *The Roy Rogers Show,* sponsored by Goodyear which appeared on the Mutual network on Tuesday evenings. The show co-starred Bob Nolan and the Sons of the Pioneers, female vocalist Pat Friday, Perry Botkin and his band, and announcer Vern Smith. The showed ended in late spring 1945 when the sponsor, Goodyear, did not pick up its option. In November 1946, Rogers's wife died after giving birth to their third child. A little over a year later, on December 31, 1947, Roy Rogers and Dale Evans married.

Although country music was popular during World War II, there was no country singer during World War II to rival Frank Sinatra, called "Swoonatra," "The Voice," and the "King of Swoon," who performed at the Paramount in New York while 10,000 teenage girls (called bobby soxers) screamed for tickets, held back by 700 policemen called in to keep order.

Country singer Jimmy Davis was elected governor of Louisiana in 1944; he also appeared in the movie *Cyclone Prairie Ramblers.* Eddie Dean became a singing cowboy in the movies while Roy Rogers remained the top western star when Gene Autry was in the Army Air Corps flying cargo planes. At Capitol Records, formed in April 1942, Lee Gillette was hired to head country

A&R; he signed a number of West Coast country acts, including Tex Williams, Jack Guthrie, Merle Travis, Jimmy Wakely, and Tennessee Ernie Ford.

In 1944, Cliffie Stone started the *Dinner Bell Round-Up* on KPAS (later KXLA) in Pasadena, California, as well as a production company and Lariat Records. In Chicago, Wilma Lee and Stoney Cooper lost their jobs at WJJD when the station decided to just play phonograph records. The decision came after the musicians union demanded that the station double its staff of musicians and play no recordings.

V-DISCS

Although American recordings were sold abroad before World War II—there are examples of songs, musicals, and artists having an international impact—it was this war that made American music truly international. Ironically, it did not come from the American record labels—who could not record from May 1942 until the end of 1944 due to a strike from the American Federation of Musicians—but from V-Discs, sent abroad to American servicemen during the war.

As part of the military buildup in the United States before it entered the war, a Morale Branch was created in July 1940 for the purpose of building the morale of soldiers who were away from home. In March 1942 this section was renamed the Special Services Division; in July the V-Disc Program where popular music was sent to troops was initiated. The first V-Discs were issued in October 1943.

Musically, the V-Discs were dominated by popular music with big bands and vocalists supplying the bulk of the offerings. Bing Crosby, the Glenn Miller group, Duke Ellington's orchestra, and others heard regularly on network radio were the most popular choices for V-Discs. Country music was represented, but it was a distinct minority. In the first V-Discs sent in October 1943, there were two songs from Gene Autry, "You'll Be Sorry" and "Goodbye, Little Darlin'," two cowboy songs, "Home on the Range" and "Take Me Back to My Boots and Saddle" by John Charles Thomas, and "Pistol Packin' Mama" from Al Dexter. The next month there were four songs from Elton Britt, "There's a Star Spangled Banner Waving Somewhere," "Buddy Boy," "When the Roses Bloom Again," and "I Hung My Head and Cried."

In December 1943 there were three songs from Texas Jim Robertson: "Red River Valley," "Ridin' Old Paint," and "In Texas for the Round-Up in the Spring." This emphasis on cowboy songs during the first year of the V-Discs reflected the popularity of the singing cowboys from the movies. These movies were shown in Europe before World War II.

In January 1944 there was a V-Disc of Bob Wills and His Texas Playboys doing "San Antonio Rose" and "New San Antonio Rose" and Texas artist Bill Boyd doing "The Train Song." In February 1944 there was a V-Disc of

Roy Acuff singing "The Great Speckled Bird" and "Low and Lonely." The following month, March 1944, there was another Acuff offering, "Pins and Needles," as well as Carson Robinson doing two songs, "1944 Nursery Rhymes" and "The Charms of the City Ain't For Me." That same month there was a recording by Bing Crosby singing "Ridin' Herd on a Cloud."

The importance of Bing Crosby to country music has often been overlooked; however, it was Crosby who recorded a number of country songs and helped establish country music as a legitimate source of material. Particularly during World War II, Crosby used material originally recorded by country artists and written by country writers; further, he did not look down his nose at the material or thumb his nose in a condescending manner. For Bing Crosby these were good, solid songs, and pop music audiences accepted them as such. For those reasons, Bing Crosby provided an invaluable service to the country music industry, giving it, in a sense, his stamp of approval and acknowledging its legitimacy. Other country songs done on V-Disc by Bing Crosby include "The Last Round-Up," "You Are My Sunshine," a medley of "I'm an Old Cowhand" and "I Can't Escape from You," a medley of "Empty Saddles" and "Mr. Paganini," "Sioux City Sue" and "On the Sunny Side of the Street."

In April 1944, Wade Mainer released "Sparkling Blue Eyes" and Bill Boyd released "New Steel Guitar Rag" on V-Discs. There were no country releases in May or June but in July 1944, there were V-Discs of Gene Autry singing "After Tomorrow" and "It Makes No Difference Now" and Ted Daffan's Texans performing "No Letter Today" and "Born to Lose." The August 1944 V-Discs also did not contain any country recordings but in September there was a release of the Light Crust Doughboys performing "Bartender's Daughter" and "The Little Bar-Fly." In October there was "Salt Water Cowboy" by Barry Wood; in November there were no country V-Discs, and in December there were two songs by Bob Wills and His Texas Playboys, "Miss Molly" and "Home in San Antone."

In 1945 there were no country V-Discs in January or February but in March there were two songs by folksinger Josh White, "Cottoneyed Joe" and "One Meat Ball" and two songs by Al Dexter, "Rosalita" and "So Long Pal." In April there were "Hoe Downs" by the Cactus Cowboys and in May there were V-Discs of Burl Ives doing "Big Rock Candy Mountain" and "Blue Tail Fly"; Susan Reed, a folk singer from Asheville, North Carolina, who appeared at Cafe Society Uptown and Downtown in New York 1945–1946, doing "I Know My Love," "Green Sleeves," "Black Black Black," and "I Know Where I'm Going"; and the Light Crust Doughboys performing "Sweet Sally" and "Zip Zip Zipper."

In June 1945, there were V-Discs by the Hoosier Hot Shots doing "A Sentimental Gentleman from Georgia" and "Is It True What They Say About Dixie" and Ted Daffan performing "Bluest Blues" and "Look Who's Talkin'." In July there were releases of Elton Britt singing "Someday You'll

Want Me" and "I'm a Convict with Old Glory in My Heart," and in August a release by The Korn Kobblers, a novelty group that appeared at Rogers Corners Club in New York, performing "Sylvia" and "Pollywolly Dooddle." There were no country releases on V-Discs during the rest of 1945, but in December there was a V-Disc of folksinger Josh White performing "The Riddle Song" and "The House I Live In."

In addition to the V-Disc program, the Armed Forces Radio Service was created during World War II and used transcriptions and shortwave broadcasts to provide over 50 hours of programming each week, and the United Service Organization (USO) was created and sponsored tours of performers who entertained troops.

COUNTRY MUSIC AFTER WORLD WAR II

At the end of World War II country music was headed in five different musical directions. The most commercially popular was western swing, led by the groups of Bob Wills and His Texas Playboys and Spade Cooley. This was the big band sound in country music. Next was the Singing Cowboys in the movies. Gene Autry, Roy Rogers, Tex Ritter, and the Sons of the Pioneers were all still popular at the end of World War II on the silver screen, and they were all producing hit records, both with western themes and more pop-oriented topics. These two types of country music were both based in California.

The third type of country music was what later became known as bluegrass. The person acknowledged as the founder of bluegrass is Bill Monroe whose band, The Bluegrass Boys, created a hard driving, string band sound. The defining sound of bluegrass today is the five string banjo played in the "three-finger" or "Scruggs" style that was popularized by Earl Scruggs, who joined Monroe's band in Nashville at the end of 1945. Scruggs and Monroe's lead singer, Lester Flatt, split off after a few years and formed Flatt and Scruggs and the Foggy Mountain Boys, which became the most commercially successful bluegrass group in the 1950s.

Bluegrass evolved into a separate genre under the country music umbrella as the twentieth century progressed. The sound of bluegrass remained essentially unchanged as it stayed true to its musical roots but was never as commercially successful as the mainstream country music that developed.

The fourth type of sound in country music was the honky tonk sound, later referred to as traditional country music that came out of the bars of Texas where people came on the weekends to drink and dance. Led by Texas artists such as Ernest Tubb, Ted Daffan, and Al Dexter, this music became a benchmark for country music in the coming years as commercial country music increasingly moved in a pop-oriented direction until it lost its core audience. At that point, country music always returned to this "traditional" sound in order to reestablish its working class roots and recapture its core audience.

The fifth type of country music was the type of country music that prevailed throughout the twentieth and twenty-first centuries. This is the pop-oriented country music that is influenced by the pop market as it seeks to capture a larger, nontraditional audience. The leading proponent of this pop-oriented country at the end of World War II was Red Foley, although Gene Autry moved in this direction as well. By the end of the 1940s Eddy Arnold was the most commercially successful country artist and his recordings were in this country-pop vein.

In 1946, the year after the War, there were eight million records sold; country music accounted for 13.2 percent of sales—topped only by "popular" with 50 percent and classical with 18.9 percent.[1] The 550,000 jukeboxes, which before the war accounted for most of the sales of country records, still accounted for a significant amount of sales but consumers increasingly purchased country records on 78 rpm discs. Part of the reason for increased country record sales to consumers was the exposure country music received from disc jockeys on local radio shows, barn dances, on network radio shows, and songs heard on jukeboxes.

There was high employment during World War II in the defense-based economy and people made money they could not spend because of the rationing of goods, the limited availability of consumer items, and the heavy encouragement of savings by the government through War Bond drives to finance the war. The pent up savings and demand when the war ended in 1945 resulted in a huge number of radio sets sold in 1946–1947. By the end of this two-year period 93 percent of American households owned a radio. But 1947 saw the introduction of television to American consumers; at a time when radio was at the height of its popularity, TV made its first inroads to replace it as the dominate mass medium in the United States.

In a 1946 poll of record label A&R men, Chicago was named as the best place to find country musicians; the A&R men considered Chicago the hub of the hillbilly side of the music business because WLS and *The National Barn Dance* had established Chicago as a country music center. Chicago was also a center of pop music with record label offices, recording studios and popular venues for pop and jazz musicians. There were also recording studios in Dallas, Cincinnati, and Los Angeles where country acts recorded.

In 1946 *The National Barn Dance* lost its national sponsor, Alka-Seltzer, and its star singer, Red Foley, who left to join the *Grand Ole Opry* in April, replacing Roy Acuff as host of the NBC network portion of the *Opry* sponsored by Prince Albert tobacco. In May, *The National Barn Dance* lost its NBC connection; by this point they had also lost a number of their top stars although Lulu Belle and Scotty, one of the most popular acts in the history of *The National Barn Dance*, returned to the show after leaving briefly. This was the beginning of the end for Chicago as the capital of country music. After World War II the country music industry was increasingly centered in Nashville.

Roy Acuff left the *Grand Ole Opry* and the *Prince Albert Show* because he was frustrated with the *Opry's* requirement that he return to Nashville every Saturday night to perform on the *Opry*. Saturday nights were the biggest nights for personal appearances and Acuff's popularity kept him in constant demand for appearances—at much higher fees than what the *Opry* paid. So Acuff left and went to the West Coast to tour and appear in movies. There was some dissension and grumbling amongst the *Opry* regulars when the top brass went outside the fold to recruit Red Foley for the network show instead of promoting from within the ranks.

RED FOLEY

Red Foley, born June 17, 1919, in Blue Lick, Kentucky, began his career as vocalist with the Cumberland Ridge Runners on WLS's *National Barn Dance* in the 1930s, then hosted the WLS road shows in the late 1930s and early 1940s. In 1941 he began recording for Decca and his first hit was "Old Shep." Red Foley was more popular with *Opry* audiences than with *Opry* members when he started the *Prince Albert* segment, but the WSM brass knew Foley had network experience; furthermore, the advertising executives with the Prince Albert account wanted Foley and they got him. Foley represented the smooth sound of a country crooner who was popular with city audiences as well as rural customers.

Playing guitar for Foley was Chet Atkins, who worked for Johnny and Jack in Raleigh, North Carolina, before joining Foley at WLS in Chicago. Another guitarist, Hank Garland, was in the Arkansas Cotton Pickers before he left to join Cowboy Copas's band on the *Opry*. Two other guitarists, Billy Byrd and Harold Bradley, taught him the rudiments of jazz. Bradley returned to Nashville after his discharge from the Navy and joined his brother Owen's dance band; he also traveled to Chicago and played on his first recording session for Pee Wee King's Golden West Cowboys. Guitarist Grady Martin replaced Garland in Paul Howard's western swing group, the Arkansas Cotton Pickers. These guitarists were key players in Nashville's studios as the city became a recording center beginning in the late 1940s.

NASHVILLE

The beginning of Nashville's emergence as a major recording center came in 1946 when three engineers at WSM, Aaron Shelton, Carl Jenkins, and George Reynolds, began recording sessions at the radio's studios in the old National Life Building at 7th Avenue N. and Union but soon moved their studio to the Tulane Hotel on Church Street, between 7th and 8th Avenues N. Using a Scully lathe and Ampex recorder, with a mixing board designed by the engineers, the Castle Studio (named because WSM called itself the "Air Castle of the South") did local advertising jingles and recorded radio shows for regional networks but also did sessions for every recording label except RCA, which had an exclusive contract with the National Association of Broadcast Employees and Technicians to provide engineers for their sessions.

The first million-seller recorded in Nashville hit the stores in 1946. "Near You" was written and produced by Nashville big band leader Francis Craig who recorded the song in the newly formed Castle Studio. It was released on Bullet Records, a small independent company formed by Jim Bulleit and remained number 1 on the *Billboard* Pop Chart for 17 consecutive weeks.

HOLLYWOOD

In Hollywood, Roy Rogers starred in eight singing cowboy movies, but Gene Autry only starred in one—a result of his disagreement with Republic, his movie studio. The top moneymaking female at Republic Pictures, Judy Canova, continued to star in hillbilly movies, releasing *Singin' in the Corn* in 1946. *The Roy Rogers Show* debuted on the NBC radio network on Saturday nights in 1946, sponsored by Miles Laboratories. The show featured Bob Nolan and the Sons of the Pioneers, Gabby Hayes, Dale Evans, and Country Washburn and His Orchestra; however, at the end of the season the show was cancelled. *Gene Autry's Melody Ranch* radio show on CBS resumed after the war and remained popular on Sunday evenings.

Spade Cooley fired vocalist Tex Williams in California, and Williams took most of Cooley's band with him, forming the Western Caravan. Tennessee Ernie Ford was discharged from the Air Force in 1946 and settled in San Bernardino, California, then joined KXLA in Pasadena as an announcer before becoming a regular on *Hometown Jamboree*.

BARN DANCES

The *WWVA Jamboree* in Wheeling, West Virginia, had a lineup that included Doc Williams and his Border Riders with Chickie Williams the featured vocalist and William "Hiram Hayseed" Godwin doing comedy. On July 13, 1946, the *Jamboree* began playing for a live audience at the Virginia Theater. Added to the lineup were Hawkshaw Hawkins, Wilma Lee and Stoney Cooper, Roy Scott, and Lee Moore (who was also the all-night DJ).

In September the *Old Dominion Barn Dance* was established in Richmond, Virginia. The Saturday night show was broadcast over 50,000-watt WRVA from the Lyric Theater at Ninth and Broad Streets. The show was organized by C.T. Lucy, general manager of WRVA, who built the show around the Workman family: Sunshine Sue, her husband John, and his brother Sam who were known as Sunshine Sue and the Smiling Rangers.

In Dallas, the *Texas State Barn Dance* was created by radio personality Uncle Gus Foster and club owner Slim McDonald; the show was held in the Sportatorium, where co-producer Ed McLemore held wrestling matches. In Washington, DC, the *Town and Country* show, produced by Connie B. Gay, began on radio.

HANK WILLIAMS

In September 1946 Acuff-Rose signed Hank Williams as a songwriter and publisher Fred Rose soon obtained a recording contract for him.

King Hiram Williams was born September 17, 1923, in Mount Olive, Alabama. Hank's father was confined to a veteran's hospital when Hank was six because of a brain aneurysm, and his mother, a strong, domineering woman, moved the family to Montgomery in 1937. For the next 10 years Hank lived in Montgomery; he formed a band and developed his songwriting and performing skills. Hank had a show on WSFA in Montgomery from July 1941 until August 1942 but was fired for habitual drunkenness—a problem that plagued him his entire life.

During World War II Hank worked at a shipbuilding company in Mobile, Alabama; also during this period he met Audrey Sheppard and the two married in December 1944. Hank met several country performers while he was in Alabama, including Roy Acuff, and in 1943 sold Pee Wee King a song, "(I'm Praying for the Day That) Peace Will Come," for $50. King assigned the song to Acuff-Rose Publishers in December 1943.

In 1945, back in Montgomery, Hank published his first songbook, *Original Songs of Hank Williams,* and began to perform again on WSFA, where he developed a large following. Hank had come to Nashville to audition for the Opry—but was turned down—before he came to Nashville on Saturday, September 14, 1946, to audition his songs for publisher Fred Rose. Rose signed six of Williams's songs, then obtained a recording contract for Williams with a small, New York-based label, Sterling Records. Rose also served as Williams's unofficial manager.

Hank Williams's first recording session occurred on December 11, 1946, when he did "Wealth Won't Save Your Soul," "Calling You," "Never Again," and "When God Comes and Gathers His Jewels." When the year ended Hank Williams was still living and performing in Montgomery, Alabama.

HIT SONGS: 1946

In 1946 there were more divorces recorded than any year in American history up to that time, a result of veterans returning from World War II as changed men, as well as quickie wartime marriages. Since country music articulates the thoughts and feelings of the white working class, this trend was reflected in songs such as "Divorce Me C.O.D." in 1946 by Merle Travis. The fact that there were also a number of unhappy marriages was reflected in songs such as

"One Has My Name (The Other Has My Heart)" by Jimmy Wakely and the first cheating song, "Slippin' Around," written by Texas artist Floyd Tillman and recorded by Jimmy Wakely and Margaret Whiting, which became a huge hit although it was banned on some radio stations.

For some people, the image of country music is cheatin' and drinkin' songs. That image of country music comes originally from the decade after World War II when the white working class was going through divorces, and country music was heard on jukeboxes in bars, although most artists did not record drinking songs because they could not be played on the radio. However, there were a number of songs aimed for the jukebox crowd who gathered in bars during the evenings.

EDDY ARNOLD AND STEVE SHOLES

In 1945 Steve Sholes was released from the Army, where he had worked compiling V-Discs, and rejoined RCA Victor Records. Sholes had first joined Victor as an errand boy in 1929, right after his high school graduation. Sholes was born in Washington, DC, on February 12, 1911, and lived there until he was nine when the family moved to Merchantville, New Jersey. After high school, he attended Rutgers University and continued to work at RCA Victor part time; beginning in 1935 he joined the firm full time and worked first in the factory storeroom of the radio department and then in the sales department at RCA Victor under label president Edward Wallerstein.

Sholes came of age in the Big Band era and played saxophone and clarinet in local bands. This musical background was advantageous when he moved from the radio to the record department in 1936, taking a $25 a week cut in salary to do so. Here, he worked as a sales clerk and was assigned to listen to test pressings (recordings were made direct to disc at this time) to ensure quality control on the records.

Eli Oberstein came from the accounting department at OKeh Records to RCA Victor's sales accounting department through Ralph Peer, but an enmity developed between Oberstein and Peer over Peer's publishing interests and outside income that led to Peer's departure from the company. Oberstein remained and in October 1936 he was promoted to head of the Artists and Repertoire (A&R) Department where he was in charge of signing and recording talent. In this role he traveled the country recording country and blues acts. He also allowed Sholes to record some jazz artists.

The departure of Oberstein left RCA Victor without a strong presence in the country music field. This remained Victor's position until after the war when Steve Sholes rejoined the label and was put in charge of country and blues music.

To be put in charge of hillbilly and race music was not a high honor for a New York record man at the time; the prestige and power were in pop music. The Big Band era was coming to a close and the solo vocalists emerged as major stars after Frank Sinatra exploded as a bobby sox idol in 1943. To be put in charge of hillbilly and race music was the bottom rung in the pecking order for A&R men, and most turned up their noses and barely tolerated it. But Steve Sholes was a rare man; he developed a love and respect for the people in country music as well as for the music itself. His first success was Eddy Arnold.

When Frank Walker signed Eddy Arnold unseen and unheard in 1943, RCA Victor desperately needed a successful country act. Victor had led the way for country music, beginning with Uncle Eck Robertson's fiddle tunes, then Vernon Dalhart, and through the 1930s with Jimmie Rodgers. But it was in danger of being replaced by Columbia, who had Gene Autry, Bob Wills, and Roy Acuff, and Decca, who had Ernest Tubb, Red Foley, and Bill Monroe, as the top country label. Eddy Arnold changed all that.

Arnold had done two recording sessions for Victor—both in Nashville at the WSM studio—before Steve Sholes called him in 1946 and invited him to record in Chicago. Arnold and Sholes chose some songs, among them "That's How Much I Love You" written by Arnold and Wally Fowler. Since country recordings did not use drums at the time and Arnold wanted more "bottom" to his sound, he invited a piano player to come along; this was Owen Bradley's first recording session for a major label. "That's How Much I Love You" was released in late 1946; it soon became apparent that the public loved the singer and the song and it became the first of a string of hits in Eddy Arnold's career.

On May 24, 1947, Eddy Arnold had the number 1 record in the nation with "What Is Life Without Love," which only stayed number 1 for one week. A record by Bob Wills, "Sugar Moon" held the number 1 slot for one week and then "Smoke! Smoke! Smoke! That Cigarette" by Tex Williams reached number 1 and remained in that position for 16 consecutive weeks. This was followed by Eddy Arnold's hit, "I'll Hold You in My Heart (Till I Can Hold You in My Arms)" which reached number 1 on November 1 and remained in that position for 21 weeks, followed by "Anytime," which stayed number 1 for 9 weeks, then "Bouquet of Roses," number 1 for 19 weeks, "Texarkana Baby," number 1 for 3 weeks, "Just a Little Lovin' (Will Go a Long, Long Way)," number 1 for 8 weeks, and then a Jimmy Wakely song, "One Has My Name (The Other Has My Heart)" which stayed number 1 until Arnold's "A Heart Full of Love (For a Handful of Kisses)" became number 1 at the end of 1948. That meant that during those 95 weeks, Eddy Arnold had the number 1 country record for 65 weeks. Further, for 60 consecutive weeks—from November 1, 1947, until November 13, 1948—Eddy Arnold had the number 1 country record in America. His sales were so strong that in 1948 Eddy Arnold outsold the entire Pop Division at RCA Victor. Eddy Arnold was managed by Colonel Tom Parker, who established himself as a manager with strong contacts at RCA Victor Records, Hill and Range Publishing

Company, and the William Morris Agency through his management of Eddy Arnold; he later used these same contacts when he managed Elvis Presley.

THE INTRODUCTION OF TAPE

A great leap in recording technology came at the end of World War II when the head of the Russians Radio Berlin unit showed some Americans a captured German magnetophon in September 1945. This tape machine had 14-inch reels which produced symphonic works on magnetic tape with such fidelity that they could not be distinguished from the actual concert. It was also used for Hitler's speeches, so he could be miles away from where listeners believed he was giving a speech.

The importance of this discovery was not immediately apparent to the recording industry, who felt the future belonged to wire recorders. Sears had one on the market for $169 and some predicted wire recordings would eventually replace records. However, the magnetized wire was fragile, had poor fidelity, and tended to rust—all of which was overlooked at this time. For this reason, recording sessions were direct to disc. This meant that if a mistake was made, the musicians had to start over again from the beginning. There was no tape splicing, overdubbing, or "mixing" after the song was recorded. It all had to be done right on a single take.

Tape technology received its biggest boost from Bing Crosby in 1946. Crosby was negotiating with NBC for his radio show, and wanted to tape record his show, sponsored by Kraft, so the shows could be edited. Also, it would leave him more time to play golf because he could tape several shows at a time, freeing up days for the golf course. NBC objected but ABC accepted the offer. This allowed ABC to repeat the program and saved over-time costs. The other networks soon saw the advantages of taped shows and followed suit.

1947–1949

In 1947 the record industry recorded sales of $214.4 million at retail—which exceeded the 1921 figures for the first time. There were 3.4 million record players produced.

In August 1947, Paul Cohen, who was head of Decca's country division, came to Nashville because his two top selling country stars, Red Foley and Ernest Tubb, were on the *Grand Ole Opry,* and held a recording session at the Castle Studios in the Tulane Hotel. WSM musicians Beasley Smith and Owen Bradley helped Cohen schedule times and musicians. From this time on, Cohen established a practice of recording in Nashville in two- and three-week sessions, with Smith and Bradley helping him. This marked the beginning of regularly scheduled recording sessions by major labels in Nashville.

On September 17 and 18, Ernest Tubb headlined a *Grand Ole Opry* show at Carnegie Hall in New York featuring Minnie Pearl, Radio Dot and Smoky Swann, Rosalie Allen and hosted by emcee George D. Hay. This was one of the last appearances by Hay with the *Opry* group. On October 31 Eddy Arnold headlined a country show at Constitution Hall in Washington, DC, promoted by Connie B. Gay, that featured the Willis Brothers, Minnie Pearl, Rod Brasfield, T. Texas Tyler, Cowboy Copas, and Kitty Wells on the bill. Unlike the Carnegie Hall Show, this was not open to the public—it was an invitation-only affair for congressmen, senators, and other Washington VIPs. The Carnegie Hall and Constitution Hall shows indicated that country music was moving uptown, able to attract an audience in cities whose populations considered themselves cultured and sophisticated.

On April 3, 1948, the *Louisiana Hayride* was first broadcast from 50,000-watt KWKH in Shreveport, Louisiana. That station was owned by a newspaper, the *Shreveport Times,* which was owned by the Ewing family. The commercial manager of the station was former Vagabond member Dean Upson, who secured sponsors with Johnnie and Kyle Bailes working as announcers and talent recruiters. Producer and emcee of the show was Horace Logan, who introduced a lineup of Harmie Smith, Hoot & Curley, Pappy Covington, Tex Grimsley, Johnnie & Jack with Kitty Wells, and the Bailes Brothers that night. In August, Hank Williams made his first appearance on the *Hayride,* then became a member.

In California Roy Rogers starred in seven movies that year and began a radio show on the Mutual network in the fall, sponsored by Quaker Oats on Sunday evenings. Gene Autry starred in only one singing cowboy movie, continued his *Melody Ranch* show on CBS radio sponsored by Wrigley's Doublemint gum, and began a series of tours. These one-night stands featured two-shows a day and demonstrated the appeal of Autry, who was one of the most popular touring acts at that time, consistently selling out shows. Autry's first tour of the year began in January and the fall tour usually ended at the Madison Square Garden and Boston Gardens rodeos. Each performance was a full two-hour show with music interspersed with comedy, rope tricks, acrobats, dog acts, and his horse Champion, who performed tricks.

In 1948 radio was still the dominant mass medium in the United States; by the end of 1948 94.3 percent of American families owned a set. But there were changes at the network level for country music on radio after the war.

By 1945 *The Boone County Jamboree* in Cincinnati had been renamed *The Midwestern Hayride,* and in 1948 it began to be featured on TV. The *Dixie Jamboree* on WBT in Charlotte appeared on the regional CBS network during World War II; it evolved into the *Carolina Hayride* and from 1946 was broadcast over the CBS radio network on Saturday nights.

In the fall of 1948 the *Big D Jamboree* began in Dallas, an outgrowth of the *Texas State Barn Dance* and *Lone Star Jamboree* (established in 1946 and 1947, respectively). The original host for the *Texas State Barn Dance,* KLIF DJ Big Al

Turner, was joined by KRLD's Johnny Hicks, who co-produced the show. Turner was replaced by John Harper. The show featured the Callahan Brothers, Riley Crabtree, and Gene O'Quin; the house band was the Light Crust Doughboys, who were billed as the Country Gentlemen.

On December 18, 1949, the *Hometown Jamboree* premiered at the American Legion Stadium in El Monte, California. Cliffie Stone and Steve Stebbins produced the show each Saturday night under the Americana Corporation umbrella. The show was broadcast on KLAC-TV from 7 to 8 p.m., then a dance followed until 1 a.m. with the 10 to 11 p.m. segment broadcast locally over KXLA radio. The show was an outgrowth of Stone's *Dinner Bell Round-Up* with Molly Bee, Bucky Tibbs, Ferlin Husky, Gene O'Quin, Dallas Frazier, Jonie O'Brien, and Jonell and Glennell McQuaid added to the cast.

Hank Williams had his first number 1 record in 1949, "Lovesick Blues," which, ironically, he did not write. In June he made his debut on the *Grand Ole Opry* and was an instant success. For the next three and a half years his star burned brightly in country music but he was unable to deal with his stardom and his personal life became as dark as his professional life was bright.

Gene Autry's biggest hit came in 1949 but it was not a western song; "Rudolph the Red-Nosed Reindeer" became a number 1 hit in both the pop and country fields thus establishing that song as a Christmas standard.

RADIO AND PUBLISHING

An important reason for the rise in the sales of hillbilly and race records were the disc jockeys, particularly at small radio stations, who grew in stature and importance after World War II. Disc jockeys didn't just cue up records and play them any more, now they made comments about the song or artist, thought about format and pacing, and had special programs for requests, new releases, a single vocalist, or oldies.

Publishing was becoming increasingly important to Nashville because of the increasing power of BMI over ASCAP, who still shunned hillbilly and blues music, and the decline in sheet music sales in the publishing industry. Monies from record sales and radio airplay were becoming the way publishers and songwriters made most of their money. Also, the country music industry was growing and needed new, fresh songs for the increasing number of country recordings released.

COUNTRY MUSIC ON TV: 1948–1955

The era of TV began in 1941 when the Federal Communications Commission authorized the broadcast of commercial television; however, World War II stopped the development of TV for American consumers until the end of the war. On April 13, 1946, the DuMont Television Network went on the air; however, that year only 6,476 sets were produced. In 1947 there were 178,571 sets produced, mostly 10-inch screens that cost from $225–$2,500 plus a $5 antenna installation fee. In 1948, the first full year of TV programming, there were four networks: ABC, CBS, NBC, and DuMont. During the first six months of the year there were 350,000 sets in American homes; Milton Berle became the first TV star with his show, *Texaco Star Theatre.*

There were four shows that featured country music on the networks during prime time (7 to 9 p.m.) in 1948. The first to appear was *Village Barn,* which debuted on May 17 and ran until May 29, 1950, on the NBC network. *Hayloft Hoedown* appeared on the ABC network on Saturday nights beginning July 10 and ending September 18. On September 29 *Kobb's Corner* appeared on the CBS network on Wednesday evenings; this show ran until June 15, 1949. *Saturday Night Jamboree* debuted on December 4 and ran until July 2, 1949, appearing on Saturday nights on the NBC network.

The TV shows were presented in a variety show format. *Village Barn,* which was broadcast from the Village Barn in New York on West 8th Street, featured Pappy Howard and His Tumbleweed Gang, Harry Ranch and His Kernels of Korn, and Bill Long's Ranch Girls. *Hayloft Hoedown* was broadcast from Town Hall in Philadelphia and was only a summer show. The regulars were Elmer Newman, Jack Day, the Murray Sisters, Jesse Rogers, the Stuff Jumpers, Wesley Tuttle, the Ranch Square Dancers, and the Sleepy Hollow Gang. The show was hosted by "Pancake Pete" (Elmer Newman) and was a radio show on WFIL in Philadelphia; it had appeared on the ABC radio network since 1945.

Kobb's Korner was broadcast from Shufflebottom's General Store, USA, (actually, a studio in New York) and starred Stan Fritts and His Korn Kobblers, Hope Emerson, Jo Hurt, and Betty Garde. *Saturday Night Jamboree* was also a New York-based program, emceed by Elton Britt, known for his World War II hit, "There's a Star Spangled Banner Waving Somewhere." Others on the show included Chubby Chuck Roe, Sophrony Garen, Ted Grant, Eddie Howard, John Havens, Edwin Smith, and Gabe Drake. In 1949 Boyd Heath replaced Britt as host.

Important local programs included Pee Wee King's show over WAVE-TV in Louisville and Connie B. Gay's *Radio Ranch* in Washington, DC.

The following year, 1949, was a little better, with the introduction of the *ABC Barn Dance.* This was actually Chicago's *National Barn Dance* on TV. A half hour show on the ABC network, it appeared on Monday nights beginning February 1949 and lasted until November of that year. Emcees were Hal O'Halloran and Jack Stillwell; the Sage Riders were an instrumental quartet and regulars included Lulu Belle and Scotty, Cousin Tifford, the De Zurick Sisters, John Dolce, and Holly Swanson.

Eddy Arnold appeared on Perry Como's NBC pop/variety show on December 10, 1949. Arnold had an appeal that extended beyond country music; his smooth vocals and nonwestern garb appealed to the urban and suburban audience.

In 1950 there were three shows on prime time TV: *Country Style,* which featured a lot of square dancing, *Rhythm Rodeo* and *Windy City Jamboree,* both broadcast from Chicago. At this point country music on TV still had a long way to go; the "country" shows originated from Chicago or New York—because that's where the TV studios were—and were yokel type shows that emphasized rube comedy. But in 1951 the first significant country music show began on TV which became the forerunner for real country music on television.

The *Midwestern Hayride* began on June 16, 1951, on the NBC network; it lasted until September 6, 1959. At first it was broadcast on Saturday night, then Tuesdays; in July 1957 it switched networks, going over to ABC, where it was broadcast either Saturday or Sunday evenings. Hosts for the show were Bill Thall (1951–1954), Bob Shrede (1951), Hugh Cherry (1955–1956), Paul Dixon (1957–1958), and Dean Richards (1959). The regulars included the County Briar Hoppers (1951–1952), Slim King and the Pine Mountain Boys, Zeke Turner, Bonnie Lou Weins (1952–1959), the Midwesterners (1954–1959), and the Hometowners (1957–1959). It was broadcast from either Dayton or Cincinnati, Ohio, and proved to be a summer standby.

The first country music show hosted by a country star was *The Eddy Arnold Show,* which premiered July 14, 1952, on the CBS network. The show appeared for 15 minutes on Mondays, Wednesdays, and Fridays, then moved over to NBC where it appeared on Tuesdays and Thursdays. In April 1956 it became a half-hour show on ABC and stayed on that network until it ended on September 28, 1956.

During the run of Eddy Arnold's show, several other country music shows came on TV. *The Old American Barn Dance* appeared in the summer of 1953; this show, emceed by Bill Bailey, featured artists such as Pee Wee King and Tennessee Ernie Ford. On October 15, 1955, the *Grand Ole Opry* began broadcasting regularly on the ABC network with regulars Carl Smith, Ernest and Justin Tubb, Hank Snow, Minnie Pearl, Chet Atkins, Goldie Hill, Marty Robbins, Rod Brasfield, Cousin Jody, Roy Acuff, June Carter, Jimmy Dickens, and the Louvin Brothers. The show lasted about a year, ending on September 15, 1956.

The presence of television grew dramatically during the 1948–1953 period; in 1948 only 1 percent of American homes had a TV while 50 percent had a TV by the end of 1953.

COUNTRY AND WESTERN

In the July 25, 1949, issue of *Billboard,* the name of the country charts in *Billboard* were changed from "Most Played Juke Box Folk Records" to "Most Played Juke Box Country and Western Records" while the "Best Selling Retail

Folk Records Chart" was changed to "Best Selling Retail Folk (Country and Western) Records." The term "country and western" seemed more appropriate for the genre than "folk." The charts based on jukebox play continued until June 1957, and the "Best Sellers" charts ended in October 1958. The airplay chart, which began in December 1949, ended in October 1958; that month the "Hot C&W Singles" chart began, which determined radio airplay for country songs. The "Hot C&W Singles" chart became the "Hot Country Singles" chart on November 3, 1962, and the genre, which was known as country and western began to be called "country," although many continued to refer to the music as country and western.

NASHVILLE SONGS

In 1950 there were two songs which had a significant impact on the future of Nashville. "Tennessee Waltz" was written by Pee Wee King and Redd Stewart on the back of a match box as the two drove back to Nashville from Texas. "Kentucky Waltz" by Bill Monroe was on the radio and Stewart noted there was no "Tennessee Waltz," so the two wrote one that night in the car.[2] The song was published by Acuff-Rose and originally released in the spring of 1947 by Pee Wee King and His Golden West Cowboys on RCA Victor and reached number 3 on the country charts.

Fred Rose had good connections with New York A&R men, especially Mitch Miller with Mercury Records. Rose sent "Tennessee Waltz" to Miller, who produced the song on Patti Page. The song entered the pop chart on November 18, 1950, and rose to number 1 where it remained for 13 weeks. This song made the pop world aware that Nashville was a "song town" and pop producers began to look at Nashville as a source of songs.

"Chattanoogie Shoeshine Boy" was written by Fred Rose, using the melody to "Darktown Strutters Ball," although the names of Jack Stapp and Harry Stone are listed as the writers. Stapp and Stone were on their way to see Rose when they stopped to get their shoes shined; when they saw Rose, Stapp told him he had a great idea for a song: "Boogie Woogie Shoeshine Boy." Rose wrote the song and put Stapp's and Stone's name on it as a favor, said Stapp, who was program director at WSM.

Owen Bradley had worked with Paul Cohen with Decca for several years, organizing musicians for recording sessions when Cohen came into Nashville. On this particular date, Cohen could not be there so Bradley was in charge of the session. He recorded "Chattanoogie Shoe Shine Boy" (the title was changed at Foley's insistence, according to Stapp, because Foley had good luck with "Tennessee songs" (prior to "Chattanoogie Shoe Shine Boy" Foley had hits with "Tennessee Saturday Night," "Tennessee Border," "Tennessee Polka," "Sunday Down in Tennessee," and "Tennessee Border No. 2").

The song entered the country chart in January 1950 and rose to number 1, where it remained for 13 weeks. It reached number 1 on the pop charts and remained there for 8 weeks. So the year 1950 began and ended with a Nashville song at the top of the pop charts.

The title "Music City U.S.A." was given to Nashville by WSM announcer David Cobb in 1950 as he spun records on WSM, and the first full-time song-writers in Nashville, the husband-wife team of Felice and Boudeleaux Bryant, moved to Nashville in 1950. Boudleaux Bryant was a classical violinist who played with Hank Penny's Radio Cowboys at WSB in Atlanta and then with Gene Steele and His Sunny Southerners in Memphis at WMC. He toured with a jazz group in the summer of 1945 and met Felice Scaduto when the group played in Milwaukee; five days after they met they were married. They began writing songs—Felice loved to write poetry, which became the basis of their songwriting partnership—and their first hit was "Country Boy" by Little Jimmy Dickens in 1949. The song was published by Acuff-Rose and Fred Rose encouraged the Bryants to move to Nashville, which they did. After the move Dickens recorded the Bryants's "I'm Little But I'm Loud," "Take Me As I Am," "Out Behind the Barn," and "Hole in My Pocket" while Carl Smith recorded "Hey, Joe," "Back Up, Buddy," and "It's a Lovely, Lovely World."

Mercury Records, based in Chicago, became the first major label to have an office in Nashville when they hired Dee Kilpatrick in 1950. Kilpatrick did sales, promotion, and A&R for the label; he recorded Johnny Horton, Jimmy Dean, Carl Story, and Bill Carlisle.

5

Country Music in the 1950s

1950

The Singing Cowboys were still making movies on the West Coast in the early 1950s but TV was in the future for Roy Rogers and Gene Autry as both saw the end of the singing cowboy movie era approaching. Each of the singing cowboys had a network radio show as well. At Capitol Records in Los Angeles, Ken Nelson took over the A&R duties for that label while Jim Beck, a studio owner in Dallas, recorded Lefty Frizzell and Ray Price. Hank Williams had three number 1 hits in 1950 ("Long Gone Lonesome Blues," "Why Don't You Love Me," and "Moanin' The Blues") and five other songs that reached the top ten. Hank had the number 1 country song for 19 of the 52 weeks in 1950. Eddy Arnold continued his string of hits with seven in the top ten and made two movies in Hollywood. Hank Snow had his first big hit in 1950, "I'm Moving On," which remained a number 1 record on the country charts for 21 weeks as well as "The Golden Rocket," which also reached number 1 in 1950. Lefty Frizzell had his first number 1 records in 1950, "If You've Got the Money I've Got the Time" and "I Love You A Thousand Ways."

KITTY WELLS

The first female superstar in country music emerged during the early 1950s and paved the way for future female performers in this genre. It all began with a hit song by Hank Thompson, "Wild Side of Life," released in early 1952 and which remained number 1 on the *Billboard* chart for 15 consecutive weeks. Answer songs were popular and a song that spent 15 weeks at number 1 which asserted that a married woman "would never make a wife" because she was too attracted to "the wild side of life" demanded an answer from the female point of view.

A female audience wants a female singer to be a spokesperson for their thoughts, feelings, and concerns; in other words, a female audience wants a female singer to articulate a female point of view. Many female singers want to be appealing to men—to be sexy and desirable—but no woman wants to take her husband or boyfriend to a concert and have him ogle the woman on stage. Kitty Wells was the first female to present a woman's point of view to the female country music audience and that audience felt comfortable with her and rewarded her with their loyalty.

Kitty Wells was not destined to be a controversial figure; the mild-mannered lady was born Muriel Deason in Nashville on August 30, 1919. She came from a musical family; her mother was a gospel singer and her father and uncle were country musicians. Wells dropped out of school to work at a clothing manufacturer but with her two sisters and a cousin also performed on the radio as the Deason Sisters. In 1937, at the age of 19, she married Johnnie Wright and the two performed with Wright's sister, Louise, as Johnnie Wright and the Harmony Girls. In 1939 Wright teamed with Jack Anglin to form Johnnie and Jack. The duo was popular; in 1951 they had top five country hits with "Poison Love" and "Cryin' Heart Blues" and in 1952 had a top ten hit with "Three Ways of Knowing."

Muriel traveled with Johnnie and Jack and performed on their radio shows during the 1940s; during this time Wright began to refer to his wife as "Kitty Wells," which was the name of an old folk song recorded by the Pickard Family. During World War II Johnnie and Jack split but reunited after the war and joined the *Louisiana Hayride* in Shreveport. Kitty recorded for RCA in 1949 and 1950 but had no chart hits. In 1952 Johnnie and Jack joined the *Grand Ole Opry* during a time when "Wild Side of Life" was a huge hit.

Producer Owen Bradley convinced Wells to record the answer song, "It Wasn't God Who Made Honky Tonk Angels" on May 3, 1952; Wells relented because she received $125 for the session. It entered the *Billboard* charts in July and was number 1 for 6 consecutive weeks. The song was controversial and Wells wasn't allowed to sing it on *Grand Ole Opry* broadcasts because the NBC radio network executives felt it was "suggestive." The message in the song was that God didn't make honky tonk angels; instead, "too many times married men think they're still single" that caused "many a good girl to go wrong."

Kitty Wells's career was helped by her ability to tour. It was not deemed proper for a woman to tour with a group of men in those times; she would be considered a loose woman. But Kitty Wells was married to Johnnie Wright so it was perfectly alright for her to tour with his group.

DISC JOCKEY CONVENTION

In November 1953 a number of disc jockeys from around the country came to Nashville to celebrate the *Grand Ole Opry*'s 25th anniversary—or 27th, depending on if you counted from 1925 when the *WSM Barn Dance* was first on the air or 1927 when the show was renamed *Grand Ole Opry*. In Nashville they formed the Country Music Disc Jockeys Association. The *Opry* wanted to keep a distance from this organization and made it clear that the *Opry* and the Association were not linked. However, it was a good business move that eventually helped the *Opry*. First, having all of those country music business people in Nashville helped the Opry Artists Bureau, headed by Jim Denny, make personal contacts with buyers of country talent. Most of the country DJs promoted shows in their area in addition to their DJ duties.

At this initial meeting, Carl Haverlin, president of BMI, spoke. This showed the importance of country music to BMI, whose early success stemmed in large part from the enormous amount of country songs which they licensed. Further, the future success of BMI and country music were linked; if more stations played country music, then BMI collected more money for country music songwriters and publishers—expanding the horizons of both BMI and the country music industry.

The Country Music Disc Jockeys Association marked the beginning of a booster organization for country music. Although there was a close connection with the *Opry*—the *Opry*'s birthday was the reason for inviting everyone to Nashville—the organization operated independently of the *Opry*. Five years later this organization evolved into the Country Music Association. During the 1953–1958 period the Grand Ole Opry Birthday Celebration became the major convention for those involved in country music. All the major disc jockeys, talent bookers, and other business people—as well as country artists—came. It was a gathering of the tribes for country music and became a major reason that Nashville increasingly served as a focal point for the business of country music.

RADIO AND BARN DANCES

In 1952 there were still more listeners to radio than there were viewers of television, and country music continued to be heard on barn dances until the mid-1950s. In 1952 there were 176 stations carrying the *Prince Albert Show* from the *Grand Ole Opry* over the NBC radio network each Saturday night. In July 1954 *The Ozark Jubilee* began on KWTO in Springfield, Missouri; it was broadcast over the ABC radio network, then became a TV show on ABC. There were also barn dances or country jamborees throughout the country: The *Big D Jamboree* was on KRLD in Dallas and the *Saturday Night Shindig* was on WFAA, also in Dallas; Houston had the *Hometown Jamboree* on KNUX, while the *Hollywood Barn Dance* came from Los Angeles on KNX. The *Hometown Jamboree*, began in 1949 by Cliffie Stone on KXLA in Los Angeles, and the *Hayloft Jamboree* from WCOP in Boston also began in the 1950s. One of the most popular country music shows was the *Town Hall Party* from Los Angeles, which was carried by the NBC network.

Other barn dances were *Hayloft Hoedown* from WFIL in Philadelphia; *Hoosier Hop* from WOWO in Fort Wayne, Indiana; *Roundup of Stars* in Tampa over WDAE; and the *Old Dominion Barn Dance* on WRVA in

Richmond, Virginia. Other cities with regular radio barn dances included Cleveland; Indianapolis; Yankton, South Dakota; and Omaha, Nebraska.

The year 1955 marked a turning point in radio. A number of well-known radio network shows ended, including *The Jack Benny Program* (which began in 1932), *The Lone Ranger* (which began in 1933), *Lux Radio Theater* (1934), *Sergeant Preston of the Yukon* (1947), *The Hallmark Hall of Fame* (1948), and *The Whistler* (1947). The importance of network radio was winding down as sponsors and programs shifted to television.

By this time the economics of broadcasting dictated a change in programming. The high dollar national sponsors moved over to TV for the national audience; radio increasingly became a local, rather than a national, medium. Further, the shift in national sponsors precipitated a drop in income. With the loss in income radio could no longer afford to produce live shows or keep a staff band on the payroll. Increasingly radio substituted records for live shows. Although radio had played records on the air since World War II, after 1955 the airwaves were dominated by recorded music.

ROCK 'N' ROLL

Musically, there was about to be a huge shift in the tastes of the population. In 1955 Bill Haley's recording of "Rock Around the Clock" reached number 1, marking the official beginning of the rock 'n' roll era. The next year, Elvis Presley sold 10 million records as teenagers became the dominant record buyers. This shift in taste cost the major labels a great deal; until 1955 the six major record labels dominated the pop music charts. However, in 1956 small, independent labels—who invested in rhythm and blues when the major labels stuck with white pop singers like Perry Como and Eddie Fisher—usurped the power of the big labels to dominate the singles charts. By the end of 1956, 25 different labels had placed hits in the top 50 recordings.

This shift in radio programming and corresponding record sales hurt country music a great deal. In 1951 Patti Page sold 2.2 million copies of her recording of "The Tennessee Waltz," a song published by Acuff-Rose, and Nashville felt like it was on top of the world. A number of songs from country music songwriters at Nashville publishing companies were recorded by pop acts. The biggest single beneficiary was Acuff-Rose and their songwriter, Hank Williams, who had hits recorded by Tony Bennett, Jo Stafford, and Rosemary Clooney. In 1951 over a third of the sales of recordings were country; Tennessee Ernie Ford, Red Foley, Ernest Tubb, Hank Williams, and Little Jimmy Dickens all averaged about 750,000 in sales per release while Eddy Arnold's record sales topped a million for each release. At Columbia Records about 40 percent of all their sales of singles were to the country market while at Decca about half of their sales were attributed to country.

But in 1956, according to Nashville executives, the bottom fell out. Elvis Presley was signed in Nashville and originally considered a country artist but his success soon transcended the country music field. Other young performers like the Everly Brothers, Carl Perkins, Jerry Lee Lewis, and other rockabilly pioneers all had roots in country but again their appeal went beyond the traditional country music audience.

From a business perspective, rock 'n' roll was fueled by the growth of independent labels, who recorded music (primarily rhythm and blues music) that the major labels weren't recording. The small labels were aided by AM radio, which played the new music. It was important that the music was on AM radio because the signals for AM reached long distances at night, bouncing off the ionosphere. Thus the sounds of a big city could penetrate rural and small town areas; the tastemakers of the rural and small-town areas may have wanted to keep rock 'n' roll out of their town—and, in many instances, did keep it off their local radio stations—but they could not keep it off the radios tuned into distant signals.

As radio became local instead of national it had to target a market better. For most of its history radio had presented a smorgasbord of programs to appeal to a broad cross section of the American public. But television replaced radio as the medium for the masses and so radio had to increasingly find an audience that television did not reach. The audience that radio found in the 1956–1958 period was young teenagers who wanted to hear rock 'n' roll and rhythm and blues records. Many young country performers moved into rock and roll and the young white working class audience, who might have become country music fans, shifted over to rock 'n' roll. Older country artists, or those uncomfortable with the new sound and new audience, could not and would not make the shift to rock. Radio increasingly abandoned country music in favor of rock music and thus country music was left without significant exposure to the mass audience. The jukeboxes were loading their machines with rock 'n' roll records. Television was not particularly interested in country—although there were a few shows on the air (most significantly, *The Ozark Jubilee*) and radio didn't see the country market as particularly lucrative.

Country music had been hit by the perfect storm: as the national sponsors left radio for TV, the radio stations abandoned live talent for records so the barn dances began to leave the air. Since TV aimed its programs at families, teenagers found a home at radio, which played rock 'n' roll records. The result was that country music almost disappeared from the radio airwaves. Or, rather, the music that country performers increasingly played did not sound like the country music of old.

BILL HALEY AND THE COMETS

Bill Haley, who had what most consider to be the first rock 'n' roll hit, had his roots in country music. After World War II, Haley was a country music disc jockey on WPWA in Chester, Pennsylvania, and had a band, the Four Aces of Western Swing, who played locally and recorded for Cowboy

Records. The group's first record, in 1948, was the Hank Williams song "Too Many Parties, Too Many Pals," b/w "Four Leaf Clover Blues." Their second release was a cover of George Morgan's "Candy Kisses" on one side with Red Foley's "Tennessee Border" on the other.

After these releases, Haley changed the name of the band to the Saddlemen and had a string of releases, including a cover of Roy Acuff's "Wreck on the Highway." In February 1951, Haley recorded a cover record of "Rocket 88" by Jackie Brenston which was produced by Sam Phillips in Memphis and was a hit on the R&B label Chess. Haley's version was released on Holiday Records.

In 1953 Haley got rid of his sideburns and cowboy hat and renamed his group Bill Haley and the Comets. They recorded "Crazy, Man, Crazy," a song filled with jive phrases and buzz words, which became a hit in the summer of 1953. Veteran songwriter Max Freedman had written a song with Jim Myers, "Rock Around the Clock," that was a proven crowd pleaser when Haley played it during 1953. In 1954 Haley signed with Decca Records and recorded "Rock Around the Clock" on April 12, 1954, in New York. The record sold 75,000 copies. Haley then recorded his follow-up, "Shake, Rattle and Roll." Meanwhile, Myers sent copies of his song to producers and directors in Hollywood and the record ended up in the movie *Blackboard Jungle,* which was the first movie to use a rock 'n' roll song for a theme.

After the film was released, Decca reserviced the record to radio stations where it became a huge hit, landing at the number 1 spot on *Billboard*'s pop charts, and sold over six million copies. This event is considered by many to be the start of the rock 'n' roll revolution. Haley celebrated by buying five Cadillacs for his band and a yacht for himself.

By the end of 1955 rock 'n' roll was a household word and its most famous practitioner was Bill Haley and the Comets.

ELVIS AND NASHVILLE

In Memphis, Sam Phillips owned a small recording studio and record label. On July 5, 1954, 19-year-old Elvis Presley, along with Scotty Moore and Bill Black, spent the evening in Sam's studio trying to record a 1948 pop hit, "Harbor Lights" and a 1950 country hit, "I Love You Because." It wasn't quite working so they took a break. During the break, Elvis began pounding his guitar and singing the old Arthur "Big Boy" Crudup hit, "That's All Right, Mama." Sam felt an excitement and told them to work up the song so it could be recorded. They also recorded the old Bill Monroe bluegrass hit, "Blue Moon of Kentucky" in the same frenzied, souped-up style.

"That's All Right" b/w "Blue Moon of Kentucky" was released as Sun #209 on July 19, 1954. Things happened quickly. On October 2 the group performed "Blue Moon of Kentucky" on the *Grand Ole Opry* in Nashville, but *Opry* manager Jim Denny wasn't impressed; the wild-haired kid just didn't seem to fit the *Opry* mould. On November 6 Elvis signed with the *Louisiana Hayride* for a year's worth of appearances. By January 1955, Sam Phillips had virtually quit recording other artists and concentrated on Elvis.

Elvis's records were selling briskly, but a big hit causes a problem for a small label. Phillips didn't make much profit on each single sold, and he had to plow that money back into more pressings while hoping distributors paid. The cash flow problem was enormous. Distributors would not pay before 90 days, and then perhaps only a partial payment to keep the product coming. Meanwhile, Phillips had to pay all his creditors—from publishers to pressing plants to trade papers. He was successful, but felt like he was going under.

About 200 miles east, in Nashville, the end of 1954 marked the end of a golden era in country music, and the beginning of some dark days. Hank Williams had died at the beginning of 1953 and Fred Rose died on December 1, 1954. In Memphis the rockabilly sound of Elvis Presley was starting to catch on. This would shake, rattle, and roll the country music industry into the doldrums for the rest of the 1950s.

Sam Phillips and Sun Records experienced success with Elvis as well as a new singer, Johnny Cash, who released "Cry, Cry, Cry" b/w "Hey Porter" early in 1955. The cash flow problem was putting Sam Phillips on the edge of being out of business but there was hope on the horizon—several major labels were interested in purchasing Elvis's contract.

At the 1955 DJ convention in Nashville, Elvis met with Steve Sholes, who was head of RCA's country division, as well as Colonel Tom Parker, a manager and booking agent who had been working with Hank Snow, and Julian Auberbach, head of the Hill and Range publishing company. Parker structured a deal whereby Sam Phillips received $40,000 for Elvis's contract. This enabled Phillips to carry on with Sun Records.

In January 1956 Elvis went into the RCA Victor studios in Nashville, located in the building they shared with the Methodist TV, Radio and Film Commission at 1525 McGavock Street and recorded "Heartbreak Hotel," a song published by Nashville-based Tree Publishing. Tree was started by Lou Cowan and Jack Stapp after Stapp saw the royalties from "Chattanoogie Shoeshine Boy" where Fred Rose had listed him as co-writer. Since there was no hope of Stapp writing any more songs, he decided to start a publishing company with Lou Cowan, an Army buddy.

"Heartbreak Hotel" became Presley's first major hit and in 1956 Presley zoomed to superstardom, selling 10 million records and appearing on the Ed Sullivan, Steve Allen, and Dorsey Brothers TV shows. The world would never be the same—and neither would Tree. The success of Elvis led Jack Stapp to resign as program director at WSM to work with the publishing company. Actually, Stapp had hired Buddy Killen to run the publishing company so after Stapp left WSM he only stayed exclusively with Tree for a few months before he moved over to another radio station, which allowed him to own a publishing company on the side. Since he could not pay Killen a big salary he gave him part of the company.

NASHVILLE STUDIOS

Jack Stapp's resignation came as a direct result of a memo sent by Jack DeWitt, president of WSM, on August 2, 1955. The memo addressed a problem at WSM: a number of employees had businesses on the side. In that memo DeWitt told his employees they must chose whether to give up their outside business and stay with WSM or leave WSM. Three WSM engineers, Aaron Shelton, Carl Jenkins, and George Reynolds had Castle Recording Studio which did a brisk business; in addition to recording local radio commercials, the studio recorded artists for the King, Dot, Bullet, and Decca labels. The hits "Chattanoogie Shoeshine Boy" by Red Foley and "You Win Again" by Hank Williams were both recorded there.

The studio was an excellent facility—the engineers were top notch and produced quality recordings. But when DeWitt's directive was issued, they elected to stay with WSM, which had obtained a TV station the year before. There were other studios outside Nashville competing for the business of country music; Jim Beck had an excellent studio in Dallas, King Records had a studio in Cincinnati, and Springfield, Missouri, was host to *The Ozark Jubilee*, the hottest country music TV show on ABC.

OWEN BRADLEY

Owen Bradley was a well-known big band leader in Nashville. Bradley was born in Westmoreland, Tennessee, and moved to Nashville with his family when he was young. A natural musician, Bradley worked professionally when he was a teenager and then led his own band, with Snooky Lanson and Kitty Kalen as vocalists, at the end of the 1930s. His band broadcast on WLAC and then, in 1940, he joined WSM. From 1947, when Paul Cohen began recording Decca acts in Nashville, Bradley worked with Cohen, hiring the musicians, setting up the sessions, and even auditioning songs.

In addition to his work with Cohen and leading his big band, Bradley recorded as Brad Brady and His Tennesseans for Bullet Records and had two hits on Coral in 1949. Bradley also co-wrote "Night Train to Memphis," a hit for Roy Acuff.

Bradley approached Cohen with an offer: he and his brother, Harold, would build a studio in Nashville if Cohen commited Decca to record 100 sessions a year there. Owen and Harold had already owned two studios, one on Second Avenue and another in Hillsboro Village. Owen Bradley saw the potential of Nashville as a recording center and wanted to be part of that. The Nashville music business was centered downtown at the time; WSM was on Seventh Avenue North, the *Grand Ole Opry* was held at the Ryman Auditorium on Fifth Avenue North, and a number of publishing companies and booking agencies were in the Cumberland Lodge Building on Seventh Avenue North. The Bradleys wanted to build a studio in the Cumberland Lodge Building, but the owner and tenants would not allow that so Owen used his life insurance policy to obtain the down payment for a house at 804 Sixteenth Avenue South in 1954. The following year he bought a Quonset Hut, a popular building for the Army during World War II, from Army surplus and built a film recording studio there. Paul Cohen promised to invest $12,000 in the enterprise, but he never paid up. Still, he committed to recording a number of sessions at the Bradley Recording Studio, owned by Owen and Harold Bradley.

Paul Cohen actually preferred the Dallas studio of Jim Beck; however, a tragedy sealed the deal for Nashville to obtain Cohen's business. Beck had recorded Lefty Frizzell, Ray Price, Billy Walker, and other acts. In addition to Cohen, Don Law, head of A&R for Columbia, also recorded a number of sessions with Beck in Dallas. But in May 1956 Beck died after cleaning his recording equipment with carbon tetrachloride; he had not provided ventilation and the chemicals poisoned his system.

The house that Owen Bradley purchased and renovated as a recording studio became the first studio—or any kind of business associated with the music industry—on what later became known as Music Row. The next business on that street to house a music business came from Jim Denny a little over a year after Jack DeWitt issued his ultimatum for WSM employees with outside businesses.

COUNTRY SHOWDOWN IN NASHVILLE

The big showdown the entire country music industry was watching culminated on September 24, 1956, when Jim Denny, manager of the *Opry* and head of the Opry Artists Bureau, which booked *Opry* acts, was called into WSM President Jack DeWitt's office and fired after he refused to give up Cedarwood, his publishing company. The head-to-head confrontation between Denny and DeWitt was a power struggle; DeWitt was the president of WSM but Denny felt he was responsible for the success of the *Opry* and the Opry Artists Bureau, which made WSM a lot of money. A few days later Denny called a meeting of the artists he had represented and outlined his plans to set up an outside booking agency. The artists, whose income depended on their bookings, agreed to go with Denny. They knew and trusted Denny, and knew he could get them work; further, they were concerned about an inexperienced person being named to the Opry Artists Agency which might put their livelihoods in jeopardy. (Dee Kilpatrick replaced Jim Denny as *Opry* manager.)

The artists sent a telegram to DeWitt and told him of their plans; DeWitt's response was that if they went with Denny, there would be no *Opry* for them.

Denny controlled about 70 percent of the top talent in country music and the *Opry* could not afford to lose them but both men were headstrong and obstinate. The artists were obviously nervous and caught in a quandary; they did not want to lose their *Opry* affiliation but the *Opry* provided mainly exposure, and they had families to feed. Further, Jim Denny had negotiated with the Philip Morris Tobacco Company for a package tour of *Opry* acts while still employed at the *Opry;* the tobacco executives were impressed with Denny and decided to continue to work with him on the tour. The result was that Denny booked a hugely successful tour that lasted 16 months and established his firm, The Jim Denny Agency, as the premier booking agency for country music. It also broke the back of the *Opry*'s hold on country music in Nashville. After this point, the *Opry* was never the dominant force in country music like it had been; attendance during the late 1950s was a fraction of what it had been and now, there was outside competition. Thus, the way was paved for independent entrepreneurs to set up shop and create a country music industry outside the *Opry*. Jim Denny set up his shop in a former furniture store on 16th Avenue directly across from the Bradley Recording Studio.

NEW BEGINNINGS

There was both a blessing and a curse in the events of 1955–1956. On one hand, these events led to Nashville becoming a more diverse city with country music and broke the hold of the *Opry*. On the other hand, the success of Elvis and the rock revolution seemed to almost put country music out of business. The *Opry* suffered declining attendance for a number of years, unable to attract new, young followers. Radio stations that programmed country switched to rock, the young artists who would have sung country now sung rock, and the audiences for country switched to rock. There was money generated by publishing which kept the industry alive. A number of the young rock acts—such as Elvis, the Everly Brothers, Roy Orbison, and others—had strong Nashville connections in publishing so the money from a number of early rock hits came back to Nashville. Still, it was getting increasingly difficult to hear country music on the radio and if radio stopped playing country records, that could mean the death of a genre.

Once again a perfect storm confronted the country music industry. The showdown created when WSM ordered its employees to give up their outside interests created a situation where Owen and Harold Bradley established the first studio on what became known as Music Row, Jim Denny established a booking agency independent of the *Grand Ole Opry*, TV forced radio to reinvent itself as a media for records instead of live talent, and rock 'n' roll forced country music to regroup. Although it looked like the end of country music at the time, the success of Elvis in 1956 (as well as the previous success of Eddy Arnold in the late 1940s and early 1950s) led RCA Victor to build a studio and establish a permanent office in Nashville. RCA Studio B opened for business in November 1957; it was located just a block away from the Bradley Recording Studio. These two studios recorded a number of pop, rock, and country hits during the following years.

GRAMMYS

The first Grammy Awards were presented in 1958. The awards came from the newly formed National Academy of Recording Arts and Sciences, formed in Los Angeles as a reaction to the decline in sales of middle-of-the road music after rock 'n' roll hit.

The question of "criteria" came up and record sales were immediately dismissed; instead, the awards were formed to reward "artistic creativity" in the recording field. This was an award for excellence, voted on by its members, and not an award based on sales. In May 1958 the first awards were presented in Los Angeles. Given awards were artists Frank Sinatra, Ella Fitzgerald, Henry Mancini, Count Basie, and Domenico Mondugno. The top song was "Nel Blue Dipinto di Blue" ("Volare"). The first Grammy for "country" music was given to the Kingston Trio for "Tom Dooley." Ignored were Elvis Presley, the Everly Brothers, and songs like "Hound Dog," "Teddy Bear," and "Wake Up Little Susie."

The awards soon proved popular and grew; in 1958 there was a second awards show in November. The second Grammy for country music went to Marty Robbins for his hit, "El Paso."

RADIO VS. TELEVISION

In the mid-1950s radio was fighting for its life; in fact, many thought radio was on its deathbed and would soon disappear. The key factor in all this was the rise in television and the decline in network radio. Although television has received credit for being a revolutionary technology, changing American family life with its entertainment, the fact is that radio was equally revolutionary. In its fight for survival, radio created a "new" medium, dominated by recordings and aimed at young people. While the American family became increasingly sedentary in front of the television, teenagers became increasingly active with the radio, changing their dress, behavior, and language because of the music they heard.

COUNTRY ON TV IN THE MID-1950s

The most important early country music show on TV was *The Ozark Jubilee*, broadcast on the ABC network on Saturday nights beginning January 22, 1955. Hosted by Red Foley, the show featured top country talent such as Webb Pierce, Jean Shepard, Hawkshaw Hawkins, Porter Wagoner, the Oklahoma Wranglers, Bobby Lord, Marvin Rainwater, Wanda Jackson,

Billy Walker, Norma Jean, Leroy Van Dyke, Smiley Burnette, and Lew Childre. The theme song for the show was "Sugarfood Rag," written and played by guitarist Hank Garland.

The show became *The Country Music Jubilee* in July 1957 and then *Jubilee U.S.A.* beginning August 1958. The show ran until September 24, 1960, when it was abruptly cancelled by ABC, although it was still popular. The reason ABC gave for cancelling the show was because it had the rights to the Gillette boxing fights; however, the real reason was that Red Foley had been indicted for tax fraud and was preparing to stand trial as the 1960 season began. (Foley's first trial ended in a hung jury; his second in 1961 resulted in an acquittal.)

The major competitor to the Springfield show was the syndicated *Stars of the Grand Ole Opry,* which began on ABC on October 15, 1955, and ran until September 15, 1956. However, the Opry did not concentrate on TV the way the Springfield group did, preferring to stick with radio and its live shows. Another show, *Talent Varieties,* was broadcast on the ABC network from Springfield, Missouri, beginning in 1955, but that show only lasted a few months. *The Pee Wee King Show* broadcast from Cleveland, Ohio, also broadcast for a few months in 1955.

The next major country music show was *The Ford Show, featuring Tennessee Ernie Ford,* commonly called *The Tennessee Ernie Ford Show* and sponsored by the Ford Motor Company. This show debuted on October 4, 1956, and ran until June 29, 1961, on Thursday nights on the NBC network.

The Jimmy Dean Show had a major impact on country music on TV. This show debuted on June 22, 1957, and ran until April 1, 1966. It first appeared on Saturday nights on CBS during the summer of 1957, then switched to the ABC network where it appeared first on Thursday nights, then finished its run on Friday nights. Dean's show was originally broadcast from Washington, DC, but in its final season was broadcast from a variety of venues, including one broadcast from the Grand Ole Opry in Nashville. The show introduced "Rowlf," a muppet by Jim Henson which served as the launching pad for Henson's career.

Although there was country music on network TV in the 1950s, the genre experienced its greatest success in local and syndicated programs. This parallels the story of country music on radio, where a handful of country shows appeared on the network yet numerous cities had a country music program broadcast as a barn dance as well as numerous early morning and mid-day programs. By and large, these local programs were broadcast in the Southeast.

The Southeast tended to lag behind the rest of the country in purchasing TV sets; in the mid-1950s about 75 percent of the households in the Northeast and Midwest had TV sets while only about 50 percent of southern households had sets. Also, people in cities were more likely to own a TV set (ownership ranged from 50 to 80 percent) while rural households were less likely (ownership ranged from 42 to 61 percent).

COUNTRY MUSIC AND POST–WORLD WAR II AMERICA

The year 1945 was the last year of World War II and a pivotal one for country music. At this point, American country music was dominated by western swing—particularly Bob Wills and Spade Cooley—and by West Coast country music. Of the top songs in 1945 only one, "It's Been So Long, Darling" by Ernest Tubb, was by a Nashville act. The year 1946 would be a virtual repeat of 1945 with western swing still dominating country music. The top country recording acts, Bob Wills and His Texas Playboys, Tex Ritter, Al Dexter, and Merle Travis were all West Coast acts. While Nashville was important for its radio broadcasts from the *Grand Ole Opry* on WSM, it was certainly not a recording center nor were its acts well known for their success on records. But that was beginning to change.

Nashville had all the musical elements that would guide the future of country music by the end of 1945 performing on the *Grand Ole Opry*. On the *Opry* was Bill Monroe with his group the Blue Grass Boys; by the end of 1945 his group included Lester Flatt and Earl Scruggs, and this sound defined bluegrass in the coming years. There was also Ernest Tubb, and his Texas honky tonk sound showed another direction country music took, especially into the 1950s as this hard driving, barroom sound virtually defined the sound of "hard" or "traditional" country for the coming years. Hank Williams and Webb Pierce later represented that "traditional" country music, which stayed close to its rural roots.

The star of the *Grand Ole Opry* was Roy Acuff, whose mountain image fit the *Opry*'s image of country music from folk roots in the southern area of the United States and whose full throated sound was a prime example of the untrained vocal singing style. Uncle Dave Macon, with his vivid showmanship and vaudeville background also connected country music to its folk and live performance roots, but his sound and style were already part of the past, although a past that would be treasured and revisited time and again in the future.

Also on the *Opry* was Pee Wee King and his Golden West Cowboys whose tight organization headed by manager J.L. Frank, pioneered business practices in country music artist management and bookings in the years to come and whose outfits—they dressed in snappy cowboy clothes—defined the country music "look" after the mountaineer image was shunned and discarded (except by Acuff) after World War II.

Then there was Eddy Arnold, whose smooth vocal style—reminiscent of a country Bing Crosby—led country music to a commercial sound and whose image pulled country music away from the rural, hayseed image towards a more urban, urbane, sophisticated look. Of all the acts on the *Opry* at the end of 1945, it was Eddy Arnold who had the greatest impact on commercial country music and the establishment of Nashville as the center for the country music industry in the following years.

There is a difference between what is influential and what is popular. The criticism of what is most popular is that it satisfies only the current tastes of the public, often at the expense of artistic integrity or breaking new ground musically. The theory is that for something to be popular it must appeal to the lowest common denominator, the basest tastes of the public, and hence is discardable.

On the other hand, in an open market capitalist economy, what is most commercial defines popular culture. In business—and the music industry is a business—record companies must achieve success from sales of recordings in order to be profitable. The incentives for recording an act or a genre of music rests with the profit motive. Thus the capitalist system serves as a gatekeeper for which musical acts become available to the public.

Since World War II, country music has proven itself to be commercially successful. In fact, even before World War II, going back to Fiddlin' John Carson in Atlanta, to Vernon Dalhart in New York, and through Jimmie Rodgers and the Carter Family, as well as the singing cowboys Gene Autry, Roy Rogers, and Tex Ritter, country music has done well as a business. This led major recording corporations to record and release this music. This, in turn, has led to the opportunity for broad exposure for the music and access to the electronic media and distribution network that brings the product to consumers.

But some country music has proven itself to be more commercial than others. Bluegrass, although it is a vibrant, important music, has never been particularly commercial. Consequently, this field is dominated by small, independent labels who record and release this product; the major labels generally avoid it. The same fate has befallen western music since World War II; outside of a few acts like Gene Autry and the Sons of the Pioneers (who always transcended the genre and recorded songs that were not just "western") this type of music is primarily recorded and released on small, independent labels. Even western swing and honky tonk, although reissued on major labels because it was originally recorded there, doesn't really have a place in contemporary country music. They were important in their day, but somehow their day passed. What did not pass, but grew, was commercial country music.

Prior to World War II there were two distinct images for country—the singing cowboy and the musical mountaineer. But another image gradually evolved—that of a sophisticated singer who had a country background but assimilated the ways of the city. A singer who did not sing with a twang, who sang with violins instead of fiddles, and who dressed in tasteful sports coats and slacks (and later, tuxedoes). This is what Eddy Arnold, Red Foley and, later Jim Reeves did for country music—they moved it up town and into the middle class.

Just as the country's population shifted from rural areas to urban areas, especially beginning in World War II, country music shifted—both musically and visually—from the rural, country image to one of the suburban gentleman who kept his down home roots and rural values but acquired some city sophistication along the way. That is the story of a generation that grew up in rural America during the Depression and then left the farm during World War II. They were proud of their heritage, but wanted something more—they wanted respect, wanted to be part of mainstream America, and wanted to join the American middle class; in short, they wanted to be more worldly and less provincial.

The country fan was a man moving up in this world—a country boy who was not a hick, someone who came from the farm but was not a rube, someone who sang country music but was not a hillbilly, and someone who'd been in the hay fields, but was not a hayseed.

The story of country music from before World War II until the present time mirrors, in many ways, the story of the United States itself. While this country had been changing from a rural, agricultural-based nation into an urban, industrial based nation before World War II, the war certainly sped up this process and brought it to fruition. During the war, the population shifted from rural areas to cities, where defense plants were established. It was not unusual for people from the South—still recovering from the Great Depression—to move to a major city during the war for jobs in defense or defense-related plants. In the Armed Services, Southerners were mixed with others from other parts of the country so country music reached a wide variety of people. Also American music became an international music during World War II, primarily through the V-Discs sent out during the war to servicemen and Armed Forces Radio. Country music left the South for good and became a national music because southern servicemen exposed others to country music in the Armed Forces, and because Southerners moved out of the South in large numbers and fanned out across the country in search of defense-related jobs.

The city exerted a strong pull on rural Americans throughout the twentieth century. It was the place of bright lights so people were not chained to the cycles of the seasons and daylight. In the city there was action, excitement, and entertainment around the clock and the city person was viewed as cosmopolitan: cultured, sophisticated, and worldly wise. The rural person was often viewed as a country bumpkin, a rube, a hayseed—all the uncool things nobody wanted to be. Still, in the city there were jobs and for someone raised in the country doing farm work, it seemed like these jobs did not involve backbreaking work for easy money, so rural people moved to cities in large numbers throughout the twentieth century, particularly from World War II.

Rural people reacted to their move to the city in two ways. First, they wanted to keep some of their rural roots and so they planted gardens, read stories about idealized country life illustrated by Norman Rockwell with his idealized view of rural and small town life, and listened to country music. But rural people who moved to the city also bought suits and ties, attended social functions, and attempted to join the middle class. This middle class was defined not only in terms of income, but also in values: the Protestant work ethic, hard work, independence, material possessions, and, increasingly, a ranch house in the suburbs.

Part of the story of country music is a fight for respect. For a number of years the performers and fans of country music were subject to stereotypical images of poor white trash. Those who loved the music were often embarrassed by their own tastes. They were both proud and ashamed—proud of their rural past and proud of their taste and connection with country music, but ashamed that the music was linked with so many negative cornpone images. Country fans looked for artists who made them proud to be country music fans, who moved country music uptown, gave it self-respect and dignity.

The period 1957–1963 saw Nashville emerge as the undisputed center for country music. By this time the Singing Cowboys were gone from the silver screen, although Gene Autry and Roy Rogers had TV shows. Most of the barn dances were either gone or on a local station; Springfield, Missouri, ceased to be a country music stronghold after *The Ozark Jubilee* ceased production in 1960; Jim Beck's death meant that major labels no longer went to Dallas to record. RCA set up a studio and permanent office in Nashville in 1957 and named Chet Atkins to head that office; Atkins produced many of the country hits on RCA in the following years and became one of the founders of "The Nashville Sound." The other founder, Owen Bradley, was named head of Decca's country division in 1958. In 1962 Owen and Harold Bradley sold their studio to CBS, and Columbia Records established permanent headquarters in Nashville under A&R country head Don Law.

Three of the biggest hits to come out of Nashville during this period were "El Paso" by Marty Robbins and "Battle of New Orleans" by Johnny Horton, both in 1959, and "Big Bad John" by Jimmy Dean in 1963. Johnny Cash established himself as a top country artist during this period of time, and Jim Reeves wore tuxedoes as he sang country songs with his smooth, velvet voice. Owen Bradley produced hits on Patsy Cline and Brenda Lee while Chet Atkins showed his versatility by performing at the Newport Jazz Festival in 1960. BMI constructed a permanent home and ASCAP opened an office in Nashville in 1963.

But there was tragedy as well. Johnny Horton died in a car accident in 1961; Patsy Cline, Hawkshaw Hawkins, and Cowboy Copas died in a plane crash in March 1963, and Jim Reeves died in a plane crash in 1964.

In 1964 the music industry ushered in a new era when The Beatles appeared on *The Ed Sullivan Show* and the "British Invasion" began. In Nashville there was a new era as well because on the same charts as The Beatles was Roger Miller, who recorded his first hit "Dang Me" that year. Miller became the biggest country-pop music star of that period while Jimmy Dean continued to bring country music to a national audience with his television show on the ABC network.

6

Politics and Country Music

POLITICS AND EARLY COUNTRY MUSIC

Country music was the counter to the counterculture in the 1960s. This counterculture tends to dominate the stories of the 1960s, a youth-oriented era that spawned the image of "sex, drugs, and rock 'n' roll" for a number of young people, and an image of long-haired scruffy hippies usually comes to mind. It was the Beatles and the British Invasion, the acid rock of Jimi Hendrix, and the free love of Woodstock. Country music entered this era when many in "the silent majority" found that the sounds of country connected with their life. It was also an era when country music first became connected with politics on a national level, initially through the presidential candidacy of George Wallace.

Music has a long history of involvement with politics; in colonial times, a musician (usually a fiddler) attracted and entertained a crowd before a politician spoke. Country music has a long history with politics in the South, with numerous politicians using country musicians to show they were part of the "common man."

Some politicians running for office were musicians who used their musical skills to attract voters and votes. In the 1886 race for governor of Tennessee, two brothers, Alf and Bob Taylor, ran against each other; Alf was a Republican and Bob was a Democrat. Their campaign became known as the "War of the Roses" because people related it to the York and Lancaster families fighting for the English crown. Both brothers played the fiddle and they fiddled across Tennessee, campaigning for votes until Bob won that election. Bob was elected to the United States House of Representatives in 1878 and served one term; after his election to governor in 1886 he was reelected in 1890 and 1896, then served in the United States Senate from 1907 until his death in 1912. Alf was elected to the United States House of Representatives in 1888 and served in that office until 1895; he was elected governor of Tennessee in 1920.

Fiddlin' John Carson aligned himself with Eugene Talmadge when the Georgia politician first ran for state commissioner of agriculture in 1926. Carson played his fiddle and sang at political rallies, and Talmadge won that election and was reelected to that post in 1928 and 1930, then was elected governor of Georgia in 1932 and reelected in 1934. In 1940 he was elected governor again but was defeated in his bid for reelection in 1942. In 1946 Talmadge ran for governor on a segregation platform and was elected; however, he died before taking office. The Georgia General Assembly then elected Talmadge's son, Herman Talmadge, as governor. Herman Talmadge only served as governor from January until March when the state Supreme Court ruled against his election. In 1948 Herman Talmadge was elected governor of Georgia during a special election, then reelected in 1950 for a full four-year term. When Fiddlin' John Carson died in December 1949, he ran the elevator in Georgia's Capitol Building, his reward for his long-time support of the Talmadges.

Some early country musicians ran successfully for office. W. Lee O'Daniel moved to Fort Worth from Kansas and joined the Burrus Mill and Elevator Company where he was promoted to general manager. In 1930 he formed The Light Crust Doughboys and served as emcee on the radio show and during their personal appearances and even wrote some songs for the group, including "Beautiful Texas." In 1935 O'Daniel left Burrus Mill and started the Hillbilly Flour Company, which sponsored a show with musical entertainment by the Hillbilly Boys. "Pappy" O'Daniel was such a smooth announcer and radio salesman that he was elected governor of Texas on the Democratic ticket in 1938. He was reelected in 1940, then was elected to the United States Senate in 1941 in a special election when he defeated Lyndon Johnson.

In 1938, the same year O'Daniel was elected governor of Texas, Stuart Hamblen, a popular performer on Los Angeles radio, ran for Congress but did not win. Down in Louisiana, Jimmie Davis, who first recorded for Victor in 1928 and recorded a number of songs in the decade before his election (including "She's a Hum Dum Dinger from Dingersville," "Tom Cat and Pussy Blues," "Organ-Grinder Blues," and "Mama's Getting Hot and Papa's Getting Cold" in addition to future standards like "Nobody's Darlin' But Mine"), was elected clerk of the criminal court in Shreveport. In 1940 Davis was elected to the Louisiana Public Service Commission then, in 1944, was elected governor of Louisiana on the Democratic ticket. Davis recorded his biggest hit, "You Are My Sunshine," in 1940 and sang it at his political rallies; during his campaign for governor he was backed by a band that included pianist Moon Mullican, mandolinist Joe Shelton, and steel guitarist Charles Mitchell. In 1945, his first year as governor, Davis had a number 1 song, "There's a New Moon Over My Shoulder."

In 1959 Davis ran again for governor of Louisiana and was elected; during his time in office he had a chart record, "Where the Old Red River Flows."

Davis ran again for governor in 1971 but finished fourth in the primary. In 1972 Davis was elected to the Country Music Hall of Fame.

There were some country musicians who did not fare as well running for political office. Roy Acuff, a star on the *Grand Ole Opry,* ran for governor of Tennessee in 1944 as a Republican and lost, then ran for the United States Senate in 1948 but lost that election, too. Perhaps an early lesson here is that Democrats had a much better chance of being elected to public office in the South than Republicans during the first half of the twentieth century. That was because the South was overwhelmingly Democratic due to the fact that Abraham Lincoln—who waged war on the South and freed the slaves—was a Republican. It was Republican administrations who administered the era of Reconstruction, which allowed carpetbaggers from the North to go south and pick the spoils. Later, in the twentieth century, the Republicans were blamed for the Great Depression, which began under the presidency of Republican Herbert Hoover after a decade under Republican Presidents Warren Harding and Calvin Coolidge.

By the time Franklin Roosevelt won the 1932 election there were, in effect, two Democratic parties. The northern, or liberal Democrats believed in an activist government while the southern Democrats were much more conservative. President Franklin Roosevelt received much of his most implacable opposition to the New Deal in the South from politicians like Senators Carter Glass and Cotton Ed Smith and from conservative planters and businessmen. Although the South was overwhelmingly Democratic to the point of many areas being a one party region, southern Democrats were overwhelmingly conservative, against the New Deal and for segregation. However, President Roosevelt was idolized in the South by many of the working class.

Roosevelt united the Democratic Party during his 12 years in office, although the northern liberal wing did not agree with the southern conservative wing; however, they were united because Northerners hated Herbert Hoover and blamed the Republicans for the Great Depression while the Southerners hated Abraham Lincoln and supported segregation. In 1941 FDR invited country performers to the White House to perform for the King and Queen of England; among those performing were Wade Mainer and the Coon Creek Girls. Roosevelt also invited Gene Autry to the White House to perform. First Lady Eleanor Roosevelt attended the National Folk Festival and encouraged folk music and folk art.

There were three seminal events that caused many southern Democrats to look favorably to the Republican party during the late 1940s and early 1950s. The first occurred in the 1948 election when Hubert Humphrey spoke on behalf of civil rights at the Democratic Convention, a plank embraced by President Harry Truman, who integrated the armed forces in 1949. A contingent of southern Democrats, led by Strom Thurmond, split from the Democratic Party and formed the Dixiecrats who won the presidential vote in Alabama, Louisiana, Mississippi, and South Carolina. After the election of Harry Truman, the Dixiecrat Party disbanded and most Dixiecrats reluctantly rejoined the Democratic Party, although groundwork had been laid for a later split from the Democrats because of Civil Rights.

The second event was the firing of General Douglas MacArthur by President Truman in 1951. There was much support for the popular MacArthur and many viewed Truman's action as wrong. MacArthur returned to the United States and gave a speech before Congress where he invoked the famous phrase, "Old soldiers never die, they just fade away," before starting a campaign to capture the Republican nomination for president. But when MacArthur's political views became known it was obvious the country would not accept them.

The third factor was the election of Dwight Eisenhower to the presidency in 1952. General Eisenhower was a World War II hero, the commander in chief of allied forces who oversaw the D-Day invasion. Fifty percent of Southerners voted for Eisenhower in 1952 and he won Florida, Tennessee, Texas, and Virginia, although he lost Arkansas, North Carolina, Alabama, Mississippi, Georgia, South Carolina, and Louisiana. However, in 1954 the Supreme Court declared segregation illegal in the *Brown vs. Board of Education* decision which caused southern conservatives to turn against him. During Eisenhower's second term he ordered the National Guard to protect nine black children integrating Central High School in Little Rock, Arkansas, which further eroded Republican support in the South.

The Democratic party of the 1960s lost many southern Democrats—or at least lost them on national issues. The local Democratic organizations were still strong and in many southern elections the Democratic primary was, in essence, the general election, since there was little if any Republican opposition. The presidential campaign of 1960 between John Kennedy and Richard Nixon saw the South keep its Democratic leanings, but country music did not fit with the wine sipping elegance of the Kennedy White House, which was connected to the northeast intelligentsia of Harvard and Yale more than with southern good ole boys. Kennedy's promotion of Civil Rights caused blacks to vote Democratic—they had traditionally been solidly Republican— and southern whites to wonder if they fit in the Democratic party.

Kennedy was succeeded by Lyndon Johnson, a Southerner from Texas, who understood the power and importance of country music. Johnson invited Eddy Arnold to his ranch and to sing for the president of Mexico and Gene Autry visited the White House. But Johnson struggled to attract the votes of white Southerners; in the 1964 election more southern whites voted for Barry Goldwater, the Republican nominee, than for Johnson.

The white Southerners' distrust of the national Democratic Party solidified when Johnson signed the Civil Rights Act in 1964 which cast the Democratic Party on the side of Civil Rights for African-Americans and alienated many white Southerners.

GEORGE WALLACE, CIVIL RIGHTS, AND COUNTRY MUSIC

The issue of Civil Rights made Alabama Governor George Wallace a national candidate, first vying for the Democratic nomination for president and then as a third-party candidate. The candidacy of Wallace also brought country music into the national spotlight.

In his first inauguration speech on January 14, 1963, as Alabama's governor, Wallace proclaimed, "Segregation now...segregation tomorrow ...segregation forever." After that speech, Wallace became the most prominent anti-civil rights leader of his time, governing a state whose population was 30 percent black. Later in 1963 he made good on his promise to "stand in the schoolhouse door" when a Negro student tried to enroll in the University of Alabama. Federal officials intervened and the student was enrolled.

Wallace touched a sympathetic chord in whites all across the country with his tirades against hippies and communists and for the rights of private property, community control, and neighborhood schools. By the 1968 election, millions of Americans despised antiwar demonstrators, civil rights, the sexual freedom displayed by young people, and the decline of "fundamental values." America, they felt, had lost the cultural compass that guided it towards God, family, and country. For these Americans, what was most important was the sanctity of the traditional family, the importance of hard work and self-restraint, an autonomous local community, and the centralism of Christian religious beliefs. Uniting all of this was a muscular anticommunism; it was widely believed that antiwar protestors and civil rights activists were inspired and directed by Communists.

Americans began to hate the federal government because it was too intrusive—enforcing school integration with the U.S. Army, the Supreme Court's ruling against prayer in schools and free speech, and the intrusion of the federal government in state governments—especially when it defended civil rights activists against the state's political hierarchy.

The movement Wallace led stirred racial fears, patriotism expressed as anticommunism, a cultural nostalgia, and right-wing economics. There was an emphasis on "good country people" throughout the rural South who were hardworking, law-abiding, churchgoing, soft-spoken, and poor. The South had long prided itself on "the southern way of life," which demanded subordination of all issues to that of white supremacy.

Wallace expressed a widely held view about Negroes when he said, "I don't hate them.... The colored are fine in their place, don't get me wrong. But they're just like children, and it's not something that's going to change. It's written in stone."[1] Throughout the South it was commonly accepted wisdom that blacks were an inferior race and that whites understood "their Negroes" in their area and took care of them in a paternal manner. White supremacists not only accepted this view but also accepted that law and order, safety, and traditional values were part of this. For many white southern Christians, it was part of God's plan and to go against this was to go against God's will.

Anti-integrationist racism did not begin with George Wallace; he emerged at the front of a long parade that had been marching since Reconstruction. During his lifetime, Wallace saw firsthand the fears that integration brought to Southerners. In 1954, just after the Brown decision, white business and civic leaders in Indianola, Mississippi, began a grassroots organization, the Southern White Citizens' Council, which was headquartered in Jackson. This idea caught fire and spread across the South; the Alabama Citizens' Council grew from a couple hundred to 20,000 between October and December 1955. By the spring of 1957, there were 80,000 members.

Mississippi also laid the groundwork for opposition to federal mandates when it issued a "Resolution of Interposition" which claimed a state government could block any federal decision—with the implication that it could also block any federal law—which it disagreed with. It was the old Civil War assertion all over again: are we a nation of sovereign states or one single united nation? In the halls of Congress over 90 percent of southern congressmen and senators signed a "Southern Manifesto" drafted by South Carolina Senator Strom Thurmond which asserted that the Supreme Court's decision in the Brown case was federal power overriding the law.

During the 1950s, a number of right-wing organizations emerged, including Joseph Welch's John Birch Society, the Reverend Carl McIntire's Twentieth Century Reformation, Dr. Fred Schwarz's Christian Anti-Communism Crusade, Reverend Billy James Hargis's Christian Crusade, Edgar Bundy's Church League of America, Dean Clarence Manion's Forum, and Texas oilman H. L. Hunt's Life Line Foundation. Most of these organizations linked Christianity, patriotism, and anticommunism in such a way that enabled true Christians to be patriots who hated and feared Godless communism and wanted to uphold family values and the rule of law. The main "rule of law" that they upheld were those laws that banned integration. Southern voters sent a number of men to Congress who supported and proclaimed these views: among the notable examples were Mississippi's James K. Vardaman and Theodore Bilbo; Coley Blease, Ellison (Cotton Ed) Smith, and Strom Thurmond from South Carolina; Eugene Talmadge from Georgia; and Thomas (Tom-Tom) Heflin from Alabama.

By 1968 the Democratic Party was considered by many southern whites as too tolerant of civil rights activists whose activism led to street riots and burning cities, too tolerant of antiwar marchers and campus demonstrators, too tolerant of criminals who threatened the idea of law and order in peaceful communities, and advocates of too many social programs that gave handouts to the lower classes that were paid for by the hard-working middle class.

Wallace played on the fears of whites, weaving a tapestry of respect for the law and Christianity against communism, degeneracy, unbathed beatniks, socialists, atheists, sign-carrying degenerates, homosexuals, drugs, pornography, permissiveness, riots, and the backlash of kids against parents in the "generation gap," which led to an erosion of cultural values. White working class Americans felt powerless and afraid of all the changes that threatened their stable world. There was a sense of anguish and betrayal that America had gone from being a God-fearing nation that upheld family values to one headed down a slippery slope to degeneracy, lawlessness, crime in the streets, and lack of respect for the traditions and traditional values which made America great. The voice of the hard-working white man had been drowned out by unwashed hippie protestors and an overbearing government that sent bureaucrats into cities and towns to usurp the authority of local community leaders. Wallace's rhetoric convinced the white working class that they—not blacks or the young men being sent off to war in Vietnam—were the "victims" because everything they held dear was being swept away. The enemy behind all of this was Communism; in 1968 half of all Americans believed the Communist Party played a significant role in the civil rights movement and antiwar protests.

Country music played a part in all this because of its southern roots, the fact that so many artists came from the South, and the audience was either southern or had family roots in the South, and because country music is, essentially, the music of the white working class.

Southern politicians had long used country music in their campaigns; many began each political rally with a country music band—usually local talent—who played some big country hits, a patriotic song or two, and a gospel hymn. It was a way for these politicians to reach "the common man" and infuse a "common touch" into a campaign. It was also a good way to gather a crowd and keep them entertained as a warm-up for a political speech.

George Wallace began his political career in Alabama in 1938 when he was 19; he was elected to probate judge, then, in 1946, won a seat in the Alabama House of Representatives. He was considered a moderate in terms of segregation at the time because, although he opposed the Democratic Party's platform for Civil Rights in 1948, he did not walk out of the Convention with the Dixiecrats. In 1958 Wallace ran for governor but was defeated by John Patterson, who had the support of the Ku Klux Klan, a group Wallace had spoken against. Following that lost election Wallace reportedly told an aid, "I was outniggered by John Patterson. And I'll tell you here and now, I will never be outniggered again."[2]

In addition to his personal revelation about campaigning heavily on segregation, Wallace also had a revelation about country music when, after scoffing at the idea of country performer Webb Pierce warming up the crowd for him, saw Pierce draw a huge crowd for his opening political rally. From that point forward Wallace used country and gospel performers in his political campaigns.

During the 1968 presidential campaign, a number of country music stars—including Hank Snow, Hank Williams, Jr., and Stuart Hamblen, as well as southern gospel groups such as the Oak Ridge Boys, Hovie Lister, and the Statesmen and Wally Fowler—openly supported George Wallace.

In the 1968 election, Richard Nixon was elected president with 43.4 percent of the vote; George Wallace received 14 percent while Democratic nominee Hubert Humphrey received 42.7 percent in a close election. However, if you combine the votes of Nixon and Wallace they total 57.4 percent—a harbinger of the coming trend in American politics.

In his book, *The Nashville Sound,* published in 1970, author Paul Hemphill describes a typical Saturday night crowd at the *Grand Ole Opry* in the late 1960s as "white lower-middle-class people who drive trucks and keep house and work in factories, and most of them are somewhere between 30 and 45 years old. Their politics is simple and conservative, and in '68 they were voting for Wallace."[3]

Hemphill notes, "During the 1968 Presidential campaign, Music Row was practically a battlefield command post for George Wallace, who drew supporters there while he ran [Hank Snow and Doyle Wilburn of the Wilburn Brothers both stood up for George on a paid national telecast] and mourners when he lost. ('Just think, he'd have been the biggest country music fan we ever had as president,' said Lou Stringer, who runs a small music publishing company and once moonlighted as a weekend preacher)."[4]

Bill Malone, in his book *Don't Get Above Your Raisin',* notes that the connection between Wallace and country music wasn't just about politics. Malone writes, "Wallace's appeal among country musicians also came from the fact that he actively courted their support as no other candidate had done. This was important for a musical form that was self-conscious about its alleged inferiority and anxious for acceptance....Wallace and the country musicians shared a common ground, apart from ideology, in their origins in the southern working class with their common accents, religion, food tastes and social memories."[5]

POLITICS AND COUNTRY MUSIC: 1963–1974

While rock 'n' roll represented liberalism during the 1960s, country music represented a conservatism; while the youth movement represented a revolution in America, heralded by big changes in society, country music represented a desire to stem the tide of those changes, to look at yesterday instead of tomorrow for hope and solace.

What has come to be known as "the sixties" may be defined as the period from 1963 to 1974, or from the year of the assassination of President John Kennedy to the resignation of President Richard Nixon. During this period the two biggest political issues were civil rights and Vietnam; the biggest cultural and social issues centered on the "generation gap" between the Baby Boomers and their parents. Raised on big band and pop music of the 1940s and early 1950s, the parents believed in unquestioned patriotism, authority, a social hierarchy, and self-restraint. Their children, raised on the Beatles and rock music, believed in permissiveness, freedom, self-expression, and questioning authority.

The politics of this era represented a clash of cultures; being "liberal" meant a pro-civil rights stance. After Kennedy's assassination, Lyndon Johnson presented "The Great Society" and an escalation of the Vietnam War. While John Kennedy inspired youth to be active and involved and Lyndon Johnson sought to bring the poor and disenfranchised into the political mainstream, Richard Nixon sat clearly on the side of the World War II era generation, against the Baby Boomer's liberalism while at the same time overwhelmed by it. Nixon responded by dividing the country to unite his supporters; the result was a social revolution amongst the young who challenged the middle class's ideas, values, and leadership. But the middle class had a backlash of its own.

Although "white supremacy" was a term used by many to characterize the base of George Wallace's support, he argued that it was "middle-class" supremacy that he was after, a rebellion against the elites who ran the media, business, and government. In this light, George Wallace was one of the founders of the conservative movement that nominated Barry Goldwater for the presidency in 1964 and elected Richard Nixon in 1968 and 1972 and Ronald Reagan in 1980 and 1984.

COUNTRY MUSIC: 1963–1974

Looking at country music between 1963 and 1974 it is interesting to examine the songs on the *Billboard* country singles charts because these songs achieved significant airplay and thus reached a large listening public. Album cuts and songs that were sold under the counter (such as the racist country releases sold in the South) are not considered although, in some cases, they represent important cultural statements. However, by examining the songs that were commercially successful, an accurate reading about the public's tastes as well as the tastes of the companies that market country music may be gained. All of the songs discussed achieved enough radio airplay to be on the *Billboard* country singles chart, and emphasis has been given to songs that reached the top 15 positions.

Because country music is part of the commercial music industry and "love" is perennially the most popular topic with the radio-listening and record-buying public, it is not surprising that most of the songs on the country charts during the 1963–1974 period were about love—getting it, losing it, or keeping it. There are too many "love" songs to list but the clear message is that members of the country music audience preferred songs about their personal lives, not about social conditions or political trends. Approximately 80 percent of the songs charted during the 1963–1974 period were about love or, more accurately, relationships.

Most of the country songs that dealt with political, social, or cultural issues had either an underlying or overt patriotic theme; in general, country music is not protest music except when it protests protestors. There were a number of songs in which country artists exerted pride in themselves as country people and in country music. These include "Bright Lights and Country Music" by Bill Anderson (1965); "I Take a Lot of Pride in What I Am" by Merle Haggard (1968); "Are You from Dixie (Cause I'm from Dixie Too)" by Jerry Reed (1969); "I'm Just Me" by Charley Pride (which reached number 1 in 1971); "You're Lookin' at Country" by Loretta Lynn (1971); "Listen to a Country Song" by Lynn Anderson (1972); "Southern Loving" by Jim Ed Brown (1973); "Rednecks, White Socks and Blue Ribbon Beer" by Johnny Russell (1973); "Hank and Lefty Raised My Country Soul" by Stoney Edwards (1973); "Country Sunshine" by Dottie West (1973); "Country Bumpkin" by Cal Smith (which reached number 1 in 1974); and "Country Is" by Tom T. Hall (which also reached number 1 in 1974).

Most political/social/cultural commentary in country music during the sixties came from the perspective of a working man trying to make ends meet, shown best by a series of records by Jim Nesbitt: "Livin' Off a Credit" (1963), "Looking for More in '64," "Still Alive in '65," and "Heck of a Fix in '66," released in their respective years.

Other songs with political/social/cultural overtones were "The One on the Right Is on the Left" by Johnny Cash; "History Repeats Itself," Buddy Starcher's 1966 song about the similarities between Presidents John Kennedy and Abraham Lincoln; "Gallant Men" by Senator Everett McKinley Dirksen, "Day of Decision" by Johnny Sea; "Skip a Rope" by Henson Cargill (1967); and "You Better Sit Down Kids" by Roy Drusky (a 1968 remake of a pop hit by Cher). In 1969, songs such as "This Generation Shall Not Pass" by Henson Cargill; "In the Ghetto" and "Clean Up Your Own Back Yard" by Elvis Presley; "These Are Not My People" by Freddie Weller; and Tommy Cash's "Six White Horses"—about John and Robert Kennedy and Martin Luther King—fit this category.

Continuing in this vein, in 1970 Johnny Cash released "What Is Truth?" while Tommy Cash had "The Tears on Lincoln's Face." In 1971 Johnny Cash sang "Man in Black" and Eddy Arnold released "A Part of America Died," a song about policemen being killed. The next year, 1972, saw the release of "The Monkey That Became President" by Tom T. Hall; "Made in Japan" (number 1) by Buck Owens; and "The Lawrence Welk–Hee-Haw Counter-Revolution Polka" by Roy Clark. In 1973, socially conscious songs such as "Americans" by Byron MacGregor and "The Americans (A Canadian's Opinion)" by Tex Ritter hit the charts. "Ragged Old Flag" by Johnny Cash and "U.S. of A." by Donna Fargo were hits in 1974.

Some of the hardest hitting social commentary came from women in country music. Loretta Lynn became a spokeswoman for women's rights with songs like "Don't Come Home A Drinkin' (With Lovin' on Your Mind),"

"Rated X," and "Fist City." Bobbie Gentry performed "Ode to Billie Joe" in 1967; Jeannie C. Riley released "Harper Valley P.T.A." (number 1) and "The Girl Most Likely" in 1968; and Bobbie Gentry sang "Fancy" in 1969. These songs challenged the social status quo and while most country fans (and female country singers) did not call themselves feminists, they certainly stood up for themselves. These "feminist" country songs focused on the hypocrisy of judging women one way and men another—especially regarding sex and independence where a woman lets her man (and others) know she is no shrinking violet. Tanya Tucker, who began having country hits when she was 13 years old, released "Delta Dawn" in 1972; "What's Your Mama's Name" and "Blood Red and Going Down" were both number 1 hits in 1973; and "The Man That Turned My Mama On" in 1974.

A hawkish attitude toward Vietnam pervaded country music songs during the first half of the 1960s, evident by Johnny Wrights's number 1 song, "Hello Vietnam," which reached the peak position on October 23, 1965, and stayed there for 3 weeks. In November, Dave Dudley's "What We're Fighting For" reached number 4. The next year, Ernest Tubb reached number 48 with "It's for God, and Country, and You Mom (That's Why I'm Fighting in Viet Nam)." In January 1966 "Soldier's Prayer in Viet Nam" by Benny Martin with Don Reno reached number 46; the next month, Loretta Lynn's "Dear Uncle Sam" reached number 4. Perhaps the biggest Vietnam "hit" was "The Ballad of the Green Berets" by S. Sgt. Barry Sadler, which reached number 2 on the country charts and number 1 on the pop charts in the spring of 1966. Also that spring, "Private Wilson White" by Marty Robbins reached number 21, "Viet Nam Blues" by Dave Dudley reached number 12, and "The Minute Men (Are Turning in Their Graves)" by Stonewall Jackson reached number 24. "Distant Drums" by Jim Reeves, which does not mention Vietnam specifically but deals with leaving a loved one to go to war, reached number 1 on May 21 and stayed 4 weeks at the top of the charts. In 1967 Johnny Darrell's version of "Ruby, Don't Take Your Love to Town," about a Vietnam veteran whose wife is running around, reached number 9 and "The Private" by Del Reeves reached number 33. In 1968 "Little Boy Soldier" by Wanda Jackson reached number 46; "Ballad of Two Brothers" by Autry Inman reached number 14 (and number 48 on the pop charts); "My Son" by Jan Howard (whose son was killed in Vietnam) reached number 15; and "Galveston" by Glen Campbell was number 1 for 3 weeks in 1969. But there was a slight turning against the war in John Wesley Ryles's song "Kay"—about a taxi driver who lost his love to Nashville stardom—which contained the line "two young soldiers from Fort Campbell told me how they hate that war in Vietnam."[6]

The most popular statement against the counterculture occurred with two Merle Haggard songs: "Okie from Muskogee," which reached number 1 on November 15, 1969, and remained there for 4 weeks, and "The Fightin' Side of Me," which hit number 1 on March 14, 1970, and stayed at the top of the charts for 3 weeks. Both songs seemed to imply a hawkish view of Vietnam but were actually protest songs about antiwar protesters. Bobby Bare's "God Bless America Again" reached number 16 in 1969, and in 1970 Bill Anderson's "Where Have All the Heroes Gone" reached number 6. Also in 1970, Jeannie C. Riley's "The Generation Gap" reached number 62.

In 1971 Merle Haggard's "Soldier's Last Letter," a World War II song, reached number 3, while "Battle Hymn of Lt. Calley" by C Company featuring Terry Nelson—a song in support of the leader of the My Lai massacre—reached number 49 (and 37 on the pop charts). Also in 1971 Johnny Cash's "Singing in Viet Nam Talking Blues" reached number 18.

But in 1972 an anti-Vietnam sentiment emerged slightly in country music with Skeeter Davis's "One Tin Soldier," which reached number 54 on the country charts after the original version by Original Caste was a hit on the pop charts. Another cover release, "Tie a Yellow Ribbon" by Johnny Carver reached number 5 (Tony Orlando and Dawn had the pop hit).

While country music never quite embraced "flower power," there were some songs that promoted a general cosmic goodness. Examples are "It Takes People Like You (To Make People Like Me)" by Buck Owens (1967); "I Wanna Live" by Glen Campbell (1968); "I Believe in Love" by Bonnie Guitar (1968); "Less of Me" by Bobbie Gentry and Glen Campbell (1968); "Try a Little Kindness" by Glen Campbell (1969); "Everything Is Beautiful" by Ray Stevens (which reached number 1 on the pop charts but only number 39 on the country charts in 1970); "Let's Get Together," a remake of the Youngbloods's pop hit by George Hamilton IV and Skeeter Davis (1970); "Bridge Over Troubled Water," a remake of the Simon and Garfunkel hit by Buck Owens (1971); "I Wanna Be Free" by Loretta Lynn (1971); and "I'm Just Me" by Charley Pride (1971). In 1973 "I Love" by Tom T. Hall hit number 1. In 1974 songs such as "Love Is Like a Butterfly" by Dolly Parton (number 1) and "I Care" by Tom T. Hall hit the country charts.

Mainstream country music generally avoided the racial issue, although Kenny Rogers's "Ruben James," a song about a white child being raised by a black woman, reached number 46 in 1969 and "Irma Jackson," a song about interracial love written by Merle Haggard reached number 67 on the charts in 1970 by Tony Booth.

Songs addressing the working life in the early 1960s include "Get a Little Dirt on Your Hands" by Bill Anderson, which reached number 14 in 1962; "Busted" by Johnny Cash, which rose to number 13; "Detroit City" by Bobby Bare (which made it to number 6 on the country charts and number 16 on the pop charts); and "Last Day in the Mines" by Dave Dudley (1963). In 1967 Tex Ritter had "A Working Man's Prayer," a song that went to number 59. Merle Haggard, country music's chief social commentator, presented an anthem to the working class with "Working Man Blues," which reached number 1 in 1969.

Other songs that addressed the working life include "If I Were a Carpenter" by Johnny Cash and June Carter (1970); "I Never Picked Cotton" by Roy Clark (1970); "Oney" by Johnny Cash (1972); "Working Class Hero" by Tommy Roe; "If We Make It Through December" by Merle Haggard; and "That Girl Who Waits on Tables" by Ronnie Milsap, all in 1973. The most significant of these is the number 1 hit "If We Make It through December," which tells of a man facing Christmas with his family after being laid off during an economic downturn.

Truck driving songs, which became anthems to the blue collar working man, were popular in country music during the 1960s. In 1963 Dave Dudley released "Six Days on the Road," which reached number 2 on the country charts and number 32 on the pop charts, and Hank Snow saw his "Ninety Miles an Hour (Down a Dead End Street)" go to number 2. In 1964 George Hamilton IV went to number 11 with "Truck Driving Man." In 1965 Del Reeves's "Girl on the Billboard" reached number 1. That same year, Dick Curless released "A Tombstone Every Mile," which went to number 5, and Dave Dudley came out with "Truck Drivin' Son-of-a-Gun," which peaked at number 3.

The popularity of Red Sovine's "Giddyup Go," which reached number 1 in January 1966 and remained in that position for 6 weeks, led to two answer songs: Minnie Pearl's "Giddyup Go—Answer," which reached number 10 and Don Bowman's "Giddyup Do-Nut," which reached number 49. Also in 1966 Red Simpson—who made a career out of singing trucking songs—released "Roll Truck Roll" (number 38), "The Highway Patrol" (number 39), and "Diesel Smoke, Dangerous Curves" (number 41). Kay Adams's trucking song "Little Pink Mack," which reached number 30, was also released in 1966.

Several trucking songs made it into the top 15 positions in 1967: "Phantom 309" by Red Sovine (number 9), "How Fast Them Trucks Can Go" by Claude Gray (number 12), and "Anything Leaving Town Today" by Dave Dudley (number 12). Trucking songs that landed in the top 15 in 1968 include "There Ain't No Easy Run" by Dave Dudley (number 10) and "Looking at the World Through a Windshield" by Del Reeves (number 5).

Dave Dudley reached number 12 in 1969 with "One More Mile" and number 8 in 1971 with "Comin' Down." Also in 1971 Red Simpson's "I'm a Truck" hit number 4. In 1973 Dave Dudley topped the charts again with "Keep On Truckin'" (number 10). Finally, C.W. McCall's "Wolfe Creek Pass" peaked at number 12 in 1974.

During the 1963–1974 period only two songs mentioned welfare. One, "Waitin' in Your Welfare Line" by Buck Owens (1966), is a semi-humorous attempt to compare his undying love to welfare stereotypes. The other, Guy Drake's number 6 hit "Welfare Cadillac" voices the idea that those on welfare are driving Cadillacs—a forerunner to the view of "welfare queens" who collect welfare checks while living an affluent lifestyle. (The image was popular but no one found an actual example of this.)

The issue of class is evident in country songs throughout 1963–1974 with the country singer generally being poor and up against the rich or privileged. In 1963 Lester Flatt and Earl Scruggs had a number 1 hit with "The Ballad of Jed Clampett," the theme song to the television series *The Beverly Hillbillies*. The theme of a poor but proud country native who, while naive, possesses a native intelligence that allows him to take advantage of a rich man's greed is also central to the song "Saginaw, Michigan" by Lefty Frizzell, which reached number 1 in 1964. In 1964 Johnny Cash had a hit with "The Ballad of Ira Hayes," which tells the tale of a Native American who helped hoist the flag at Iwo Jima but is an outcast back at home.

Two other songs of the period are also strong examples of class struggle: "Coal Miner's Daughter" by Loretta Lynn, which reached number 1 in 1970, and "Coat of Many Colors," released by Dolly Parton in 1971. In both of these songs the singer is proud of her heritage, while at the same time acknowledging the pain of poverty.

The idea of family values was prevalent in country music throughout the 1960s and early 1970s. In 1962 Jimmy Dean had a hit with "To a Sleeping Beauty" about a father's love for his daughter. In 1964 Porter Wagoner offered "Howdy Neighbor Howdy," which welcomes visitors to a country home. In 1965 Ned Miller offered fatherly advice in "Do What You Do, Do Well"; Jimmy Dean sang a love song to his wife, "The First Thing Ev'ry Morning (And the Last Thing Ev'ry Night)," which reached number 1; and Sonny James had "True Love's a Blessing." Meanwhile, Loretta Lynn gave a warning to her wayward husband in "The Home You're Tearin' Down." In 1968 Glen Campbell had a number 3 hit with "Dreams of the Everyday Housewife"; Bobby Goldsboro sang "The Straight Life"; and Eddy Arnold sang "They Don't Make Love Like They Used To."

In 1969 Johnny Cash had a number 1 hit with "Daddy Sang Bass," about a family that sang together and stayed together, while Merle Haggard had a number 1 hit with "Hungry Eyes," about love defined through a family's poverty.

In 1971 two songs about children, "Watching Scotty Grow" by Bobby Goldsboro and "Two Dollar Toy" by Stoney Edwards, were released. That year also saw the release of "Daddy Frank" (number 1) by Merle Haggard; "Take Me Home, Country Roads" by John Denver; and "One's On the Way" by Loretta Lynn, which reached its number 1 position the following year. Three family- or home-oriented songs hit number 1 in 1972: "Bedtime Story" by Tammy Wynette; "Grandma Harp" by Merle Haggard; and "Happiest Girl in the Whole U.S.A." by Donna Fargo. In 1973 Loretta Lynn released "Love Is the Foundation" (number 1) as well as "Rated X," a feminist plea to not judge a woman by appearances. Strong family values messages are also evident in other artists' releases of 1973, including

"Kids Say the Darndest Things" (number 1) by Tammy Wynette; "Kid Stuff" by Barbara Fairchild; "We're Gonna Hold On" (number 1) by George Jones and Tammy Wynette; and "Daddy, What If" by Bobby Bare with Bobby Jr. In 1974 songs such as "(We're Not) The Jet Set" by George Jones and Tammy Wynette; "They Don't Make 'em Like My Daddy" by Loretta Lynn; "Country Bumpkin" (number 1) by Cal Smith; "No Charge" (number 1) by Melba Montgomery; and "Back Home Again" by John Denver (number 1) dealt with themes of home and family.

Although country music may be labeled conservative when measured against the liberal ideas of civil rights, anti-Vietnam War protests, feminism, and criticism of society in general and the United States in particular, an examination of the songs of this 1963–1974 period show a mixed bag. In general, country music songs were more conservative through the 1960s but seemed to become more liberal as the 1970s began. Part of this increased liberalism was likely the result of growing dissatisfaction with the Vietnam War. The middle and working classes turned against the war not only for political reasons but for personal reasons as well: Most of the young men who served were from poor, working-class families. These families were often country music's audience.

After the first wave of anti-integration sentiment led by George Wallace had passed, it was hard to be against addressing the injustices brought to light by the civil rights movement. While most Southerners who came of age during this era privately carried the racist baggage of their parents to some degree or another, those who continued to be staunchly racist could no longer voice those views to wide support in the public arena. Moreover, the creative community tends to be more tolerant than society at large, and the musicians, songwriters, and singers who make up the country music community tended to be more open to a racially mixed society, especially since many of them had grown up enjoying integrated music like rock 'n' roll, were influenced by rhythm and blues, and cheered black sports stars. Also, many Southerners were appalled by the violence of anti-integrationists and wanted no part of that. Once the barriers of segregation came down, people realized that the imagined horrors of blacks and whites eating in the same restaurant or working together wasn't as bad as they had imagined.

There is no doubt that country music in general rejected the counterculture during the years 1963–1974. Yet this fact was expressed most vociferously in country musicians' casual conversations, rather than in their songs. Hints of it can be seen in occasional public documents like Paul Hemphill's book *The Nashville Sound* and Robert Altman's 1975 film *Nashville*. By and large, most singers were more interested in releasing a hit record than in making a social statement—and when making a social statement threatened to get in the way of their career, they were likely to keep their views to themselves.

7

Country Music and the National Media

The national print media wrote basically the same story about country music over and over during the 20-year period after World War II (1945–1965). Country music, it seems, was always just being discovered and was better than the reader thought and you're not going to believe this but a lot of people actually like it so well that country artists sell a lot of records!

An article from *Time* in 1941 about the hit song "New San Antonio Rose," written by western swing legend Bob Wills and recorded by Bing Crosby, sets the tone. It states, "This song, 'New San Antonio Rose,' may baffle or even irritate fastidious rhetoricians, and its tune is strictly golden bantam. Yet last week Decca Records reported that in January alone the song had sold 84,500 disks."[1]

In 1943 that same magazine headlined an article "Bull Market in Corn" where it states, "The dominant popular music of the U.S. today is hillbilly." The article continues that "this constituted the biggest revolution in U.S. popular musical taste since the 'swing' craze began in the middle 30s." In describing country songs it states, "Preserved in the U.S. backwoods by generations of hard-bitten country folk, the old hillbilly ballads are sometimes of rare melodic beauty. But most of them hew closely to a few homely, foursquare formulas. The songs get their quality, if any, from their words— long narrative poems evolved by generations of backwoods minstrels."

It mentions the recording "It Makes No Difference Now" by Jimmie Davis and says this record "really started the corn sprouting on Broadway." It then concludes, "Almost any simple soul might write hillbilly words and the composition of hillbilly music has always been regarded by Tin Pan Alley as a variety of unskilled labor."[2]

In an article in *Life* in 1943 which discussed the immensely popular country song "Pistol Packin' Mama" during the war, the magazine describes the song as a "raucous little item" and "obnoxious." Elaborating on the record by Al Dexter, the articles says the song "is naive, folksy, and almost completely devoid of meaning. Its melodic line is simple and its lyric rowdy and, of course, monotonously tautological" before concluding that the record "promised to become even more of a national earache than it is at the moment."[3]

In an article titled "Hillbilly Boom" by Maurice Zolotow in the *Saturday Evening Post,* the writer cites the sales figures of "Pistol Packin' Mama" "which proves that hillbilly music has come into its own." The writer notes that other million sellers during this same time include country songs like "There's a Star-Spangled Banner Waving Somewhere" by Elton Britt and "No Letter Today" by Ted Daffan and his Texans. It notes that, "On the road, hillbilly troupes will consistently outdraw legitimate Broadway plays, symphony concerts, sophisticated comedians and beautiful dancing girls" and observes that Roy Acuff will draw large crowds while others, like Betty Grable and Bob Hope, "would only succeed in drawing boll weevils."

The article talks about Art Satherley, one of the pioneers in field recordings of country music and states that he will travel "into regions where no city shoes have ever trod before." In an attempt to show a little respect for the diversity of country music, the article concludes "Although all hillbilly music sounds monotonously alike to the urban eardrum, it includes many types of music."[4]

In an article in *Collier's* in 1946 titled "Whoop-and-Holler Opera," writer Doron K. Antrim begins, "There's a moanin' and a wailin' throughout the land as the resurgent hillbillies whang away at their doleful tales of love and woe." The writer states that country music is "the epidemic of corn that is sweeping the country today" and describes country musicians as "barefoot fiddlers who couldn't read a note but who could raise a voice on endless tunes, especially with the aid of corn liquor."[5]

In a review of a performance by Bob Wills in California in 1946, *Time* notes that Wills's song, "G.I. Wish" "had the same kind of whine, the same kind of maudlin lyrics that put his 'Stars and Stripes on Iwo Jima' and 'Smoke on the Water' among the nation's top-selling folk records last year." In this article *Time* called Wills a "backwoods Lombardo."[6]

In 1948 the *Christian Science Monitor* ran an article titled "Hillbilly Phenomenon." Writer Robert Schermann notes, "Cowboy music is paying off in a big way. In the past year its chief exponent, the hillbilly singer, has been the biggest money maker in show business." The writer continues that during country shows audiences "whoop, stomp, jump and generally raise the roof" while the band consists of "an ill-tuned fiddle, a couple of raspy guitars, perhaps a bass fiddle, and a delicate little instrument known as the steel guitar, from which there can be coaxed anything from the croak of a bullfrog to the clang of a cowbell."[7]

In an article titled "Corn Of Plenty" in *Newsweek* in 1949, the magazine states, "'The corn is as high as an elephant's eye—and so are the profits.'

A hard-bitten Tin Pan Alley character shook his head in amazement, for he was talking about hillbilly songs—the current wonder of the music world.... Hillbilly music is now such a vogue that it is just about pushing popular tunes, jazz, swing, bebop, and everything else right out of the picture."

The article continues that, "While the rest of the music business remained in its chronic fluttery state, the hillbilly output remained fairly constant. But the demand for it has multiplied fivefold since the war. This week the industry was still moving in concentric circles and nothing was dependable—except hillbilly music."

The article gives some grudging respect, stating, "Once a specialty product marketed in the Deep South, it now has a nationwide sales field" before concluding "it would seem that all a singer needs is a hoedown fiddle, a steel guitar, a mandolin, and a new inflection in his voice—and he's set for the bonanza."[8]

In an article in the *New York Times Magazine* in 1951 titled "Tin Pan Alley's Git-Tar Blues," writer Allen Churchill states, "New York's writers of pop tunes look in envy and calculation at the 'Country' songsmiths now outsmarting the city slickers," and continues, "Adding insult to misery is the fact that the bellwether song of the folk music trend seems destined eventually to unseat the Alley's favorite—Irving Berlin's 'White Christmas'—as the top popular tune of our time." The song he was discussing was "Tennessee Waltz," recorded by Patti Page but written by country songwriters Pee Wee King and Redd Stewart and published by the Nashville firm of Acuff-Rose.

The article continues, "New Yorkers have long been blissfully unaware of the fact, but this country contains two great song-buying areas. One is the city field, which goes for 'pop' songs from Tin Pan Alley, Broadway shows, and Hollywood musicals. The other is the country field, the territory outside cities, especially in the South, where music is taken more seriously than anywhere else. Music enjoyed in this vast area consists of all types of hillbilly, mountain, Western and old-time folk tunes, jumbled together under the encompassing name of country music." The article also notes that "the financial success of top country singers has aroused the envy of city folk."[9]

In an article titled "Hillbilly Heaven" in *American Magazine* in 1952, writer Don Eddy begins the article, "If you don't mind, I will write this report lying down. I feel giddy. Before my eyes are funny little men chasing each other with pitchforks and banjos. In my ears ring mournful sounds such as never were before on land or sea. No, it's nothing I et. It's because I have been exposed, in person, to a national phenomenon called Grand Ole Opry, and I'm afraid it bit me."

The writer continues in this smarmy, cutesy vein, stating, "This noteworthy nation has been taken down bad with an epidemic called hillbillyitis" and notes there's lots of money in country music with the observation, "For guys who were skinning mules not too long ago, this is a lovely bale of hay."[10]

In *Cornet Magazine* in 1952 an article titled "Nashville, Broadway and Country Music" by writer H.B. Teeter talks about the large amounts of money country stars are making while an article in *Newsweek* that same year entitled "Country Music is Big Business and Nashville is Its Detroit" states that, "Country music has become more than a regional manifestation; it has become a national desire." It describes country music as "this twang-wail-and-howl division of the electronics industry" and notes, "Whether heard on TV, radio, jukebox, phonograph, or by orchestra, this shouting or moaning from an old transatlantic past is doing a sturdy fifth of the dollar volume of the music for which the United States pays money to hear."[11]

In *Nation's Business* in 1953 an article by Rufus Jarman titled "Country Music Goes to Town" notes that country music is an industry grossing an estimated $25 million a year and observes, "These country glamor boys are as big—sometimes bigger—in record sales and juke box popularity as Bing Crosby or Frank Sinatra....They live in mansions with swimming pools attached in Nashville's fashionable suburbs, drive immense automobiles bearing their initials in gold, and wear expensive Western getups."[12]

In "Hillbilly Music Leaves the Hills" in *Good Housekeeping* in 1954, the article states,

> Who would have thought ten years ago that a group of country singers and a few musicians playing guitars, banjos, and fiddles could fill the auditoriums of big cities? What, no tricky pianist, no singer with sexy eyes, no smooth star belting the latest Broadway ballad! No, just simple songs and dances performed in homespun style—and all over the country people are "naive" enough to pay money to hear it.
>
> As a matter of fact, country-music concerts have become astonishingly popular in the last three years. Most curiously, they've been particularly popular in the big towns—in Cleveland, St. Louis, Baltimore, Philadelphia, Cincinnati, San Francisco, and even conservative Boston. In fact, about the only big town hillbilly music has not invaded is New York City. Small groups performing such music are traveling to America's small towns, playing jamborees. Mountain music has left the mountains and gone down to the plains.[13]

In a review of a Broadway attempt at a country musical in 1954 called "Hayride," reviewer Maurice Zolotow, who had earlier been to Nashville and written about the Opry, states, "In the fashionable circles in which I move, hillbilly music is considered almost as 'degage' as wearing cloth coats or smoking those old-fashioned unfiltered cigarettes."[14]

In *House & Garden* in 1954 the article "Folk Songs" by Roy Harris states, "Hillbilly music emphasizes the lovelorn, the country fiddler, the camp meeting and occasionally the goings-on of country bumpkins (both sexes and all ages). The tunes and the harmonies are all about the same, rearranged to fit the words, some fast, some slow. The hillbilly racket begets some of the poorest music that ever entered human ears and yet it seems to give pleasure to many people."[15]

In "Country Music: The Squaya Dansu from Nashville" by Eli Waldron in *The Reporter* in 1955, the writer states, "In our own land, hillbilly music seems to be tremendously popular everywhere but in Manhattan" after observing "Hillbilly music is a booming business at the present time and its popularity is widespread. It is highly regarded in Japan and flourishes in many parts of Europe and Africa." In discussing country music, the articles states, "Present-day hillbilly music seems to be woven around three main themes— death (very often on the highway), unrequited love, and religious gimmickry such as the use of telephones and other modern technological devices in an effort to get in touch with the Beyond.... The stanch hillbilly fan also requires monumental dosages of sentimentality at regular intervals.... There is no sign of abatement among the whining guitars and mandolins and the shouts of square dancers around the world."[16]

In 1956 *Life* ran an article titled "Country Musicians Fiddle Up Roaring Business" that states, "Up until a few years ago one half of the popular music fans of America had no idea what the other half was up to. One half listened to slick songs from Hollywood and Broadway. The other—mostly from rural districts—was devoted to a brand of music loosely known as hillbilly."

The article continues, "This year some 50 million country music records will be sold, which is 40% of the total sales of all single popular music records," and that, "Nashville has become the country's third biggest record-making center, just behind New York and Hollywood." It observes that country stars "own comfortable homes, spend most of their social life visiting each other and generally spend money on expensive cars, fancy electrical appliances and thoroughbred horses."[17]

In "Country Sweeps the Country" by Goddard Lieberson in the *New York Times Magazine* in 1957, the writer, who later became head of Columbia Records, states, "One of the reigning artists recently floored a *Wall Street Journal* man by professing ignorance of his exact income, but allowing as how he had paid $48,000 in taxes for the preceding year." In discussing the music Lieberson states, "Country music is often pervaded with a strong melancholy, placing much lyric emphasis on ill-fated love, death, economic insecurity and even sibling rivalry. But it also has great streaks of just plain old homespun fun and native wit.... It has been observed by philosophers of the country field that singers are better off (1) when they can't read music (because they shouldn't sing it exactly the way it's written anyhow), and (2) when their voices don't become too polished."[18]

In 1960 *Time* published an article, "Hoedown on a Harpischord" about country music that states, "Its demise has often seemed near, but it is now going stronger than ever, and Nashville has even nosed out Hollywood as the nation's second biggest (after New York) record-producing center." It notes that "One out of every five popular hits of the past year was written and recorded in Nashville, and, discussing the "Nashville Sound," observes, "As nearly as anybody can define it, the Sound is the byproduct of musical illiteracy."[19]

In the article "Country Music: Nashville Style" by Richard Marek in *McCall's* in 1961, the writer notes that country is "the most popular music in America today" although "the new sound at the Opry is less authentic country music, more akin to the popular styles of today (although not strictly pop songs)."[20]

The observation that country music is absorbing the sounds of popular music is a common one that began in the early 1960s, as the "Nashville Sound" was developed and promoted and right after the first rock 'n' roll revolution. This observation always carries the underlying message that country music isn't as bad as you think it is. The simple fact is that country music has always been influenced by popular music from its earliest recordings. When Fiddlin' John Carson recorded "The Little Ole Log Cabin in the Lane" in Atlanta, Georgia, in June 1923 and began what became the country recording industry, he recorded a song written by Will Shakespeare Hays for minstrel shows—the popular music of its day. And Jimmie Rodgers, the "father of Country Music" who first recorded in August 1927 and, with the Carter Family, was most instrumental in creating the commercial country music industry, was heavily influenced by popular music and never really considered his songs "hillbilly," although he appealed primarily to rural audiences. Bob Wills was a country boy who grew up in the Jazz Age and had a swing band with traditional country instruments but was always insulted when people confused his music with "hillbilly" music. The earliest Opry shows often began with a string band doing "There'll Be a Hot Time in the Old Town Tonight." The list can go on to performers who became popular after World War II or even into the twenty-first century, but the point is clear: country music on recordings has never been an exclusively rural, isolated folk music dominated by British ballads collected in the mountains and sung by illiterate yokels. Still, the image persists.

And so does the image of country set to become "the next big thing." The major media routinely ignore the fact that country music is an ongoing phenomenon, that it consistently sells well—always has and always will. Still, the major media periodically "discover" country music and announce it to the world. An article from the *Toronto Daily Star* in 1964, "Make Way for the Country Sound" by Morris Duff, is indicative of this. In this article the writer states, "It looks as if the new zipped-up, country music is going to be the next big sound." He observes "At a time when many other clubs are pushing panic buttons, those featuring country and western are doing business, even when it rains or snows," and "Record stores that a year ago couldn't be bothered stocking country discs today are selling them in abundance." He gives the example of a record salesman: "A year ago, when he tried to sell country discs, he was given every excuse in the book.

Today almost all buy them eagerly." The article concludes, "Big reason for the boom is that people who formerly couldn't stand the country sound are now listening with relish. In fact, many fans don't even realize that's what they're enjoying."[21]

In that same year (1964) *Time* published a major article titled "Country Music: The Nashville Sound" that states, "Country and Western music, known in the trade as C&W, has never been more widely popular." It notes that "Nashville, with 21 recording studios, produces 30% of the nation's hit singles," and "the tenacious loyalty of C&W fans, who through the years have made country music the most durable sound on the popular market." In attempting to define the Nashville sound it notes, "More than the drawling, sow-belly accents and nasal intonations of the singers, it is the background music provided by the sidemen on twangy electric guitars."[22]

In "Country Music Snaps Its Regional Bounds" in *Business Week* in 1966 the magazine notes, "The 'Nashville Sound' has hit the $600-million popular music business, and it's the hottest thing around. The fiddles, the guitars, and the nasal Southern wail, which once assailed Northern ears only as their owners passed through on the way to Miami, have become part of the national idiom, every bit as important as rock 'n' roll."

The magazine continues that "Country music is substantially more important than the traditional Tin Pan Alley trade," and that, "Four out of every 10 records sold are either country music, or show its influence."[23] That same year (1966) *Newsweek* ran an article titled "The Gold Guitars" that states, "Last year country music raked in $70 million, or about 10 percent of the total sales of all records. About 25 percent of major labels releases are country." It observes that "Sooner or later, the fever of country music was bound to spread to epidemic proportions," and that, "What has made the Nashville Sound an all-American sound is the evolution of country music toward popular taste. The raw, nasal 'hillbilly' sound, alien to urban ears, has gradually been discarded."[24]

Also in 1966 *The Saturday Evening Post* published a long article, "That New Sound from Nashville" written by Charles Portis that states, "Country music is prospering, and so is Nashville's recording industry, which now does a brisk non-country trade." This article does provide an insightful observation that most outsiders miss when it states, "Few country singers manage to get themselves taken seriously in Nashville...generally, the Athenians of the South go one way, and the country-music people another."

Portis writes that, "Hillbilly is characterized by a squonking fiddle introduction, a funeral steel guitar and an overall whiney, draggy sound that has never set well with urban ears," but then notes, "This music has a new acceptance and a new dignity....It's not, you know, the old hillbilly stuff, the nasal voices, those guitars thumping and all."

Portis continues, "The songs have been scorned and ridiculed so long by outsiders that the performers themselves have come to place little value on them. A good many of the singers, one gathers, would turn to pop music tomorrow morning if they could change their accents and get booked in Las Vegas." This is indeed a legitimate point—that country music performers have often lacked self-respect when they venture towards the pop world—but this lack of self-respect is a direct result of a lack of respect from the major media who have written so derisively about country music through the years.

Portis observes that, "To many people the most interesting thing, the only interesting thing about the business is the money—the idea of all them old country boys being in the chips, driving Cadillacs with six-shooter door handles and wearing outrageous, glittering Western suits, designed by Nudie of Hollywood." And again he hits the nail on the head regarding outsiders looking into country music for a quick peek.[25]

Well, this could go on ad nauseam but the point has surely been made by now: the national print media was rather dismissive or even hostile toward country music in the 20 years after World War II and perpetuated an image that plagued country music, and its fans, for years. This image was, to a large extent, accepted even within the country music industry with the result that for most of its history those involved in the country music industry suffered a negative self-image whenever they faced New York-based media and the popular music world.

8

Country Music in
the 1960s and 1970s

BAKERSFIELD VS. NASHVILLE

During the late 1950s and early 1960s there were two sources for mainstream country music: Bakersfield, California, and Nashville. The Bakersfield sound was driven by Buck Owens, whose first chart record appeared on Capitol in 1959. Beginning in 1963 he had a string of number 1 hits, starting with "Act Naturally" and continuing through "Love's Gonna Live Here" (number 1 for 16 weeks), "My Heart Skips a Beat" (number 1 for 7 weeks in 1964), "Together Again," "I've Got a Tiger By the Tail" (number 1 for 5 weeks in 1965), and "Waitin' In Your Welfare Line" (number 1 for 7 weeks in 1966). Owens's hits continued throughout the 1960s; in 1963 he was joined on the charts by his fellow Bakersfield resident, Merle Haggard, whose first chart record was "Sing a Sad Song."

Merle Haggard hit his stride in 1966 when he began a string of hits with "Swinging Doors" and continued through "The Fugitive," "Branded Man," "Sing Me Back Home," "Mama Tried," "Workin' Man Blues," and "Okie from Muskogee." Haggard continued releasing hit singles throughout the 1970s and 1980s as the "traditional" or "honky tonk" sound of country music found a secure slot on country radio.

In 1964 the Academy of Country Music was formed in Los Angeles to promote West Coast country and Haggard was an early, consistent winner.

Meanwhile, in Nashville the mid-to-late 60s and early 1970s were the heyday for The Nashville Sound with songs like "Make the World Go Away" by Eddy Arnold (1965) and "For the Good Times" by Ray Price (1970) providing excellent examples of country music eschewing fiddles for strings and steel guitars for a smooth, tight rhythm section of piano, bass, drums, and guitars. Country music had been accepted by a broad spectrum of middle class listeners who came of age with pop music in the early 1950s but now watched country music shows in prime time on television.

COUNTRY MUSIC ON TV: THE 1960s

The early 60s did not see many country music shows introduced on network TV; *The Five Star Jubilee* began on March 17, 1961, and ended its run on September 22 that same year. In the fall of 1962 the *Roy Rogers and Dale Evans Show* was carried by ABC. The *Pet Milk Grand Ole Opry* series began in 1960.

Country artists appeared on TV folk and rock music shows *Hootenanny* and *Shindig* while Flatt and Scruggs were heard performing the popular theme song each week on *The Beverly Hillbillies* and the Dillards and the Kentucky Colonels could be heard on *The Andy Griffith Show*. (Although Flatt and Scruggs performed the TV theme song, and Lester Flatt sang the number 1 hit heard on radio in 1962, the TV theme was sung by Jerry Scoggins, formerly a member of The Cass County Boys, the backup group for Gene Autry during his last movies and tours.)

Country performers also appeared on the Grammy Awards telecasts, *The Dean Martin Show, The Joey Bishop Show,* and *The Mike Douglas Show*. Roger Miller hosted *The Roger Miller Show,* on Monday nights on NBC in the fall of 1966 but the show only lasted a few months.

The Kraft Music Hall originally ran on radio from 1933–1949 and the most famous host was Bing Crosby (1936–1946). It moved to TV in 1946 and beginning in the 1950s had a host for a season (Milton Berle and Perry Como were hosts). *The Kraft Music Hall* on NBC during the 1967–1968 season played a major role in the history of country music because each show was self-contained. In spring 1968, Dinah Shore, a Nashville native, hosted a special on *The Nashville Sound* and from April 24 to June 5 Eddy Arnold hosted the show, subtitled *Country Fair*. This show hosted the first live telecast of the Country Music Awards.

The *Country Music Association Awards Show* was first held in 1967 and hosted by Sonny James and Bobbie Gentry. The first broadcast of the show was in 1968 when Roy Rogers and Dale Evans hosted; the show was televised a few weeks later. The first live broadcast of the program occurred in 1968.

The end of the 1960s had several important country music shows on TV. Beginning in the summer of 1968, *Dean Martin Presents* appeared on NBC; in 1973, its final year, country artists Loretta Lynn, Lynn Anderson, Jerry Reed, and Ray Stevens were regulars. In the summer of 1968 Glen Campbell hosted the replacement show for *The Smothers Brothers Comedy Hour;* in January 1969 this became *The Glen Campbell Goodtime Hour* and ran until 1972. Regulars included John Hartford, Jerry Reed, and The Mike Curb Congregation.

On June 7, 1969, *The Johnny Cash Show* debuted and became a top rated show, appearing on ABC until 1971 with regulars Mother Maybelle and the

Carter Family, the Statler Brothers, Carl Perkins, the Tennessee Three, and Bill Walker's Orchestra. Cash revived his show on CBS in the summer of 1976 with regulars June Carter Cash, Steve Martin, Jim Varney, and Bill Walker's Orchestra. The show began with "Folsom Prison Blues" as a theme song and closed with "I Walk the Line"; during the program there was the popular "Ride This Train" segment.

The longest running TV show—and the one that has received the most criticism for stigmatizing country music with stereotypes it has yet to shake—began on June 15, 1969. *Hee Haw* featured top country acts but had a distinctly country yokel theme. Hosted by Roy Clark and Buck Owens, the show ran on the CBS network until 1971 when it went into syndication.

Throughout the 1960s country music also appeared regularly on TV with syndicated shows. Artists who hosted these shows included Flatt and Scruggs, Porter Wagoner, Leroy Van Dyke, Ernest Tubb, Bobby Lord, Bill Anderson, Carl Smith, Jim and Jesse, Billy Walker, Del Reeves, Billy Grammer, and Kitty Wells. Buck Owens, in Bakersfield, California, and Arthur Smith, in Charlotte, North Carolina, also starred in syndicated series. These shows were primarily half-hour programs where the star was the host and sang three or four songs, then a guest artist usually sang two songs.

In many ways *Hee Haw* was a throwback of country music from a bygone era. The radio barn dances of the 1940s featured big casts and a heavy emphasis on rube comedy and the hayseed image. But as country music emerged through the 1950s it increasingly moved away from the hayseed image into one with a more suburban appeal. Rhinestone suits replaced bib overalls and comedy was cut back. In TV the emergence of the "star" performer meant that the casts were much smaller and the old barn dance format was out. Also, throughout the 1950s and 60s country music sought to move uptown, present a more dignified and respectable image, and move away from the traditional stereotype of blue collar hicks. But *Hee Haw* had a huge cast, dressed their regulars in bib overalls, and used old vaudeville and barn dance routines in their comedy skits. It was immensely popular, both to the enjoyment and to the chagrin of the country music establishment. On one hand it proved the national appeal of country music, but it also saddled country music with an image it had been trying to deny and escape: country bumpkins down on the farm.

COUNTRY RADIO

The Nashville country music community reacted to rock 'n' roll by forming the Country Music Association (CMA) from the remains of the Country Music Disc Jockeys Association, which virtually died at their meeting in Miami in early 1958. A key part of the game plan for the CMA was an appeal to advertising agencies and sponsors to buy ads on country radio and make programming country music profitable. If there was money then programming would follow. To this extent, they were incredibly successful.

In their first official survey of country radio in 1961 the CMA discovered only 81 stations playing country music full time. However, through their efforts the number of country stations began to increase and showed a steady climb throughout the 1960s. Those who marketed and produced country music concentrated on creating a smoother sound for an adult population—The Nashville Sound—which appealed to the pop music markets. Meanwhile, country music pursued the "crossover," or a recording that appeared on both the pop and country radio formats (and also the pop and country charts). If crossover success was achieved, then big sales resulted; sticking simply to the country music market meant limited sales. Some of the crossover artists who enjoyed the benefits of this move were Roger Miller, Eddy Arnold, Ray Price, Patsy Cline, Jim Reeves, and Johnny Cash.

Country radio showed slow but steady growth in the early 1960s, rising from 81 stations playing country full time in 1961, to 97 in 1963, then 208 in 1965. During the 1966–1969 period country radio tripled so that, by the last year of the decade, there were 606 radio stations programming country music full time.

In 1970 a new booster organization for country radio appeared. The First Annual Country Music Survey Radio Seminar was held May 15–16, 1970, in Nashville. The event that later became known as The Country Radio Seminar got off to a rather inauspicious start, barely limping through the starting gate. Tex Ritter gave the keynote speech, introduced by Ralph Emery, but most of the big names in the country music industry stayed away, keeping the new organization at arm's distance.

The Seminar was the brainchild of Tom McEntee, who moved to Nashville from New York in early 1969. McEntee came to Nashville as managing editor of *Country Music Survey*, a radio tip sheet. (A tip sheet kept in contact with radio stations and reported what those stations were doing, "tipping" off the industry about breaking records, new acts, and other insider information.)

There were two major radio conferences held annually before the Country Radio Seminar—the Gavin Conference, which began in 1969, and the *Billboard* International Radio-TV Programming Forum, which began in the spring of 1969. But both of those conferences focused on pop or rock music; there wasn't much for country radio. Country radio had the Grand Ole Opry Birthday celebration, nicknamed "The Disk Jockey Convention," held each October and co-sponsored by the Country Music Association and WSM, but that convention had become an endless party that cost record labels thousands of dollars and, by 1970, had a diluted connection with country music radio because so many fans and assorted hangers-on had inundated the festivities.

In mid-November 1969, just after the conclusion of the annual Deejay Convention, McEntee met with several promotion men, including Rory Bourke (Mercury), B.J. McElwee (MGM), Jerry Seabolt (Plantation), and

Biff Collie (Liberty) at Bourke's home to discuss a possible convention for country radio.

At this point there were about 600 full-time country radio stations. The decision was made to hold the conference in the spring, to avoid the October event, and organizers began to canvas for panels and speakers. The Gavin Conference was used as a model—and an emphasis was placed on it being a conference and not a convention. The organizers set about trying to entice radio disc jockeys to come and a few responded. The first Seminar had 47 registrants who paid $35 each to be there; about 65–70 dropped by with approximately half from radio and the other half from the music industry. The Seminar concluded with its first and last awards dinner and show with Don Gibson as the main entertainment. Other entertainment included some "new faces" because well-known, established acts couldn't be enticed to perform there.

Country record companies weren't selling many records to consumers; about 85 percent of all country singles sold were sold to jukeboxes. And country music depended heavily on the crossover for major sales. Country radio was certainly important, and it grew throughout the 1960s, but it wasn't terribly significant in terms of major sales of country recordings.

By the time the second Country Radio Seminar rolled around, the Seminar had more industry support; however, a decision was made to keep it a "seminar" and not a convention, to stress education and fellowship and not make the event an industry blowout filled with self-serving promotions. The second event was officially known as the Nashville Country Music Radio Seminar; a board of directors was formed and two professors from a nearby university who staged professional seminars were hired to organize this one. It was held April 23–24, 1971, with a registration fee set at $50 and a lineup of unknown acts set for the dinner show because, like the year before, the top talent wouldn't play.

The country music industry in Nashville has always shown a willingness to pull together for the industry as a whole. In other cities music industry businessmen often competed against each other, fighting for their own self-interest. For some reason, the Nashville music business community has rallied together time and again, putting individual self-interest aside in order to promote the industry as a whole. Perhaps this is because the country music industry was rooted in the National Life and Accident Insurance Company whose executives regularly joined business booster organizations. It certainly helped that the first generation of successful country music business people— Jack Stapp, Jim Denny, Wesley Rose, Frances Preston, Owen Bradley, and Chet Atkins—all had roots at WSM and the *Opry* and saw the value of these booster organizations. The second generation of business people—most of those involved in the formation of the Country Radio Seminar—did not have roots in WSM but they saw how the Country Music Association had helped country music succeed and the value of pulling together for the industry as a whole. By this point the role models for the country music industry in Nashville were involved in booster organizations to promote country music, and they benefited collectively and personally from this involvement.

In 1972 the Country Radio Seminar was held at the King of the Road Motor Inn on May 12–13. The dinner show, officially titled *The New Faces Show* for the first time, was becoming more widely respected and accepted. There were about 150 attendees, with 55 country stations from 35 states represented. The Seminar had banned all promotional displays and handouts and the labels reluctantly agreed. So the seminar got down to the business at hand of improving country radio.

It was a time of country radio slipping backward. In 1971 the number of country stations dropped to 525, then rose to 633 in 1972. But in 1973 the number of country radio stations jumped to 764, then to 856 in 1974.[1] By this point the Country Radio Seminar had achieved a status of respect. In November 1972, the Seminar established itself as a nonprofit organization run by committees of individuals who served on a volunteer basis.

The 1974 Seminar was set for the third weekend in March at the Airport Hilton in Nashville—with the bars closed during the meetings to insure attendance—and there were 290 who attended at $60 a person. One of the areas the seminar dealt with was research—also a topic on the cutting edge at the time—and there was enough money made to begin funding college scholarships. At this point a survey of radio stations revealed that the average station played 40–70 records and that over two-thirds were by "non-country" artists.

The efforts of the Seminar, and the CMA, paid off handsomely that year and the next; in 1975 the number of country radio stations topped 1,000 for the first time (1,116). Growth slowed a bit—there were 1,140 in 1977 and 1,150 in 1978—but remained steady. The next spurt in growth for country radio came in 1979 when there were 1,434 country radio stations, then again in 1980 when there were 1,534 country stations. During the 1979 Seminar, which celebrated the tenth anniversary of the event, there were over 387 registrants, and in 1980 there were approximately 400 registrants with about 140 radio stations represented. Clearly, by this point, the Country Radio Seminar had come of age and gained respect for its promotion and development of country music radio stations.

The reason for the growth in country radio stations came because the pop/rock stations shifted to FM, leaving AM stations open for a new format. This was a direct result of a 1965 ruling by the Federal Communications Commission that required stations to stop simulcasting the AM signal on FM and develop different programming for FM.

Radio station owners usually owned the AM and FM signal but, because David Sarnoff, president of RCA, did not want radio to shift to FM after World War II (he wanted to save the FM band for TV and felt that once television arrived, radio would die), radio remained on the AM band. The owners kept their FM band but simulcast the AM program on that band so both AM and FM were broadcasting the same thing. Since there were so few FM receivers, this really didn't matter much until there was a demand for more radio stations. Since there was no more room on the AM band, the FCC required owners to program FM separately from AM.

Owners struggled to find programming for a medium that had virtually no income; since there were few FM receivers, advertisers saw no reason to advertise on the fledgling FM stations. At first the station owners tried "beautiful music" like the Montovani Strings; the reasoning was that (1) FM could broadcast in stereo so the better sound fit the beautiful music format, and (2) since FM receivers were rare, only the upper income population had them and they preferred classical and beautiful music to other types.

What emerged was underground radio, an extension of the alternative press of the 1960s that broadcast album-oriented rock, playing songs that could not be played on AM radio. The college-aged listener loved the new format; it was new, hip, and played music in stereo that complemented the hi-fi component systems in their dorm rooms and apartments. Since there were few if any advertisers for FM, the fledgling stations pioneered the idea of an hour of uninterrupted music, or music all night long or six in a row. The concept quickly caught on and the audience for FM radio grew.

As the 1960s turned into the 1970s, cars began to offer AM/FM radios for their models and major pop/rock stations switched to FM. The sound quality was much better, young audiences preferred FM, and it soon became financially profitable. The AM band, which had been home to the top pop/rock stations suddenly needed different programming and country music was there with a format that fit easily into the gap. And so throughout the 1970s the number of country radio stations increased because the pop/rock stations left AM for FM. Country would not make significant inroads into FM until the early 1980s when the format proved successful to the point where it could replace a pop/rock station that had low ratings.

THE OUTLAW MOVEMENT

While Nashville solidified its image as the Capital of Country Music, a challenger demanded attention down in Texas. Austin is home of the University of Texas and the city has always had a lively live music scene. In 1970 the Armadillo World Headquarters opened, housed in an old armory building. This venue joined the Broken Spoke, the Split Rail, Threadgill's Bar, the Vulcan Gas Company, and other venues that featured music each night.

Texas is home to cowboys—both real and self-proclaimed—as well as a spiritual center for country music. Young Texans might have loved rock 'n' roll during the 1960s, but country music was also deeply embedded in their soul so it is almost natural that the 60's counterculture met country music in Austin during the 1970s. A host of local and regional acts called the area in and around Austin home during the early 1970s and then a country music star arrived.

Willie Nelson was a widely respected songwriter and singer who had long captured the attention of Music Row in Nashville but could not catch the attention of a large public. He had written hits for Patsy Cline ("Crazy"), Faron Young ("Hello Wall"), Ray Price ("Night Life"), and Roy Orbison ("Pretty Paper") and recorded a string of chart records for Liberty and RCA Victor (21 of them between 1962 and 1972). But he never connected with the mainstream country music audience as a performer until he moved to Austin in 1970.

Nelson moved from Texas (he was born in Abbott, just south of Dallas) to Nashville in 1960 and might have remained there but his house burned down and he needed a place to stay. Since Nelson's roots were in Texas, and he regularly performed in clubs there, he decided to move to Houston, then changed his mind and went to Austin because of the lively music scene. When he arrived, as he noted, he found a parade and got in front of it.

In spring 1972, Nelson organized the first "Dripping Spring Reunion Festival" outside of Austin; on July 4, 1973, Nelson organized and hosted country music's Woodstock: "The First Annual Willie Nelson Fourth of July Picnic." Long-haired hippies and short-haired rednecks both came to Willie's Festival and communed in peace, aided by beer and marijuana. This was the beginning of the "Outlaw Movement" which brought sex, drugs, and rock 'n' roll to country music.

TIN PAN SOUTH

The Nashville Sound was more than just a "sound," it was an economic paradigm (record singles cheaply—four in a three-hour session—and if one hit, then make an album quickly and cheaply, don't spend much if anything on marketing, and let the album take care of itself) as well as a way of doing business. Led by Owen Bradley and Chet Atkins, "the fathers of the Nashville Sound," the business was conducted as an outpost of New York (or L.A.). Since singers spent most of their time on the road performing, the producers searched for songs and found them for the artists to record when they came into town. If an artist wrote or found songs on his or her own, that was great but it was the producer's responsibility to make sure there were songs to record. This was an outgrowth from the days of New York's Tin Pan Alley when there was a division of labor: singers sang and songwriters wrote. It continued through the Brill Building era in New York during the late 1950s and early 1960s. It was quite efficient as young artists were free to sing and tour while the songs were taken care of by professional songwriters back at the office.

This system was adapted by Nashville and led to Nashville becoming a songwriter's town, a place where a songwriter could make a living just writing songs and where artists had a steady stream of top-flight material to record. For the great singer who did not write this was perfect; for the singer who wrote some of his own songs, this was a great safety net which assured them that no matter what, there would always be great songs to record and sing, whether they were going through a dry spell as songwriters or not.

The major labels had a policy that all sessions were done in their studios; at this time the major labels each owned recording studios. The standard session for a single was three hours in which four songs were recorded with a minimum of over-dubbing and mixing was pretty much done off the board. An album consisted of three of four sessions, with the songs written before the session began because studio time was valuable. It was an efficient, effective way to make profitable recordings when country music did not sell in overwhelming numbers, and the New York and L.A. executives did not trust country musicians with their own careers.

Producers were assigned to artists; there wasn't much input from an artist although it was not a dictatorial situation; there was generally an amiability between the artist and label when deciding who would produce and an amiability between the artist and producer when deciding which songs to record. If an artist hated a song then the producer was not likely to force them to record it; however, in the end, it was the producer's (and record company's) decision about which songs were released.

Part of the reason for the artists deferring to producers was economic: there was no big money to be made in royalties from record sales. The artists made their money on personal appearances and personal appearance fees depended heavily on having a hit record on the radio. Since the record company dealt with radio station disc jockeys every day and therefore had a better "feel" for what radio wanted, then it made sense for the artist to defer to the record company about what fit best on country radio. If the record was a hit, the artist received more money for personal appearances so the artist toured to promote the record.

The music business grew up a great deal in the 1960s. On the rock side, musicians increasingly demanded "creative control" which echoed the freedom they experienced in their everyday life. Increasingly, they produced their own albums or decided which producer (if any) to work with. Since the record company executives were generally older—and not as in touch with the youth market as the performers who were part of the youth movement—the executives began to defer to the decisions of the artists.

That creative control came to Nashville and the country music industry a few years later. First, Willie Nelson signed with Atlantic Records, which was not a country label and did not have a Nashville office. Atlantic was an R&B label based in New York and its roster had featured Ray Charles, Ruth Brown, and Aretha Franklin. Atlantic executive Jerry Wexler, who had produced Aretha Franklin, heard Willie Nelson perform a series of songs and signed him to the label. Nelson released two concept albums, *Shotgun Willie* and *Phases and Stages*. He was given full creative control to record the songs he wanted wherever he wanted to. The singles and albums didn't achieve any great commercial success but they caught the attention of the music industry.

In 1975, after Atlantic decided to get out of the country business, Nelson signed with Columbia Records and recorded the album *Red-Headed Stranger* in a Dallas studio. The album was played for Nashville executives who felt it was under-produced; it sounded more like song demos than what was on country radio at the time. Nelson was going up against artists like Ronnie Milsap, who had "Daydreams About Night Things" and Linda Ronstadt with a remake of the Everly Brothers's song, "When Will I Be Loved." The Columbia executives were right; it was under-produced according to the sounds of that time. But they were wrong believing that Nelson's album wasn't commercial and that his spare, sparse sound would not be played on radio. "Blue Eyes Crying in the Rain" became a number 1 record in September 1975.

Meanwhile, back in Nashville, RCA artist Waylon Jennings, who was used to asking permission from RCA as to what, when, and where to record, decided to record some songs on his own at the Glaser Brothers Studio and then send RCA the bill. They paid it and the tradition was broken where an artist had to record in the label's studios with a label-assigned producer.

In 1973 Waylon Jennings recorded an album of Billy Joe Shaver songs; the single "You Ask Me To" was top ten. In 1974 Jennings had his first number 1 record with "This Time," followed by "I'm a Rambling Man." In 1975 he had "Are You Sure Hank Done It This Way," "Bob Wills Is Still the King," and a duet with Willie on "Good Hearted Woman."

In early 1976 Jerry Bradley, head of RCA's country division, packaged some recordings by Waylon, Willie, Jessi Colter, and Tompall Glaser into an album called *The Outlaws* and shipped it. It reached number 1 on the country charts and remained in that position for 6 consecutive weeks, becoming the first country album from Nashville to achieve platinum status. It changed country music in a number of ways. First, the creative freedom enjoyed by rock artists came to country music; next, it showed the New York and L.A. executives that country music, like rock, could achieve big sales.

The singer-songwriter era in rock music, ushered in by Bob Dylan and The Beatles and then popularized in the early 1970s by artists such as James Taylor, Carole King, and Billy Joel, came to Nashville in the form of a former Army Ranger and Rhodes Scholar. Kris Kristofferson left the Army and came to Nashville in 1966. It took him about five years of tough times and hard knocks but when Roger Miller recorded "Me and Bobby McGee" in 1969, Kristofferson's songs came to the attention of a host of other artists, including Janis Joplin who also recorded "Me and Bobby McGee" in 1970. Also in 1970, Johnny Cash had a hit with "Sunday Morning Coming Down," Sammi Smith hit with "Help Me Make It Through the Night," and Ray Price hit with "For the Good Times"—all songs written by Kristofferson.

A recording contract with Monument resulted in a debut album and then *The Silver Tongued Devil* which established Kristofferson as the premier singer-songwriter in Nashville. He didn't stay in Nashville long, though; soon after his songwriting success he moved to Los Angeles and began a career as a movie star in addition to his singer-songwriter career.

Nashville and country music have never been monolithic. While the Outlaw Movement (named by Nashville journalist Hazel Smith after Waylon released the album *Ladies Love Outlaws*) gained a lot of attention and attracted a number of young people to country music, the most commercially successful artist during the late 1970s in Nashville was Kenny Rogers, who added a smooth, pop sound to country music. In 1977 Rogers had his first number 1 hit with "Lucille." During the 1977–1981 period Rogers had 12 number 1 singles, including "The Gambler," "Coward of the County," and "Lady."

NASHVILLE DECLARES INDEPENDENCE

During the period of the late 1970s, the country record company offices in Nashville became more independent from their headquarters in New York. When Joe Galante came to Nashville in 1973 to work as a budget analyst for RCA "nobody had any budgets," he said. There were two big conventions—the Country Music Disc Jockey Convention in October and Fan Fair, developed as an alternative to the disc jockey convention, for fans in June—which took the bulk of Nashville's discretionary money each year.

"Everything was from New York," remembered Galante, who joined RCA as an MBA student at Fordham University and was transferred to Nashville.

> You had to borrow from Peter to pay Paul. We had a recording budget that we kind of stayed on top of and I monitored sales to see what was happening. But we weren't responsible for our advertising because that was done out of New York. The album covers and all the press was basically done out of New York. You just did local events here. The big thing at the time was people asking "Do we have enough money for the D.J. Convention in October? Is there enough for a hotel suite?" And then it was, "What are we going to do during Fan Fair? Well, we'll buy everybody breakfast and give 'em little key chains." That was about it.

If a record hit, "it was a big deal," said Galante. "That's why when we did *The Outlaws* with Waylon, it woke everybody up. People were like 'A platinum record? My God!'"[2]

Galante also pointed out that, "Because country consumers were supposedly from a rougher road in terms of living standards, prices for country albums were lower. So a pop album might have been $8.98 but we would have been $6.98 and then they might have gone to $9.98 with a hit album but we would have gone to $7.98. It wasn't until the 1980s that we got parity."

The Outlaws album changed all that and Galante remembered that by the early 1980s, "We kind of thought, 'Ah, hell, why not price the albums higher to start with.'"

CROSSOVERS

The key to big sales in country music from the 1960s until the 1980s was having crossovers; records that crossed over to pop radio, reached the pop audience, and achieved big sales by not appealing strictly to the country audience. That was the key to the success of Kenny Rogers, whose success (and sales) transcended country music. The success of Kenny Rogers, Waylon and Willie, Ronnie Milsap, and Dolly Parton marked a turning point in Nashville as a music business town instead of primarily a songwriter's town.

"We started getting our own marketing budgets in the late 70s when we had all the crossovers," said Galante. "When that happened the New York office said, 'You guys need to be able to do your own thing.' Then, in the 80s we started doing videos and we were responsible for those so all the major labels were set up as profit centers."

Prior to that, country marketing "was practically nonexistent," said Galante.

Basically, you ran a trade campaign. You would run an ad in a country music magazine and probably do some posters and a "canned" spot that you gave to the accounts because, at that time, the account used to buy advertising. That was pretty much it—it was low dough. Our most extensive campaign was with *The Outlaws* album but it was still very limited. We didn't buy TV ads because we didn't have any budgets for that. It was mostly point of sale material and you had the artist do free shows for the accounts to get them excited. Basically, you got a record on the radio and hoped people bought it. The problem with that was that we'd ship records out but we didn't know if they had sold or not for about a year when the ones that didn't sell were returned. The "Gold" and "Platinum" albums weren't really gold or platinum because those awards were based on shipments. You might ship gold and get a Gold Album Award but after the returns you'd find you'd only sold 250,000 instead of 500,000.

Until the late 1970s, country music was primarily a singles business; that's where the labels directed their efforts. Jukeboxes bought a large number of singles so labels spent time courting the jukebox buyers. "It was a cash flow business," said Galante. "It was never a profit business but nobody really understood what profit was at that point. People would say 'I sold 200,000 singles' but nobody asked 'how many albums did you sell?'" Sales of country albums in the pre-Outlaws day averaged around 50,000 or 60,000. RCA sold 250,000 on Charley Pride, Ronnie Milsap sold around 200,000, but it was rare for a country act to reach the 100,000 plateau for album sales.

Galante estimates that of the 32 acts on RCA by the mid-to-late 1970s "probably three of them sold albums and the rest of them sold singles."

The way that country records found their way into retail outlets changed during the late 1970s and early 1980s as well. There used to be a number of large, independent distributors in the nation; most major cities had a record distribution company that would take a record, make sure the radio station had a single, and get the album into retail. However, the major labels took over responsibility for full distribution, moving it in-house. The majors developed a sales force that called on accounts directly instead of using the independent distributor as a middle man. The result was that independent labels nearly disappeared in the late 70s and throughout the 1980s unless they were connected to a major label's distribution system. And the major labels increasingly dominated sales because they had the sales force and muscle to get into retail outlets by going directly to the retail accounts.

9

The 1980s and 1990s

TNN AND CMT

TV and videos became increasingly important to Nashville in 1983 when The Nashville Network (TNN) and Country Music Television (CMT) both debuted. The Nashville Network, formed by the Gaylord Corporation, which owned the Grand Ole Opry and Opryland Amusement Park, premiered on March 7 in a special telecast hosted by Ralph Emery. At this point, Country Music Television was not playing in the same league; it did not have the kind of budget that Gaylord could allocate and did not reach the number of cable households that TNN reached.

Country music came into homes through TNN and CMA during the 1980s and viewers enjoyed the chance to see country music in their living rooms every night of the week. Artists made videos and the most popular show, a talk show with Ralph Emery, featured the long-time disc jockey, local TV host, and Nashville legend, interviewing country artists, old and new.

In 1980 Alabama had their first hit, "Tennessee River" on RCA and followed that with 20 straight number 1 hits. Alabama was the first band to break in country music; previous groups, like the Oak Ridge Boys and Statler Brothers, were vocal groups but with Alabama, country music captured the trend pioneered by The Beatles and rock music almost 20 years earlier. Alabama brought a heavier beat to country music, bringing the sound of a rock band to country. This attracted fans to country who grew up on rock but, 15 years later, no longer found that current pop/rock music spoke to their life. The sounds of Alabama in 1985 were akin to the sounds of rock music in the 1970s but although they were commercially successful as country artists, the core audience for country demands a more traditional sound. This gave rise to the "New Traditionalists" in country music, led first by Ricky Skaggs, who brought his bluegrass background and love for old country songs into country music, and then George Strait, whose first hit "Unwound" was in 1981.

George Strait was signed to MCA Records after the movie *Urban Cowboy*, starring John Travolta, hit. *Urban Cowboy* was set in Houston, Texas, where a young oil field worker spent time at a local club (Gilley's) riding a mechanical bull. The Outlaw Movement had put the cowboy back into country music but with a black hat instead of a white one. However, the crossover artists stepped away from the western image. George Strait was a native Texan who wore a big white cowboy hat. He cut his teeth playing for dances in bars and honky tonks. His manager, Erv Woolsey, had lived in Nashville and worked at ABC and then MCA Records, but moved back to his native Texas, bought a nightclub, and booked local acts. One of the hot local acts was George Strait and his Ace in the Hole Band. Strait had ambitions to be a major country singer and Woolsey thought he had the potential to be a country star. With his strong connections in Nashville, Woolsey brought Strait to Nashville where he was signed to MCA Records.

In 1985 another "new traditionalist" emerged when Randy Travis had his first number 1 single, "On the Other Hand." Travis became a country music superstar in a five-year period with ten number 1's from 1985–1990. Reba McEntire had been signed to Mercury since 1976 but it wasn't until she signed with MCA in 1984 and began recording in the traditional country vein—embracing her rodeo roots—that she had major success.

Strait and Travis arrived in country music during a time when country music moved over to FM radio.

"*Urban Cowboy* hit right at the time FM radio started to do well," remembered Lon Helton, who at that time was head of the Nashville office of *Radio and Records* (R&R), a trade magazine. Helton explained,

> In the mid-70s when these big signal AM's started to program country music you had that new class of Barbara Mandrell, Don Williams, Crystal Gayle, the Oak Ridge Boys, Moe and Joe, and all of those guys. And that pretty much set the standard as FM stations started to do well in 1985 and '86 and they were competing with the rockers full bore, full personality, full contest, full promotion, full service and often times in markets they would be one of the top three in ratings. When the class of '89 in country hit and the boom really started, what happened was many of those cities with one country station that was doing well, ended up with two country stations. Most of the major markets, even the Northern markets like Pittsburgh, Detroit, Chicago, and St. Louis had two country FM stations.[1]

RECORD COMPANY CONSOLIDATION

During the mid-1980s a wave of consolidation hit the music industry. In 1987 the record division of CBS, which included the labels Columbia and Epic, was purchased by a Japanese firm, Sony, for $2 billion. That same year a German firm, Bertelsmann, purchased RCA Victor Records from General Electric for $333 million (General Electric had purchased RCA Records and

NBC in 1986). In 1990 the Japanese firm Matsushita Electrical Industrial Company purchased MCA Records for $5.7 billion. Warner Brothers, under threat of a hostile takeover, merged with Time-Life in 1989. EMI/Capitol and Polygram remained as they were; EMI/Capitol was a British firm and Polygram was a Dutch firm. The decade that began with six major labels, four of them American owned, ended with five of the six major recording labels owned by foreigners.

TECHNOLOGY

Technology had a major effect on the recording industry during the 1980s. The compact disc (CD) was introduced to American consumers in 1983; by the end of 1985, 22 million CDs were sold, which marked a turning point in the acceptance of the CD as the major format for recorded music, eventually replacing the vinyl record and the cassette tape. The long play VCR was introduced in 1977; by 1986 it was in 36.1 million homes and 10 years later was in 84.4 million homes. In 1980 cable television had 28 program networks; that same year CNN went on the air, a year after ESPN. In 1984 Congress passed The Cable Act, which established the regulatory framework for cable and led to the growth of cable television; during the 1984–1992 period the cable industry spent over $15 billion wiring America. By 1989 there were 79 cable program networks and approximately 53 million American households subscribed to cable.

With the introduction of the CD, the old problem of tape piracy had disappeared. These could not be copied and the only way someone could make a CD was to build an expensive CD plant. It was just like the old days when records dominated the musical landscape; in order to copy a record you had to build a manufacturing plant. This eliminated piracy. The record labels enjoyed record profits and consumers enjoyed a wide variety of music.

CLASS OF '89

There was a great deal of change in the world in 1989. In January, Emperor Hirohito of Japan died; Hirohito was emperor during World War II and played a major role in the decision to attack Pearl Harbor and initiate a war with the United States. In June, the Ayatollah Khomeini died; Khomeini led the revolt in Iran that ended the reign of the Shah and established a Muslim state that held American hostages in the embassy for 444 days. An uprising of Chinese dissidents in Beijing in June was put down with the Tiananmen Square massacre as the Chinese government brutally quashed dissent. On November 9, Germans sat atop the Berlin Wall before tearing it down. The image of brutal communism ended within a few days after the borders of East Germany were opened. This was the beginning of the end for the Soviet Union and communism in Eastern Europe. On Christmas day the Romanian dictator Nicolae Ceausescu and his wife were executed as dissidents stormed that government.

There were big changes in country music, too. Garth Brooks, Alan Jackson, and Clint Black all made their chart debuts in 1989. These "hat acts," as they were called because they all wore cowboy hats, represented a return to traditional country music but with a youthful twist. It also put the cowboy back in the saddle for country music. In 1989 Travis Tritt made his chart debut and Vince Gill left RCA and signed with MCA; in 1990 Gill had his first major hit, "When I Call Your Name." In 1991 Trisha Yearwood had her first hit, "She's in Love with the Boy" and in 1993 Toby Keith and Kenny Chesney had their first chart hits. During the 1990s these acts emerged as major superstars. In 1989 a country star died tragically; Keith Whitley died of alcohol poisoning while a future superstar, Tim McGraw, moved to Nashville, arriving on the same day that Whitley died.

Another perfect storm arrived in country music during the decade 1989–1999. First, a series of great artists appeared, led by Garth Brooks, Alan Jackson, Travis Tritt, Clint Black, Vince Gill, Toby Keith, Shania Twain, and Trish Yearwood. Artists such as George Strait, Randy Travis, Alabama, and Reba McEntire continued to have hits. The competition in the pop world was rap/hip hop, which had debuted on the pop charts in 1979 with "Rapper's Delight." During the 1980s the popularity of rap/hip hop amongst young people grew, but a lot of young people just didn't like it. The result was a lot of young radio listeners began to tune into country stations as the pop/rock world became inundated with rap/hip hop or music laden with synthesizers, which had come to dominate pop music in the 1980s. The CD was an accepted format and people replaced their records and cassette tapes with CDs; the labels fed consumer demand through the release of boxed sets, repackaged greatest hits, and old recordings.

In 1991 *Billboard,* the leading music trade magazine, introduced SoundScan, a bar code technology which allowed stores to keep track of what they sold and allowed the trade chart to accurately reflect what was sold. This benefited country music because it eliminated the old bias against country music from young retailers.

The information on sales of recordings is collected each week by *Billboard,* which compiles charts of the top songs and albums in the country in all music fields based on sales and airplay. Before SoundScan, *Billboard* and other trades regularly called a preselected group of record stores and distributors (called "reporters") around the country and asked a manager or assistant manager (or whoever was in charge of giving the report) to tell them the top sellers in the various categories (country, rock, rhythm and blues, and so on). Sales figures were not collected; the stores only gave a relative ranking. In other words, the top seller was such and such, the second was such and such, on down the line.

Since country music consumers generally did not shop in traditional record stores—either those in the mall or at free-standing locations—these stores didn't sell many country albums. Further, these stores generally employed young people who loved the popular music of the day but had an antipathy for country music at best and at worst a hatred. So they generally didn't report country sales along with pop sales.

Further, there was the psychological factor involved. Country music had its own section, generally at the back of the store, while pop music was in the front of the store. So country music was not even considered in "pop" sales unless an album sold so well that it was moved to the front of the store. This happened to some artists like Charlie Rich in the early 1970s and Kenny Rogers in the late 1970s. And so the key to big sales for country music was in crossovers. Not only did this mean the album was on both charts, it also generally meant that it was moved to the front of the stores and the reporters thought about it differently and reported it with the pop music releases.

Although much has been made about the success of country music on the pop charts in the 1990s, in truth the sales of country artists Waylon Jennings and Willie Nelson during the "outlaw movement" in the mid-1970s, the success of Kenny Rogers, Alabama, and Willie Nelson in the early 1980s after the *Urban Cowboy* phenomena, and the success of Randy Travis in the mid-1980s compares with country sales in the 1990s. But SoundScan wasn't in place before 1991, so there was a distorted picture of the popularity of country music. Simply put, it was generally assumed that rock ruled and country really could not compete in terms of sales.

With the advent of SoundScan, all those problems were eliminated; instead, the raw data of unbiased sales figures were reported. And it was discovered that country music competed with pop sellers; indeed, it even outsold a number of pop music sellers. This had been an open secret within the music industry for a number of years, at least among those in the accounting departments at the major labels.

COUNTRY MUSIC IN THE 1990s

The 1990s is remembered primarily as "The Era of Garth." It was hard to believe that a country artist could sell as many albums as Garth Brooks sold during the 1990s. After all, it was only about 15 years earlier when country music had its first platinum album with *The Outlaws*. Now, country acts were consistently selling Gold and Platinum albums (sales of 500,000 or 1,000,000). It looked like the gravy train would never end.

In 1979 Wal-Mart sold $1 billion worth of merchandise in its 230 stores; in 1989 there were 1,402 stores which sold $8.1 billion worth of merchandise. At the end of 1995 Wal-Mart had 1,995 stores and did $93.6 billion in business and by 1997 Wal-Mart had over 90 million customers each week and annual sales over $100 billion. These simple facts are a primary explanation for the growth of sales in country music during the decade of the 1990s. The story of retailing in the 1980s and 1990s is, in large part, the story of the phenomenal growth of Wal-Mart and other mass merchandisers during this period. Another mass merchandiser, K-Mart, overtook Sears as the nation's largest retailer during the 1980s, while Wal-Mart moved up to number 3. During the 1990s, however, Wal-Mart overtook Sears and K-Mart and became the number 1 retailer in the United States.

The reason this is important for country music is because around 75 percent of country music is sold in mass merchandisers. And nobody sells more country music than Wal-Mart. Indeed, if the truth be known, the explosion in country music in the 1980s and 1990s is due almost as much to Sam Walton as to Garth Brooks, Randy Travis, George Strait, or any other country singer.

The demographic, or age group, of country music buyers has generally been 25–50, but in the 1990s that figure expanded further in both directions. As the baby boomers aged, they continued to buy recordings so there were people in their 50s and 60s purchasing country CDs. The age for buying country recordings also dropped down into the teens—and this was important because it is young people in this country who set the trends.

For country music to reach the youth—who tend to be more prone to fads—the music had to become "hip." This happened in several ways. First, and most importantly, was the rise of new country stars, especially Garth Brooks, who grew up as a fan of rock music so his recordings captured the energy of rock and his live shows were like rock concerts with their theatrical trappings of lights, pyrotechnics, and a high energy performance by a singer who did not limit himself to standing behind a microphone. More than any other single performer, Garth Brooks brought an excitement into country music that attracted a horde of young fans who embraced his image, bought his recordings, and attended his concerts. Also important for the sales of country products during the 1990s was the rise of CMT because its emphasis on videos broadcast directly into homes broke down old stereotypes of country music. Next, record companies signed attractive young artists who appealed to young people, and finally, the term "country" changed its meaning. This came from a shift in the American population.

Before World War II the rural areas in the United States had about two thirds of the population while the urban areas had about a third. In 1940 about 23 percent of the population lived on farms, a figure which had been declining throughout the twentieth century (in 1900 the figure was 39 percent). But during this war, as defense manufacturing plants opened in cities, there was a tremendous exodus into urban areas. The cities appealed to rural folks during the entire twentieth century. With the wiring of the cities and the profusion of electricity came the beckoning of bright lights to the big cities. No longer were people tied to the daylight hours like they were on the farm. (Rural areas did not begin to receive electricity until after the Rural Electrification Bill was passed in 1936 and it was not until after World War II that rural America was fully wired for electricity.) By 1950 only 15 percent of the population lived on farms and a decade later that figure dropped to eight percent. It has continued to drop since.

Within cities, the image of the rural person was that of a country bumpkin, a hayseed, and a rube. The image of the city dweller was that of someone cultured, sophisticated, wise to the ways of the world. So the term "country" was something most people fled; they wanted to be "citified." Thus the terms "country" and "country music" had a very negative image with many in the nation.

The 1990 census showed the United States to be an urban nation. Actually, more people lived in the suburbs which surround a city than anywhere else, which means that about 80 percent live in metropolitan areas. Only about 20 percent of the nation live in rural areas, and only 4.6 million (or less than 2 percent) live on farms. By this time the cities suffered a negative image; they were often viewed as areas of widespread violence, rampant crime, crowded living conditions, and—for inner city dwellers—hopelessness. Country living, on the other hand, had gained appeal. To live in the country meant to have freedom and fresh air and be free from the inner city worries. A home in the country became a status symbol and country clothing, furniture, and music became increasingly desirable.

Leading the way for this change of image was the media, especially television, The Nashville Network (TNN), and Country Music Television (CMT), which both debuted in 1983. Originally, these were two separate companies, but in 1991 The Nashville Network, owned by the Gaylord Broadcasting Company, purchased CMT. Westinghouse purchased both networks; in 1999 Viacom acquired CMT and TNN and placed them in a group led by MTV. In 2000 TNN was renamed Spike TV and the format changed.

Sales of recordings of country music were always limited by a variety of factors: (1) lack of marketing from major labels (Nashville labels generally didn't have marketing departments until the 1980s), (2) lack of retail outlets where country music customers felt comfortable; (3) lack of accurate reporting of country sales, which distorted the picture of country sales and tended to perpetuate the stereotype of weak sales for country product; and (4) a negative image for the term "country" with a significant part of the population. During the 1980s and 1990s that all changed to the point where the country division became a profit center for major record labels. Because country music generated so much money and because New York and Los Angeles executives did not want to deal with country music (preferring to remain in pop with the greater prestige and bigger superstars), country executives, whose divisions made big profits for the labels, wielded an increasing amount of power, and thus Nashville emerged as a power center in the musical corporate world.

COUNTRY RADIO

To give an idea of the growth in income from country music, one should look at the growth in radio. In 1961, the first year the Country Music

Association compiled data for radio stations and probably the low point for country music (numerous stations had converted to rock 'n' roll programming between 1956 and 1961), there were only 81 stations programming country music full time. By the last year of that decade there were 606 and during the 1970s that figure grew to 1,434. In 1980 there were 1,534 but by the end of that decade there were 2,108. And those numbers continued to expand into the 1990s so that in 1994 there were 2,427 radio stations programming country music full time. This meant more people heard country music and since radio airplay is, essentially, an advertisement for a recording, country music reached a lot of potential buyers.

Within the country music business community, the primary beneficiaries are the publishers. That is because income from radio station airplay goes to publishers and songwriters—not record companies or artists. Record companies only receive income from the sales of recordings and artists receive their primary income from personal appearances, although they may also receive income from the sales of recordings. Since the Nashville music industry's financial backbone is in publishing, this strengthened Nashville as a center for country music.

REVENUE STREAMS

There are three entities in the music industry that generate and create the three basic revenue streams: record companies, publishing companies, and booking agencies. If you put the artist in the center (because the artist essentially generates most of the revenue), then the picture contains the three essential ways an artist is successful. First there are personal appearances. These occur in a variety of venues or places where the artist performs, everything from small clubs to large concert halls. Booking agents and concert promoters work together to put an artist in each venue with the promoters generally assuming the financial risk while the agent generates the commitment for the artist. The income is generated by consumers who purchase tickets; the artist receives either a set fee or a percentage of the gate with the booker receiving a percentage of the artist's money—usually 10 percent. The sale of merchandise—t-shirts, caps, pictures, and so on—generally comes from these personal appearances as fans purchase souvenirs of the artist. This merchandising is a lucrative business and beginning artists can often make as much or more from merchandising than from actual appearances. In fact, the money a new or mid-level artist receives from their personal appearances often covers only basic costs while the profits from personal appearances are generated by merchandising. (Obviously, this varies from artist to artist. Major acts make a great deal from personal appearances while lesser known acts must settle for less. The lesser known acts are more dependent on merchandising to supply the profits while the major acts generate more money from merchandising but also receive a healthy profit from their actual appearances.)

The second income stream is generated from the airplay—on radio and TV—of recordings. Each radio and TV station pays a certain amount of money (based on a formula compiled from the size of their market, advertising revenues, and size of audience) to the performing rights organizations, BMI, ASCAP, and SESAC. These performing rights organizations collect this money and then pay the songwriters and publishers of these songs for this airplay. Consumers pay indirectly for this when they buy products which have been advertised. Each advertised product costs more at the store in order to absorb the advertising costs; the radio and TV stations receive income from advertisers on their stations.

The final revenue stream comes from the purchase of recordings by consumers. When someone walks into a store and buys a recording, the money goes to the retailer, the wholesaler, and to the artist and recording company. For digital downloads the money goes to the carrier, the record label, artist, publishers, and songwriters. Sales of recordings, either physical or digital, are the only way the recording company makes money except for licensing recordings for compilation albums, commercials, and other uses.

All income from the music industry comes from these sources. For example, musicians who play on label releases are paid through their union by the recording company, which advances the money for production. Studios and engineers also receive income this way. Publishers record songs as "demos" and pay singers, musicians, studios, and engineers, usually at a rate less than the "master" rate for commercial recordings.

Managers receive money from artists' incomes; this is generally 10 to 20 percent, although for some ventures, like merchandising t-shirts or setting up a publishing company, the artist and manager may go into business together and split the income.

NASHVILLE AS THE CAPITAL OF COUNTRY MUSIC

Nashville became the center for country music for a variety of reasons. Some of these include the success of the *Grand Ole Opry,* which was created by an insurance company (The National Life and Accident Insurance Company) in order to help sell policies, the establishment of publishing and booking centers for country music by individuals (most connected to the *Opry*), and the establishment of Nashville as a recording center. But there were several reasons that major recording corporations chose to let recordings be done in Nashville. First, there was obviously a talent pool at the *Opry* and recording studios were built; the primary one was Castle, begun by three WSM engineers. But there was also the sense that the major label executives in New York right after World War II simply did not want to have to deal with country music or blues. These executives liked popular music, knew it, and understood it. But there was no power grab for country music; there was neither the big money nor the prestige attached to country music. And so Nashville became the center almost through default.

Still, the control from the major labels remained in New York or Los Angeles, although they continued to have an office in Nashville and someone in charge of the Nashville division. But as country music grew and prospered, the past success built on itself until a point was reached when Nashville was no longer an outpost; it was a financial center for the music industry. And when a place generates so much revenue, first with publishing and booking and then through sales of recordings, there is a shift in power in the corporate world.

Because the *Opry* was so popular and brought attention to Nashville, the National Life board decided to create an Opryland theme park. And because this was successful, plans were laid to begin a cable TV network centered on country music. Since Nashville established a strong publishing base, first with the creation of Acuff-Rose in 1943 and later with Cedarwood and Tree, more songwriters were attracted and more publishing companies were formed. This led the performance rights organizations (ASCAP, BMI, and SESAC) to establish offices in Nashville. The Country Music Association was formed in 1958 and this group served as a sort of Chamber of Commerce for country music and sought to promote the music to advertisers in order to attract radio airplay, which exposed the music. The CMA began the Country Music Hall of Fame, which led to Nashville becoming a major tourist attraction for country music fans, generating a new revenue stream connected to the music industry, and it established the CMA Awards as the premier award for country artists. The *CMA Awards* landed on national television and became a widely watched awards show that increased the exposure of country music.

THE NASHVILLE SOUND

The major labels recorded country music because it made money, especially when it was recorded in Nashville at local studios with local musicians. The development of the Nashville Sound was simply a handful of musicians who worked together quickly and efficiently to turn out albums economically. It didn't cost much to record a country album so it was easy to make a profit and major label executives didn't have to bother too much with the music or the people; they just sat back and collected the money. There was always somebody in charge of the Nashville office to oversee all this. The first executives were generally musicians in charge of hiring other musicians and organizing a session for some talent they'd found. Guitarist Chet Atkins was the first Nashville-based head of RCA Records, and band leader Owen Bradley was the first head of Nashville-based Decca Records. Gradually a support staff was hired and grew to include promotion people, publicists, a sales staff, and marketers. With greater profits coming into the Nashville office, country music executives wielded more power within the company so major labels shifted internally and gave the Nashville offices more autonomy. After all, as the old saying goes, "If it ain't broke, don't fix it."

Superstars have emerged from country music to have an impact in the pop world since Jimmie Rodgers, the Blue Yodeler, began his career in 1927. During the 1950s there were Eddy Arnold, Hank Williams, Tennessee Ernie Ford, Kitty Wells, and Elvis Presley; in the 1960s, there were Roger Miller, Merle Haggard, Johnny Cash, Charley Pride, Jim Reeves, Patsy Cline, and Loretta Lynn; in the 1970s, Dolly Parton, Charlie Rich, Waylon Jennings, and Willie Nelson; during the 1980s there were Alabama, Randy Travis, George Strait, and Reba McEntire; and in the 1990s, Garth Brooks. But during the late 1980s and 1990s there was a big difference in how these superstars emerged. Prior to this time the success of country music depended on crossover success, or an appeal to the pop market, but beginning in the mid to late 1980s, country artists could become superstars within the country music field and this subtly changed the music itself. The reason that country artists could stay within the country music field and achieve superstardom was because the business infrastructure was now in place so that enough money was generated within the country industry so that crossovers and appeals to the pop market were unnecessary.

The development of technologies for the information-based economy, specifically cable TV, bar codes and scanners, and computers which linked each company to itself as well as the company to the world, changed the country music industry. These information-based technologies showed the world the popularity and success of country music in hard numbers.

In the 1990s information and money were power. And that is why country music emerged as such a powerful force in the popular music industry during this period. Country music no longer has to be bothered by the whims, tastes, and prejudices of executives in New York and Los Angeles but can market its music self-contained. Ironically, since it is so successful, country music and Nashville has attracted a number of highly talented musicians, singers, song-writers, and executives from New York and Los Angeles who flee dirty cities filled with crime and traffic jams because they prefer country green.

SALES AND AIRPLAY IN THE 1990s

In a 1988 survey done by Arbitron for the Country Music Association, the breakdown of country radio listeners showed that 11 percent were 18–24 years old, 21 percent were 25–34, 23 percent were 35–44, 20 percent were 45–54, 14 percent were 55–64, and 10 percent were over 65, which meant that 69 percent of those listening to country music were over 35 and 89 percent were over 25. There were 2,169 country radio stations, up from 1,150 ten years earlier in 1978. In terms of sales of recordings, country music accounted for 7.4 percent of the total recordings sold in the United States or $462,855,000. There were 25 albums certified gold or platinum.

In 1989 country music recordings accounted for $921.1 million in sales; they increased to $1.380 billion in 1990, $1.425.8 billion in 1991, $1.507 billion in 1992, and $1.758.2 billion in 1993. When country was compared to other forms of music it showed that in 1989 it accounted for 6.8 percent of the total music sold that year; in 1990 it was 8.8 percent, in 1991 it was 12.5 percent, in 1992 it was 16.5 percent, and in 1993 it was a whopping 17.5 percent. Rock fell from 42.9 percent of purchases in 1989 to 32.6 percent in 1993 while adult contemporary/easy listening suffered a smaller drop, from 14.4 percent in 1989 to 11.7 percent in 1993.

Between 1991 and 1993 the audience listening to country radio increased; in 1991 34.7 percent of the population listened to country radio (verses 25.1 percent for CHR [contemporary hit radio]/rock and 29.1 percent for adult contemporary). In 1992 36.5 percent listened to country music radio and in 1993 41.6 percent listened. In 1993 country music listeners were spread out across the population. Interestingly, the 18–24 age group comprised 12.9 percent of the population and 12.8 percent of the country listeners, proof that country reached young people. The 25–34 age group comprised 23.1 percent of the population and 25.6 percent of the listeners; 17.3 percent of the listeners were 45–54, 10.4 percent 55–64, and 11.1 percent were 65 plus.

That meant that between 1991–1993 there were 3.2 million new listeners for country in the 18–24 category and 2.7 million new listeners in the 25–34 age group. In 1993 38.3 percent of country listeners earned over $40,000 a year and 42.9 percent owned their own home. During 1992 country listenership grew 7 percent in the South, 18 percent in the Midwest, 19 percent in the West, and a whopping 48 percent in the Northeast.

In the United States in 1996 over half the country radio listeners (53.6 percent) earned less than $30,000 a year; 22.7 percent earned $30,000–$50,000; 14 percent earned $50,000–$75,000, and 9.7 percent earned $75,000 and higher. This was in line with national averages; in 1996, according to an Edison survey, 54.8 percent of Americans earned less than $30,000 a year, 24.8 percent earned $30,000–$50,000; 13.6 percent earned $50,000–$75,000 and 6.8 percent earned over $75,000. Almost half of the listeners of country radio lived in the South (42.8 percent) while 26.2 percent lived in the Midwest, 19.2 percent lived in the West, and 11.8 percent lived in the Northeast. The decline in people living in rural America was even evident in country radio listeners; 71.5 percent of listeners lived in metro areas while 28.5 percent lived in non-metro areas. In terms of age, 65.3 percent of country listeners were between 25–54 years old. Only 15.8 percent were in the 18–24 demographic while the fastest growing group of listeners were 55 and over, which accounted for 20 percent of all radio listeners.

In 1997 22.8 percent of those listening to radio were tuned into country music. Mass merchandisers and discount stores accounted for 65 percent of sales; Wal-Mart stood head and shoulders above the rest, accounting for 43 percent of total country sales followed by K-Mart, Target, Musicland, and

Best Buy. Computers were popular and online shopping was a hot topic; in 1997 there were 45 million Web users in the United States or roughly 22.5 percent of the population 16 years old and over. During 1996–1997 4.5 percent of these users had shopped online; during the 1997–1998 period that percentage moved up to 10 percent. Half of country radio listeners owned a computer, and 39 percent had access to the Internet or used online services.

In 1997 a report compiled by Edison Media Research was released by the Country Music Association that profiled the country music buyer and listener. The report noted that the South had 35.9 percent of the American population and that 41 percent of that population were country listeners. In the midwest, which had 23.7 percent of the population, 27.7 percent of those people listened to country while the Northeast, with 19.2 percent of the population, had only 12.1 percent listening to country music. The West, which included everything west of the Rockies, had 21.3 percent of the population and 19.2 percent of them listened to country music. About 84 percent of those listening to country music were over 25; of the total number of country listeners, only 16 percent were in the 18–24 age group while 29 percent were 25–34, 31 percent were 35–44, and 25 percent were over 45.

In 1997 average country radio listeners considered religion very important to their life but were no more likely to be regular church-goers than the general population. They loved the NFL and NASCAR, were likely to hunt and fish, and 43 percent owned at least one gun. Their favorite artist in 1997 was Garth Brooks—31 percent liked him best—followed by Reba McEntire, Alabama, George Strait, Alan Jackson, Brooks & Dunn, LeAnn Rimes, Vince Gill, Clint Black, and Shania Twain.

A large portion of country listeners—37 percent—had been listening to country music for over 20 years. Another 18 percent had listened for 11–20 years.

In 1997 32 percent of country buyers still bought cassette tapes and about 80 percent found out about new music from the radio. They weren't much for attending concerts; 69 percent of the country radio audience had not attended a concert during the previous year and only 15 percent had attended two or more, but 80 percent watched TNN and 69 percent watched CMT. However, the most popular channel on cable for country listeners was the Discovery Channel; 89 percent of country fans watched that, followed by CNN.

In 1997 half the country listeners owned a personal computer and 39 percent had access to the Internet or used online services; only 7 percent bought CDs or tapes online. Interestingly of all the respondents, only 6 percent had purchased a CD or tape online.

MIKE CURB AND CURB RECORDS

In 1992 Mike Curb moved his home and his record company's headquarters from Los Angeles to Nashville. Curb had been in the music business since he graduated from high school in 1962. His first successes came when he wrote national jingles for Honda motorcycles ("you meet the nicest people on a Honda") and Chevrolet. In 1964 he started his own record label that was successful producing soundtracks for independent films in Hollywood as well as having hit singles on the radio. He formed the Mike Curb Congregation which toured, sang on numerous recordings, and had a hit single from the movie *Kelly's Heroes* ("Burning Bridges") and then landed on *The Glen Campbell Goodtime Hour* singing an inspirational song each week. In 1969 23-year-old Curb became president of MGM Records, the youngest president of a major label. At MGM he signed The Osmonds and from that group singled out Donny Osmond, then Donny and Marie and produced a string of hits on all of them ("Down by the Lazy River" and "Yo-Yo" for the Osmonds; "Puppy Love" for Donny and "I'm Leaving It All Up to You" for Donny and Marie).

In 1974 Curb sold his share of MGM and went into politics; he was elected lieutenant governor of California and then became Republican finance chair under President Reagan. During the 1970s Curb formed joint ventures with major labels and signed artists Debby Boone ("You Light Up My Life"), Shaun Cassidy ("Da Doo Ron Ron"), Exile ("I Want to Kiss You All Over"), and the Four Seasons ("December, 1963" aka "Oh, What a Night"). Curb signed Hank Williams, Jr., when he was at MGM and after he left that label continued with Hank Jr. through a production agreement.

By the 1990s Curb decided to leave L.A. for Nashville; he had a young family that he did not want to raise in Hollywood, the California business climate was becoming increasingly restrictive, and country music was getting hot.

Curb had already tasted success in country music; he had signed the Judds in the 1980s and brokered a distribution and marketing deal with RCA. The Judds had a string of hits, beginning in 1983 with "Had a Dream (For the Heart)" and then enjoyed a string of number 1 records, "Mama He's Crazy," "Why Not Me," "Love Is Alive," "Grandpa (Tell Me 'Bout the Good Old Days)," "Rockin' with the Rhythm of the Rain," and "Let Me Tell You About Love."

Because of the record business climate during the 1970s and 1980s, Curb needed to do joint ventures with major labels because those labels controlled distribution. However, in 1989 Curb Records became a fully independent label. His first big success came with Tim McGraw and "Indian Outlaw" in 1994. McGraw developed into a superstar with a string of hits in the 90s, "Don't Take the Girl," "Not a Moment Too Soon," "I Like It, I Love It," "She Never Lets It Go to Her Heart," and "Where the Green Grass Grows."

Curb's next big success came with LeAnn Rimes, a 15-year old singer from Texas whose first hit, "Blue" in 1996 opened the door to a string of hits, both country and pop. His third big success was Wynonna, who became a separate act after her Mom, Naomi Judd, had to stop touring because of illness. Curb's other acts—Hank Williams, Jr., Sawyer Brown, Jo Dee Messina, Lyle Lovett, and others—also had successful careers.

Throughout the 1990s Joe Galante guided BMG/RCA and Mike Curb led Curb Records to create superstars who sold millions of albums. Other key executives were Jimmy Bowen, who served as the head of Capitol and MCA and who is most responsible for bringing digital recording to Nashville; Jim Ed Norman, who headed Warner Brothers; Jim Foglesong, who signed Garth Brooks to Capitol; and Tim DuBois, who created the country division of Arista and signed artists Brooks & Dunn, Alan Jackson, and Brad Paisley.

THE BIG BOOM

Country music had success like it had never seen before during the early 1990s. Country was on more radio stations, sold more records, and received more positive national media attention than at any time in its history. The biggest selling country star of all time, Garth Brooks, emerged out of that era.

Mike Curb attributes the unparalleled success of country music to the acceptance of CDs and retail. Curb said,

> In the 1990s you had all these major accounts that aren't here anymore, like Camelot and Sam Goody and Tower. Those were the major record stores that you went to. And then you had the mass merchandisers, the K-Mart's and Wal-Mart's and Best-Buy's and Target's coming in. In the 90s you had the best of both worlds. You knew the major chains carried more catalogue and the mass merchandisers had special pricing and positioning and the ability to attract consumers to music from other products they sold. You also did not have the Internet and the illegal downloading issue in the 90s. Instead, you also had the phenomenon of the compact disc; America fell in love with the compact disc which meant that everybody was able to buy any music they'd ever loved that was on those scratchy 45's and 33's and 78's with that hiss.[2]

Lon Helton, founder and head of *Country Air Check,* attributed the boom to radio. "I believe that one of the reasons the boom happened was because there were two country stations in the market and they competed over music," said Helton. "There are lots of stories about guys getting close with their FedEx guy, when he was supposed to deliver the song by 10 or 10:30 in the morning. . . . They would meet the FedEx guy at 6 a.m. and have the new Garth Brooks song or the new whatever on before the other. Because there were two country stations they were competitive over the music."

10

Country Radio

THE 1996 TELECOMMUNICATIONS BILL

The 1996 Telecommunications Bill had a huge effect on country radio. The bill allowed consolidation of radio stations to the point where, at its peak one company, Clear Channel, owned over 1,200 stations.

Federal regulation of radio dates back to 1927 when Congress passed The Radio Act and established The Federal Radio Commission (FRC). In 1934 Congress passed The Communications Act and the FRC evolved into the Federal Communications Commission (FCC). In 1953 the FCC set a cap on ownership at 14 stations; 7 AM and 7 FM. In 1984 the cap was increased to 24 stations (12 AM and 12 FM), and in 1992 the cap was increased to 36 stations (18 AM and 18 FM); by 1994 the cap was 40 stations per company (20 AM and 20 FM). During the late 1970s and throughout the 1980s a number of industries were deregulated and an emphasis on deregulation sprang from an economic theory that the market was the best regulator of business and that government regulation and intervention was not in the public interest. Businesses argued that "economies of scale" meant that large companies were more effective than smaller ones because large companies could consolidate activities and save costs through quantity purchases and reduced operating costs.

The 1996 Telecommunications Bill opened the floodgates for the consolidation of radio ownership by large conglomerates. In 1975 there were 7,472 stations (AM and FM); in 1985 there were 9,450; and in 1995 there were 11,734 with over 6,600 different owners of radio stations.

Clear Channel was founded by Lowry Mays and Red McCombs in San Antonio in 1972 and purchased its first radio station that year. They continued to purchase radio and television stations under FCC guidelines. In Dallas the private equity firm of Hicks, Muse, Tate & Furst was formed with Tom Hicks as Chairman; in 1994 this firm formed AMFM, Inc. In 1995 Clear Channel, a San Antonio-based company, owned 39 stations; in 1999 Clear

Channel agreed to merge with AMFM with the Mays family holding top executive positions and Tom Hicks as co-chairman.

In the years after the Telecommunications Bill a number of stations were sold to a relatively small number of owners; during 1997 and 1998 over 2,100 stations were sold each year and from 1999 through 2001 around 1,700 stations changed ownership. Since 2002, about 800 stations a year have changed ownership.

At the end of 2005 there were 13,504 AM and FM stations; Clear Channel owned 1,184, Cumulus owned 295, Citadel owned 223, Infinity owned 178, Educational Media Foundation owned 138, the American Family Association owned 113, Salem Communications Corp. owned 106, Entercom owned 103, Saga Communications owned 86, and Cox Radio owned 78.

Although these numbers seem relatively tame on the surface—Clear Channel owned just 8.8 percent of the total radio stations in the country—Clear Channel purchased stations in key markets and left rural stations with few listeners alone so that by the end of 2005 the stations it owned reached 27.2 percent of all radio listeners. Infinity's stations reached 13.6 percent of listeners.

In 2005 the top four companies who owned radio stations had 48 percent of all radio listeners and the top 10 firms had almost two-thirds of all listeners. Although radio companies, who lobbied Congress heavily for this Telecom bill, promised more diversity with concentrated ownership, in reality over 75 percent of all commercial programming is made up of 15 formats; further, programming is heaviest in 8 formats. Playlists for commonly owned stations in the same format average a 50 percent overlap although they may overlap up to 97 percent.

The result is that radio, which used to be primarily a local medium with local ownership and local programming, is controlled by national companies with a broad geographical reach. The companies who purchased radio stations went deeply in debt to buy these stations, generally paying a high multiple to acquire the stations. (A multiple is the amount of annual income generated by a radio station times a number that reflects the value of a station. If a station earned $5 million a year and the multiple was 12 then the station's price was $60 million.)

A report written by Peter DiCola for the Future of Music Coalition in 2006 noted, "Radio consolidation has not demonstrated benefits for the public. Nor does it have any demonstrated benefits for the working people of the music and media industries, including DJs, programmers—and musicians. The Telecom Act unleashed an unprecedented wave of radio mergers that...worked to reduce competition, diversity, and localism, doing precisely the opposite of Congress's stated goals for the FCC's media policy."[1]

The effect of radio consolidation mirrored the effects of Wal-Mart on the national economy. Between 1987 and 1996 Wal-Mart's national retail market share (the percentage of income measured against all retailers) rose from 9 percent to 27 percent. Clear Channels' radio-revenue market share (the percentage of ad revenue income they received measured against all radio ad income) rose from 2 percent in 1995 to 28 percent by 2001.

In order to recoup their costs, Clear Channel set up a business arrangement whereby an independent promotion person became a middle-man between the station and the record company. The independent promotion person was a "bank" and the record companies paid him/her for access to that station. If the station wanted t-shirts or CDs for giveaways then the bank paid for them. The result was that only major labels could afford to obtain radio airplay because the price for entry was so high. Also, it cost the record companies an increasing amount of money in order to obtain airplay which meant that it was cutting heavily into their profits. There were creative arrangements whereby a record company bought an "advertisement" of a radio station; this "advertisement" was actually the record played on the air.

The radio conglomerates offered advertisers a national market; in the past there were a large number of radio stations appealing to the same local advertisers in a market; after consolidation several major companies approached national advertisers and guaranteed a "package" whereby they could place ads on radio stations throughout the country. The conglomerates also increased the number of ads on their stations which played a role in less and less people listening to radio.

The end result was an investigation by New York Attorney General Elliot Spitzer that resulted in large fines paid by record companies and Clear Channel for payola.

COUNTRY RADIO AND CONSOLIDATION

"Country radio might have been more affected by consolidation than any other format," said Lon Helton, founder and head of Country AirCheck. "One of the ways consolidation changed country radio is that country used to not be a demographic-driven format; it was a family reunion of people 25 to 54 years old, evenly split between men and women. That was the target and it was huge! No other radio format had that broad an appeal. The others were all targeted to 18–24 men, or 18–49 women, or whatever it was. Country was wider, broader, and deeper than any other format."

When the large entities bought radio stations they organized them in "clusters." They take this "cluster" of stations in a market and divide up that market; for example, they need a rock station, an urban station, a news/talk, oldies and country station. They may position the soft rock station for women 18–34 years old, maybe a rock station for men 18–34 or a news/talk station for men 35 plus or a hot contemporary hits format for females 12–18. Under this structure the conglomerates aimed country radio at women 40 years old and over.

Helton states,

> If the target changes, it changes everything you do. More importantly, the music changes. If I get a group of people who are 25–54 years old, half men and half women and play music for them, I'm going to get one result. If I get a room full of women who are 40 plus and play music, I'm going to get a different result to the music I play because the tastes are going to be different. If you look back at the popularity in the charts and look at the music, you can see that. You can see the shift to music that is more palatable to women 35 to 40 plus. In the past country music was this manly, outlaw, Waylon and Willie, are you sure Hank done it this way Country and *Western* music! This manly format has been transformed in the last few years primarily I believe because of the residue of consolidation and of positioning clusters. We've become something country never was before, a female oriented format.

A lot of research is done to determine what gets played on country radio. There are focus groups formed by consultants who listen to music and discuss their likes and dislikes, which are recorded and analyzed by the consultants. Auditorium music testing for country music involves renting an auditorium and inviting an audience to listen to music and register their likes and dislikes; it is primarily done with country oldies. For current music, radio stations use "call out research" where a station calls homes, plays a bit of a recording over the phone to the listener, and records their reactions.

"Many country radio stations today, when they do research, don't even include men," said Helton. "They don't ask men what they think about the radio station, or what they think about the music in the auditorium tests or in the weekly call outs of current music because they don't care what they think. They only care what women over 40 think. So you can see how that changes the end result. Think of the music you hear on country radio and you realize it's about women."

"Sippy-cup music" is a term used to denote a music that appeals to a young parent, particularly a young female parent. Prime examples are "Let Them Be Little" by Billy Dean and "Watching You" by Rodney Atkins. In the latter song, a youngster in his car seat spills something and utters a four-letter word beginning with "s." The reason: he's been watching his dad and wants to be like him. By the end of the song the youngster is saying his prayers at night because that's what Dad does. Country music is now inundated with sippy-cup songs.

"After consolidation country music was handled differently on the radio station," said Helton. "Country radio stations always had huge playlists, like 40 to 45 records. I remember when I was in Denver in 1973 we had an 80 record current playlist! One of the things consolidation did in almost every market in America was raise the whole of the market place up to another level. It put people in control who had more research to consult and a lot of other resources and they went from long playlists to much shorter playlists and country really became more like pop radio along the way in that respect."

"The people drain was huge," continued Helton.

Before consolidation there were a lot of smaller companies formed because the guy loved country music. The late Mike Oatman had Great Empire Broadcasting and owned a number of stations because he loved country music. That love came because he was on the air one day when Loretta Lynn came through his town with that first little record she made. Her husband, Mooney, drove her across the country and they looked for radio towers and when they saw one they'd stop and Loretta would go into the station and give them her record. Well, she handed Mike that single and later she became a huge star and that set the tone for Mike Oatman's whole life in radio.

Guys like Larry Wilson, who started Citadel Communications, loved country music. People within country music—Webb Pierce, Buck Owens, and Mel Tillis—owned country stations. So you had people who loved country music owning country radio stations and they did things with an eye towards country and not just towards the business. Those guys sold their companies to these big investors and you ended up with people who treated it more like a business. It didn't matter what the music was. By and large, the top echelon of management (both management and programming) of these big firms are not country music guys so country is treated very differently. Before this country radio always had guys who were passionate about the music but now that's no longer the case.

"When you have people who are in country radio because they want to be in country radio as opposed to any other form of radio then they run it with that in mind," observed Helton.

When you lose those people you really lose something whether it is on the general manager level or the owner level. This whole business loses something. You can feel it even now. We used to have general managers or program directors who were on the board of the CMA, on the board of the Country Radio Seminar, and involved in the country music and radio business. They were interactive and knew the label presidents by name and had dinner with them. Now, there is no more of that interaction. I believe that was good for the business as a whole, and now that's really a thing in the past. I think both businesses—country music and radio—benefited by having those kinds of relationships. There's no time for that now, it's really about money. In so many markets it comes down to three major owners or maybe four who own four, five, maybe six stations in a market. And they set up their clusters to deliver audiences.

"There has always been this relationship between country radio and Nashville country artists that doesn't exist in any other format," continued Helton.

What other format even to this day has a convention like the Country Radio Seminar? There was always this great relationship. We were all in this together so we had to band together because the common enemy was everybody else. Consolidation changed that. After consolidation most of the people who really like country left and the companies that took over, by and large were run by rockers in programming and management. A fiddle and steel guitar are like fingernails on the chalk board to those people, who aren't fans of this format. What is happening more and more is that pop people are having input and control over programming on country stations and when they listen to two songs and one has fiddle and steel on it and the other one doesn't, I guarantee you the one that doesn't is going to get the edge most of the time. That is why I believe the music is much softer today. You don't hear twin fiddles too much and you don't hear heavy steel guitar anymore or other sounds that are stereotypical country because it's foreign to many of the pop programmers' ears so it's just not going to get on the radio. The target has changed and the gatekeepers have changed. When the gatekeepers change and the target changes then the product is going to change.

The most common criticism of contemporary country music on radio is that it is "cookie-cutter music," but Helton says, "I don't think it's cookie-cutter music, it's just that the music played on country radio changed to fit the target of 40 plus women."

When the gatekeepers at radio changed, the gatekeepers on Music Row in Nashville changed too.

"Nashville is an entire city of gatekeepers," said Helton.

When a songwriter writes a song he or she may be their own gatekeeper because they know the songs that get cut and the ones that don't so they want to write a song that gets recorded. Then they take that song to a gatekeeper at their publishing company and the song plugger weeds out what they're going to go pitch, because they know what they can pitch to certain A&R people. Then the A&R people weed out songs because they know a song might be cut by a certain artist and this is targeted. Then jump ahead three or four steps to the promotion department which receives an album of 10 to 13 songs. The promotion department is hired, paid, and fired on the basis of how they get those singles on the radio. What song are they going to pick out of those ten for a single? They're going to pick what they believe will give them the path of least resistance to radio.

"Promotion departments don't want that creative left-field really big wow song because they're not sure they can get it on the radio," said Helton. "There are gatekeepers at every step of the way that narrow it down, filter it down, that take what you might think are really left-field creative songs that come down to the lowest common denominator, because every step of the way it has to pass through a filter to get to the next level. In the end, radio gets all the blame because in Nashville there's never been a badly written, badly sung, badly produced, or badly promoted song in the history of this town. They're all monster hits that radio screws up!"

Mike Curb looks at radio consolidation from the perspective of the owner of an independent record company and states,

> Radio consolidation really didn't impact us a lot because most of the programmers stayed local. Clear Channel didn't have one person making the music decisions for all their stations; they still had local music directors and program directors. The part that made it difficult at times was also the best thing at other times. If you had a record that was not hitting at a couple of key Clear Channel stations, that word would spread throughout all of the other Clear Channel stations. But, if you had a record that was hitting, breaking at a couple of key Clear Channel stations, then that too spread. So, it goes back to the same old story: if you've got a hit record, it's going to work and if you don't have a hit record, then it's not going to work. There is nothing worse than a mid-chart record because you promote it and promote it and even though it's not a hit it still costs you as much to promote it but it sells nothing. That's the worst!

"I do not blame radio and I do not blame consolidation," continued Curb.

> Over the years—and this is my fifth decade with a label—when we've had hit records we've had success but when we have not had hit records then we have not had success. Now, is it better if there are 40 different stations rather than five? Perhaps there are some advantages in breaking a new artist if you have more stations but consolidation is part of American business. At the beginning of the twentieth century there were hundreds of automobile companies and then there were three. There were lots of radio stations and then there were three national broadcasting corporations. America tends to consolidate because that is part of what happens when you live in a free country, and if you want to be an independent company you have to accept the fact that consolidation is going to take place. If you can't compete in that environment, then it is probably better not to start a record company because every aspect of the entertainment business, whether it's retail, concerts, radio, television, managers, or agencies, has experienced consolidation. We need to accept the fact that this is just one of the realities and there are pluses and minuses.

Erv Woolsey, manager of George Strait, echoes some of what Curb said. When asked if radio consolidation has hurt the country music business Woolsey said, "I think at times maybe it has, but other times it's been good; I can't say that it's really hurt us. At Clear Channel they all talk to each other and if somebody is playing something, word gets around and I think that's a good thing. Those guys are all accessible, you can plead your case to them. Radio relies so much on research now but sales should certainly be a factor. I think those guys are doing the best they can do with what they've got. Again, these guys, they don't have just one job; most of them are doing all kinds of things and so it's not fair (unless you walk in their shoes) to judge them, because they've got a lot of things going on."[2]

Jeff Walker, owner and head of Aristo, a promotion, publicity, and marketing firm, said,

> I think consolidation in general wasn't a good thing for radio. It stopped the small operator and stopped the localization of radio. I think that hurt the format because one of radio's charms was to turn it on and get the local weather, the local news, local dialogue, and local people calling in about issues of the day as well as music. Consolidation jacked up the price of radio because they had to sell a third of an hour for commercials, which is overkill in terms of listening. It's the same as some of these top rated television shows. People now are Ti-Vo-ing or DVR-ing and skipping through the commercials. They will actually be at home but they'll TiVo it and watch the next hour just to skip the commercials so they can watch a one hour show in 40 or 45 minutes.[3]

Executives in the music industry tend to tippy-toe around the question of whether radio consolidation is good for country music, especially when they talk on the record about Clear Channel. They are very careful about what they say about Clear Channel and consolidation because their livelihood depends on airplay on Clear Channel stations. In general, Clear Channel makes everyone in the music business nervous because, even though things may be going well today, if things go sour tomorrow they could be really bad. The advantage of a huge company having so much power in an industry is that, with the right leaders, things are less likely to go wrong; however, the problem is that if and when things do go wrong they can go horribly wrong.

11

Country Music Internationally

Country Music does not travel well; in fact, country music is the least international of all major American music genres. During the 50-year period 1945–1995 when American music became, essentially, "world music" in the sense that American popular music is the most pervasive and influential music in the world, country music somehow lagged behind. In 2006 country music accounted for 13 percent of all recordings sold in the United States; however, in the U.K. it was only 1 percent, in Germany 2 percent, in Australia 3 percent, Malaysia was 1 percent, Austria was 8 percent, the Netherlands was 3 percent and, a nice exception, Brazil was 13 percent. In the rest of the world country music didn't account for enough sales to compile a full percentage.

Mike McNally, formerly with EMI Records, lists three types of reasons why country music is not popular in Great Britain or Europe: (1) social, (2) cultural, and (3) political.

"There's a big cultural gap between country music lyrics and the lifestyles of the British," said McNally.

There are country songs about wide open spaces and cruising down the wide open highway. In England, you do not get the feeling of freedom and wide-open spaces cruising down the M1. There's a lot of references to an American lifestyle—big front yards, the mountains—those sorts of things, that we just don't have in Britain.

Socially, the sense of fashion in Britain just does not accept the clothes worn by country artists as "fashionable." Those cowboy hats and tight pants with big belt buckles. And third, the presidency of George W. Bush has really turned the world against Americans, and country music is linked to the Republican party. That party's emphasis on this blind patriotism, the war in Iraq, the whole conservative and religious movement, just doesn't play well with British audiences. It's a Republican music and, on the whole, the British don't care for the Republicans in America, personified by George W. Bush.[1]

While the British do not particularly care for President Bush, the bias against country music started long before he became president and will likely continue long after he's gone from the White House.

Craig Baguley, editor and publisher of *Country Music People,* the leading publication for country music in Great Britain and a long-time, die-hard country fan, said "the clothes!" when asked why country music isn't popular in England. He elaborated that the clothes of country music performers—generally tight blue jeans, cowboy boots, and cowboy hats for men—are not "hip" or fashionable for the British audience. "Especially the cowboy hat," said Baguley. "British consumers look at singers wearing cowboy hats and turn thumbs down. They just don't connect, except in the gay community where wearing a cowboy hat might be considered 'campy.' In general, if you see a fashionably dressed man in England wearing a cowboy hat in public, chances are he's gay."[2]

Paul Fenn, an agent for the Asgard Agency who has booked a number of country acts in Great Britain said that, "A number of country artists are red-necks who ask stupid questions like 'can American stamps mail a letter from England' and 'are there wash cloths in the hotel?' For others, the music isn't appropriate." Fenn noted that, for the most part "contemporary country music doesn't work, but there's hope for Americana" although "the major labels aren't interested in Americana." Fenn also said the days of major labels underwriting international tours for country acts "is pretty much over—the money has dried up because the labels aren't making money."[3] Fenn says that Joe Galante, the head of Sony/BMG has had bad experiences with international tours and this has led others to pull back support of country music in the international market.

Joe Galante agrees that country music doesn't have much of a presence in the international market but blamed it on artists and managers.

"Country artists went to England and Europe because there was some money—if somebody paid them, they went—but there were very few acts that really toured," said Galante. "It's a commitment. Just like we build markets here, you have to do that over there. I believe it starts with the artist. Most of them don't want to leave this country. When they finally get it made and get enough money over here, they don't want to go overseas and take less money. They don't understand that part. The managers are very content for their artist to not tour over there. They're making so much money with live performances here, so why go over there?"

Galante, who was formerly president of the Pop Division of BMG/RCA noted it was different with pop acts, who have a more global perspective. "If you're in New York or L.A. then you realize 'I can do one million units here in the states and one million units over there. I can do some dates here and do some dates over there.'"

Galante also notes there are cultural differences that stop many country acts from touring abroad. "When you get outside of the U.S. there aren't that many markets that really have country radio stations," he said. "I mean, they still think of it as hillbilly music or 'country western' music." Galante noted that,

> The women have done better. Shania, Faith, LeAnn Rimes, Dolly—those people have done better on an international basis than most of the males. Garth did it, but he only did it for a year; it wasn't what it was here so he didn't go back. He did a couple of things in England and Ireland and then said "I'm done." In order to work that market it's like anything else, you've got to keep going and you've got to be a missionary. Country artists don't have the desire and neither do the managers. And the booking agencies here don't want artists to leave the states because they could book the act in Dallas for $100,000.

Mark Hagen, executive director of BBC Music Entertainment, agrees that country acts need to tour internationally to be successful but don't make that commitment. "The country artists who have done well are the people who have come over consistently, over and over again," said Hagen. "Emmylou Harris, at one time, sold a lot more records in the U.K. than Shania Twain. Emmy has come to the U.K. consistently for 30 years. She has an audience here. Someone like Alan Jackson has been here once. George Strait was here once for one show."[4]

George Strait did indeed play one show in London and never returned for another engagement. Strait's manager, Erv Woolsey, has no regrets about that show. "I'm glad we went," said Woolsey. "We answered a lot of questions and had a great time. We really spent all of our time in England and did a lot of PR, and I think we only had one day off to see the sights. We sold out that show—it was only a 2,400 seater—and MCA was great to us. But we came home and talked about it and realized we've got everything we want right here in the United States and Canada. We don't have enough time to play everywhere, so we decided to stay here. You know, it's a long way over there and it takes a lot of time."

Woolsey noted that Strait has been to Europe and Africa since then but would rather go on his own to see the sights and not have to worry about working.

"There's sound economic reasons not to do it," said Hagen. "But if you do it early in your career, like the Mavericks, you play to audiences simultaneously. It's important to be recognized here. That's part of the reason Kenny Chesney has never sold any records over here. Because to the U.K. audience, for all intents and purposes, he's the same as all the other acts. Kenny is a boy in a hat. The only impact he made here is when he got married and then it was 'who's that?' Keith Urban is making some inroads. But to all intents and purposes he's not a country artist."

Australian born Jeff Walker spent a few years growing up in South Africa. He is the son of Bill Walker, the noted arranger and orchestra leader.

Jim Reeves had gone to South Africa to film a movie, *Kimberley Jim,* and met Bill Walker, who was the head of RCA's subsidiary label, Teal. Reeves invited Walker to move to Nashville; Walker did but on the week he arrived Reeves died in an airplane crash. Chet Atkins knew of Walker's reputation and connected him with Eddy Arnold who performed concerts with orchestras while Walker conducted. Walker also did a number of orchestra arrangements for records by Sammi Smith ("Help Me Make It Through the Night"), Donna Fargo ("Happiest Girl in the Whole U.S.A."), and others.

When Johnny Cash began his CBS TV show, he hired Walker to lead the orchestra. Meanwhile, Jeff Walker was in Australia getting an accounting degree; every week he watched as Johnny Cash said "Goodnight Bill Walker!" at the end of his show. In the mid-1970s Jeff Walker moved to Nashville and landed a job with the accounting firm Price Waterhouse. Bill Walker decided to start a record label, Con Bio, and Jeff became the controller and then later vice president of operations for the label from 1976–1979. In 1980 Jeff Walker formed Aristo Media, initially a publicity and public relations firm that has expanded into a full service independent marketing company with services that include new media, video, radio, and dance club promotions. Walker is an active member of the Nashville music community and serves as chair of the Global Markets Task Force for the Country Music Association.

Walker points out that there have been some exceptions to the notion that country music doesn't travel well. Dolly Parton, the Dixie Chicks, Emmylou Harris, George Hamilton IV, Charley Pride, the Bellamy Brothers, and Don Williams have "been going over there on a regular basis," notes Walker. "They still make huge money because they go back and back and back. Once a year they carve out four or five weeks and do international shows."

There have been a number of attempts to market country music in Great Britain. For years the Country Music Association had an office in London working to promote country music in the U.K. and Europe; in 1983 Ed Benson lived there and worked out of an office in London. He was followed by several other full-time employees of the CMA who had a London office.

Walker states that those early efforts were "quite expensive" and "ahead of their time." He notes that "about 10–12 percent of the membership" of the Country Music Association is international so they felt there could be a strong international market for country music.

"One of the measurements of how successful you are is how many records are sold or how many acts break," said Walker. "In the past there has been a disconnect between most of the Nashville-based artists and the labels in Europe and the foreign territories because these artists aren't getting released over there and consequently there are no sales." Because of the lack of sales the CMA has pulled back on initiatives but maintains PR/marketing initiatives through its ongoing awards programs and its annual Global Events like the Global Artist Party (at the CMA Festival) and The Global Markets

Showcase (during CMA Awards Week). Walker states that the CMA "has advisory groups in the U.K. and in Australia and those advisory groups get together and make recommendations to us. They are made up of domestic executives who know their market so we listen to their suggestions about marketing our product over there." Currently the CMA international director in England is Bobbi Boyce.

Mike Curb was involved with the international market when he was president of MGM Records and had the Osmond Brothers who toured internationally. As the owner of Curb Records he has had an office in London for several years and distribution agreements with major labels for other parts of the world.

"There have been a lot of organizations and groups that have been formed to try to spread country music to other countries and it has basically never worked, because people don't buy genres, they buy artists and records," said Curb. "If you have a great record like 'How Do I Live' by LeAnn Rimes then it can [be a] big hit in England and a big hit in Europe."

Curb continued, "The key to promoting records in England is to promote a hit record that you believe is right for the English market, but not assume that it can be a hit there because it has been successful in a particular genre in America. In fact, that is a negative. If we had promoted LeAnn Rimes as a country artist, we never would have had a hit because people in England don't buy an artist just because they're an American country artist anymore than they would celebrate Thanksgiving! People in England buy a record because it's a hit record and they love the record. They love records as great records, not because the artist happens to be country."

An effort to promote country music from within Great Britain came when Mark Hagen was with VH-1. Hagen said,

> What we found out is that we needed to put country in with everything else so you'd have a Mavericks or Shania Twain video or even Alan Jackson rubbing up against Madonna or any of the other pop acts. We didn't treat country any differently than pop; we just threw it into the mix. At that point there was an audience who had grown up with the Eagles and James Taylor and these Nashville acts were taking these records and making something similar. You also found a generation of dormant music fans who had gotten a bit bored with the music— how many Phil Collins albums will you buy? They didn't want to stop listening to music so what we said was, "We know you're fed up with Phil Collins—how about this? Let's check this out."

"Country music has never been and never will be that popular in the U.K.," continued Hagen.

> But people found they were enjoying the amount of country they got on VH-1 because they got everything else as well. They just didn't want to watch wall to wall country. The CMT did respectable figures—I don't think it was

stupendous—until VH-1 came on the air because people were watching it when MTV was very rap and grunge heavy and there wasn't anything for the older music fan. CMT was slightly hand-tied in that they were making their own programming and it was being imported directly from the states and none of the cultural references really translated. People like Alan Jackson and Brooks and Dunn—they needed to be contextualized. The U.K. and European audience needs to be told "these guys have sold millions of records and they're really popular and you might find them interesting" instead of just saying "here's the new Brooks and Dunn record!" I know that was a frustration of the people running CMT at the time—they weren't allowed to contextualize. If it had been a full on production operation then they might have had more success.

Talking about country music with British music executives the observation that comes through time and again is that country artists aren't, for the most part, "worldly." They know America and American ways but are just not interested in learning other cultures.

Joe Galante found this to be true. "I ran into Conway Twitty at a country music festival in London a number of years ago," said Galante. "I was talking to Conway, which was a big thrill for me, but he was just complaining, 'I just can't stand the food here. Why am I here? I don't like the food. I want to go home.'" Another label executive—who did not want to be named—talked about another prominent country artist who did one tour of England. "The thing he kept saying over and over was 'I hate the food here' and 'Boy, I can't wait to get back home.'"

It takes a certain worldliness to travel comfortably in different cultures, to be open to new ways of life, new foods and new ways of thinking and most country artists are just not made that way. In a sense, country music doesn't travel well because country artists don't travel well.

There are also legitimate financial reasons why country artists don't want to spend time in the international market. When they are starting out, they may not be able to afford an international tour because the expenses of touring abroad may be greater than the income. Also, it takes them out of the American market where they're needed for career-building exposure. Once they become "stars," they can make much more money in the United States than initially touring abroad. Besides, once they have achieved that level of success, most don't want to, in essence, start all over again and build their career from the ground up in another market.

There are other problems as well. It takes a lot of planning over a long period of time to organize an international tour. If you fly from Nashville to London, it's going to take about nine to ten hours from takeoff to landing and then you're going to land in another time zone. If you land in London at nine in the morning that's 3 a.m. Nashville time and you've got a full day ahead of you to take care of business. It's not easy.

Another problem comes from within the artist's camp. One manager noted, "We started talking about going to England and all the wives wanted to go, the kids, all these relatives—we just couldn't afford it. They looked at it like it was some big vacation. So we quit talking about it."

In a broad, general sense, getting country music exposed internationally has faced several obstacles: (1) the image of country music to the pop music consumer abroad that was often unflattering and uncomplimentary; (2) the reluctance of the international departments at major labels to promote this music abroad; (3) the reluctance of the label's branch offices abroad to release the music in their native markets; (4) the lack of international touring by country music artists; (5) the lack of commitment from Nashville executives to the international market; and (6) the inability to get country music on the mass media—radio and television—outside of the United States.

American music is marketed abroad through the international offices of the major labels, which are generally headquartered in New York. The New York executives aren't predisposed to like country music; they live in the rock/pop/urban music world. When they send samples of music abroad to their international offices they are not inclined to push country music. Each international office operates autonomously in deciding which acts/albums will be released in their home territories. Outside of artists who have contracts which specify a worldwide release—which is rare and mostly confined to "heritage" acts or acts with a long-standing appeal internationally—the office in, say, London is going to decide which acts to release based on the criteria of "do I believe this will sell in this market?" They base that decision on several factors and an act touring in that market is a key factor. Most country acts don't tour internationally so they don't have their recordings released in international markets.

On the other side of the coin, most country acts and their managers don't want to tour internationally because it isn't profitable (at least in the beginning), and it is outside of their comfort zone. Country labels based in Nashville are often hand-tied when one of their acts tours internationally. The New York office can exert pressure on the London office to push an American pop act because there's a quid pro quo; the New York office is also pushing a British pop act. But it's a one-way street with the Nashville office; they're not offering the London office anything in the way of support for a British act while asking the London office to spend money and resources to push one of their acts. There is a financial incentive—if the American act does well in another country then that office receives a profit—but, for the most part, it isn't worth it.

Finally, there are virtually no country-formatted radio stations outside the United States. Most of the major radio stations abroad are state owned and play a wide variety of music but mostly pop/rock. The marketing of country music in the United States has traditionally depended on getting a record played on a country radio station, which creates artist visibility which in turn creates a demand for personal appearances by the artist—which is how most artists make their money. That paradigm does not work in the international market.

There are some success stories of country artists doing well abroad but it is because of individual effort—and individual appeal—more than through the appeal of a genre. In the United States there is a core group of fans of the genre who identify themselves as "country fans." In the international market the fans are more likely to consider themselves "music fans" and like who and what they like regardless of genre. Shania Twain sells a great many albums in the international market; so do LeAnn Rimes, Trisha Yearwood, and Emmylou Harris but they are not labeled "country." Instead, they are viewed as great artists with great songs.

A number of British executives and fans point out that contemporary mainstream country music coming out of Nashville "does not fit" the British tastes. They don't feel like it is "authentic" and the terms "too polished" and "slick" come up over and over again.

Great Britain isn't the only international market for country music but country hasn't fared well in other countries either with the possible exceptions of Canada, Australia, and Ireland. Still, the sales of country albums are a mere blip on the radar screen when talking about the sales of albums worldwide. That seems unlikely to change although the Country Music Association has identified the Hispanic market within the United States for a future push to expand the country music audience.

There are some reasons to believe the Latin market may be more open to country music than Europe or Asia: (1) there is a musical connection, especially between music from Texas and Northern Mexico; (2) there is the cowboy tradition and image common to both; and (3) there is a large Hispanic population in the United States that would like to hear songs sung in Spanish. Another connection is that Texas, which has the largest market for Tejano music, is also important for the country music market.

On the side of "disconnections" is the fact that it is difficult for major recording labels to get adequate distribution or radio exposure for country music in Latin America.

Jeff Walker believes the future of country music in the international markets lies in the digital format. "There's going to be a lot more opportunities with digital radio and increased broadband and bandwidth," said Walker.

Services like iTunes are going to enable the globalization of music. I don't think its many years away where people can sit in Beijing, Dublin, Aukland, or Sydney and download music from Nashville. I think many executives are contemplating that direction. A lot of other industries have a global perspective when they sit down to make a marketing plan but the country music industry is very North American-centric and very radio driven. Now that model is changing and I believe there has to be a new way of doing things, and I think digital is going to help open those markets.

Not everyone agrees. "Country Music will always have a place in America just like Japanese traditional music will always have its place in Japan," said Mike Curb. "But to translate traditional Japanese music to America or to translate country music from the hills of Tennessee, North Carolina, and Virginia to Okinawa and Tokyo—well, that's not going to happen, even though a particular record might be the exception."

12

Politics and Religion

POLITICS AND COUNTRY MUSIC IN THE 21ST CENTURY

Is country music Republican music?

In his book, *Rednecks & Bluenecks: The Politics of Country Music,* author Chris Willman notes that, "The stereotype that country music has become the house genre of the GOP isn't easily or persuasively disproven."[1]

Not everyone agrees.

"I don't necessarily think so," said Joe Galante. "I mean, it revolves around the same things in terms of family, God, and country but I don't hear anybody complaining about taxes in songs. It just doesn't sound like Republican music to me, especially on the tax issue." Galante sees the connection between country music and the American political system as more a matter of opportunism.

"When Jimmy Carter was in the White House, country music was pretty strong there," said Galante. "Clinton was never a real fan so we never got asked to go to the White House. But the Republicans asked and Jimmy Carter asked."

Mike Curb has been active in the Republican Party since he joined Ronald Reagan's campaign for the presidency in 1976. Two years later Curb was elected lieutenant governor of California and became acting governor when Jerry Brown left the state in his quest for the presidency. Beginning in 1983 Curb served in the Reagan administration as finance chair of the Republican Party. He left Washington in 1986 but has retained ties with Republican politicians, primarily through fund-raising efforts for candidates.

"Definitely not," said Curb when asked if country music was Republican music.

If you look at the history of country music you'll find that it is about everything from love to cheating to heartache. It isn't tied to any one political party; people don't buy records because the artist is a Democrat or a Republican. In fact, I think it's best that artists say as little as possible about their political beliefs.

I've seen many artists destroy their careers by getting involved in political issues, and I've seen very few artists who have made their careers by getting involved in political issues. Jimmy Carter loved country music. I never got to know Bill Clinton, so I don't know what kind of music he likes. I do know Ronald Regan loved country music and so does George W. Bush, and Richard Nixon came to the Grand Ole Opry and played.

"I believe that middle American values tend to be expressed in country music," continued Curb. "And we've seen cases where Republican candidates have expressed more of the middle-America values or southern values and that's translated to country. But it's really not so much about a political party as it is about a particular candidate. If you have a candidate from New York who doesn't like country music running against a candidate from Tennessee who grew up on country music, and one is a Democrat and one is a Republican, I would have to say that the country music audience would gravitate toward the candidate from Tennessee. But I don't think it would be tied to any political party."

Although country music has traditionally embraced a "conservative" voice, it is difficult to consistently place it within a political party; as Bill Malone observes, "If any political label fits the music, it would be 'populist.'"[2]

During the 1981–1989 period country music found its populist president in Ronald Reagan, a handsome, charismatic man with a sunny smile, engaging personality, and born optimism. His successful performance as president was a turning point in the South moving from the Democratic to the Republican Party. That is not to say that the South—or the country music community—is monolithic; there are still a number of strong Democrats in the South and in country music. However, since the election of Ronald Reagan the region and the music has tended to be aligned more closely with the Republican Party.

In their book, *The Rise of Southern Republicans,* political scientists Earl and Merle Black state that over 84 million people (30 percent of the population) now live in the South and that what Southerners want is "low tax, low union, strong work ethic, strong commitment to family and community."[3] The Blacks note that in 1968, about half of southern white conservatives called themselves Democrats while only 24 percent were aligned with the Republican Party. The southern strategy of President Richard Nixon brought more white Southerners into the Republican fold, but the Watergate controversy and his resignation in disgrace embarrassed and discredited Republicans. By the 1976 election, only 30 percent of conservative white Southerners called themselves Republicans. In 1980, during Reagan's campaign for the presidency, 40 percent of southern white conservatives identified themselves as Republicans, but in 1988, at the end of his presidency, 60 percent of southern white conservatives identified themselves as Republicans. In short, it was not until the Reagan presidency that white conservative Southerners joined the Republican party in large numbers because these white conservatives identified with his values, concerns, and priorities.

There was also the issue of core beliefs versus political party. In short, southern conservatives used to belong to the Democratic Party. After the 1960s southern conservatives were faced with a dilemma: either change your political beliefs or change your party. During Reagan's presidency they changed their party.

Ronald Reagan made being a Republican in the South acceptable and respected but he did not do it by himself. By the time Reagan became president, most conservative Southerners believed the Democratic Party was hostile to their beliefs, values, and priorities. The core beliefs of these conservatives are (1) a highly developed sense of personal responsibility for one's own economic well-being; (2) the belief that individuals—acting alone or as part of a family—should be responsible for finding work and providing a good standard of living for themselves and their families. Individualism is important to this group; there are no "social" explanations for those who do not succeed, which puts them against welfare and social programs. While conservative whites may accept the need for welfare programs to handle temporary losses of income, they strongly believe that long-term welfare programs are unfair to taxpayers, violate the individualist philosophy, and are harmful in the long run to those receiving welfare.

The Blacks note that in 1994 the Republicans took control of Congress for the first time since 1952, and in 1996 Conservatives accounted for 43 percent of southern white voters and 34 percent of all southern voters. There were also some powerful social and economic forces at work.

Studies have shown that as family income increases, people are more likely to become Republicans. Studies also show that the country music listener is no longer "poor." Among working class whites, 42 percent were core Republicans while 35 percent were core Democrats; 57 percent of middle-income southern whites were core Republicans while only 27 percent were core Democrats. A large majority of upper-income whites, 64 percent, were core Republicans.[4]

Among southern white men, 57 percent were core Republicans while 49 percent of southern white women were core Republicans; on the other side, only 23 percent of southern white men were core Democrats while 31 percent of southern white women were core Democrats. If a family had an income of $75,000 in 1996, only 10 percent thought of themselves as liberal; 64 percent were core Republicans and 21 percent were core Democrats.[5]

There was an old saying in the South about "yellow dog Democrats." That meant some were so loyal to the Democratic Party that if the party ran a yellow dog, they would vote for it. The terms have changed; "core" is now the political science term for "yellow dog." In general, southern white men tend to be core Republican voters. They have shifted their loyalties from the Democratic to the Republican party since Ronald Reagan's presidency because Reagan presented an antigovernment, free-market message while the Democratic Party supported government regulations of business, affirmative action, a social safety net, and more protection for women's rights. White men tend to be the strongest anti-tax constituency; they distrust regulations for business, guns, and the environment and feel their personal freedom threatened by an activist federal government. The Republican image as tax cutters helped with this group.

Although the Republican political philosophy has been embraced by many country music fans, some note problems in this world view. In his book, *What's the Matter with Kansas? How Conservatives Won the Heart of America,* author Thomas Frank argues that conservative Republican administrations have been detrimental to the American working class in economic terms. Frank states that "over the last three decades they have smashed the welfare state, reduced the tax burden on corporations and the wealthy, and generally facilitated the country's return to a nineteenth-century pattern of wealth distribution," and concludes, "the primary contradiction of the backlash: it is a working-class movement that has done incalculable, historic harm to working-class people."[6]

Conservatives, according to Frank, have labeled liberals as "sophisticated, wealthy, and materialistic" implying that "these tastes and preferences reveal the essential arrogance and foreignness of liberalism."[7] Conservative Republicans have branded Democrats as a "wealthy, pampered, arrogant elite that lives as far as it can from real Americans" while Republicanism identifies itself with "the faith of the hardworking common people of the heartland, an expression of their unpretentious, all-American ways just like country music and NASCAR."[8] Republicans, in short, brand themselves as the true representatives of the working man because "economics do not count," according to Frank.[9]

The end result for middle Americans, according to Frank, is an experience that "has been a bummer all around. All they have to show for their Republican loyalty are lower wages, more dangerous jobs, dirtier air, a new overlord class that comports itself like King Farouk—and, of course, a crap culture whose moral free fall continues without significant interference from the grandstanding Christers whom they send triumphantly back to Washington every couple of years."[10]

SONGS OF THE WORKING MAN

The image of country music being the music of the working man or woman endures; in 1978 the classic song of the working man, "Take This Job and Shove It" by Johnny Paycheck, was released and became a number 1 song on the *Billboard* Country Singles charts. There were other songs about the working man or woman in the 1970s; in 1976 there was "One Piece at a

Time" by Johnny Cash, in 1977 there was "Working Man Can't Get Nowhere Today" by the poet of the common man, Merle Haggard, and in 1978 there was "Me and the I.R.S." by Johnny Paycheck.

In 1980 there was "Hard Hat Days and Honky Tonk Nights" by Red Steagall and "Workin' at the Car Wash Blues" by Jerry Reed; in 1981 there was "Working Girl" by Dolly Parton, "Common Man" by Sammy Johns, and a warning to the common people, "Don't Get Above Your Raisin'" by Ricky Skaggs.

In 1982 we had an answer song to Paycheck's earlier hit, "I Wish I Had a Job to Shove" by Rodney Lay as well as "Play This Old Working Day Away" by Dean Dillon; in 1985 there was "Forty Hour Week" by Alabama and "Working Man" by John Conlee; in 1986 there was "Working Class Man" by Lacy J. Dalton; in 1988 there was "I Owe, I Owe (It's Off to Work I Go)" by David Chamberlain and "Workin' Man (Nowhere to Go)" by the Nitty Gritty Dirt Band; in 1989 there was "Death and Taxes (And Me Lovin' You)" by Patsy Cole, "Hard Times for an Honest Man" by James House, and "Too Much Month at the End of the Money" by Billy Hill.

The decade of the 1990s began with "Work Song" by The Corbin/Hanner Band then "Working for the Japanese" by Ray Stevens. In 1992 there was "Lord Have Mercy on the Working Man" by Travis Tritt, "Hard Days and Honky Tonk Nights" by Earl Thomas Conley, "Hey Mister (I Need This Job)" by Shenandoah, "I'm in a Hurry (And Don't Know Why)" by Alabama, "Workin' Man's Dollar" by Chris LeDoux, "Papa Loved Mama" by Garth Brooks, and "Working Woman" by Rob Crosby; in 1993 there was "It Sure Is Monday" by Mark Chesnutt, "American Honky Tonk Bar Association" by Garth Brooks, and "Working Man's Ph.D." by Aaron Tippin; in 1994 there was "Lifestyles of the Not So Rich and Famous" by Tracy Byrd.

In 1995 there was "Workin' for the Weekend" by Ken Mellons and "Workin' Man Blues" by Jed Zeppelin; in 1997 there was "Cowboy Cadillac" by Garth Brooks; in 1999 there was "Busy Man" by Billy Ray Cyrus, "Hands of a Working Man" by Ty Herndon, and "Little Man" by Alan Jackson. In 2003 Marty Stuart brought back "Too Much Month at the End of the Money"; in 2004 Dusty Drake sang "I Am the Working Man"; and in 2004 there was "Redneck Yacht Club," a humorous look at the leisure time of the working man by Craig Morgan.

STRICT FATHER VS. NURTURANT MOTHER

George Lakoff, in his book *Moral Politics: How Liberals and Conservatives Think,* sees Americans politically divided into "strict father" and "nurturant parent" models where the Republicans have captured the "strict father" image and the Democrats appeal to the "nurturant mother" image. According to Lakoff, the "strict father" emphasizes "discipline, authority, order, boundaries, homogeneity, purity and self-interest" while the "nurturant parent" emphasizes "empathy, nurturance, self-nurturance, social ties, fairness, and happiness."[11]

In the strict-father model progressive taxation is referred to as "theft," and "taking people's money away from them." Conservatives do not see the progressive income tax as "paying one's fair share" or "civic duty" or even "noblesse oblige," according to Lakoff.[12] Both the strict father and nurturant parent view the nation as family with the government as a parent; however, liberals tend to see helping people in need as a key function of the government and thus support social programs while conservatives view requiring citizens to be self-disciplined and self-reliant as a key function of government.[13]

Music touches the emotions and the Democrats have tended to appeal to reason. Political pundits have pointed out that many programs and policies of the Democrats help middle and lower-middle class Americans more than the programs and policies of the Republicans. However, many of those who would benefit from Democratic programs vote Republican.

In his book, *The Political Mind: The Role of Emotion in Deciding the Fate of the Nation*, author Drew Weston refutes the notion of an electorate that votes by "reason" and states that "a dispassionate mind that makes decisions by weighing the evidence and reasoning to the most valid conclusions bears no relation to how the mind and brain actually work."[14]

Weston criticizes Democrats for developing "campaign strategy that... focuses on facts, figures, policy statements, costs and benefits, and appeals to intellect and expertise" because, "We are not *moved* by leaders with whom we do not feel an emotional resonance. We do not find policies worth debating if they don't touch on the emotional implications for ourselves, our families, or things we hold dear.... The more purely 'rational' an appeal, the less it is likely to activate the emotional circuits that regulate voting behavior."[15]

Contemporary liberals, according to Weston, "believe that the way to voters' hearts is through their brains" but, "In politics, when reason and emotion collide, emotion invariably wins."[16] The fact that Republicans have consistently connected with emotional concerns of the electorate while Democrats have appealed to reason and intellect is the reason that Republicans have been successful attracting voters who may vote against their own economic self-interest, according to Weston.

The lyrics of country songs generally do reflect listeners' personal views, particularly in relation to social and cultural values and especially when presented in an emotional context. This is the essential link between country music and the Republican Party since the 1980s: Both have successfully appealed to people's strongest emotions.

RELIGION AND COUNTRY MUSIC

The country music audience identifies itself as religious—specifically Christian—and the Republican Party became the party of Christian evangelicals during the 1980s, so it is natural to assume that the country audience feels comfortable with the Republican Party in terms of religious beliefs, especially during the 1990s when the Democrats were branded as secularists, antagonistic to religion.

There are some flaws in that argument. First, country radio listeners are no more likely to attend church than non-country listeners. Although they describe themselves as religious and tell survey takers that religion is very important in their lives, the country fan, in general, has a more relaxed view of religion than Christian evangelicals. Country songs are filled with moral messages as well as stories of good old boys raising hell; the country audience feels as comfortable going to a bar on Saturday night as they do going to church on Sunday morning.

Religion—specifically Christianity—is deeply embedded in country music, and during the past 30 years a number of songs mentioning "God," "Jesus," "Lord," "prayer," and "Heaven" or with an underlying Christian message have been on the country music charts.

Country music is not afraid to sing about God or Jesus and country radio is not afraid to program these songs. In 1976 there was the humorous "Dropkick Me, Jesus" by Bobby Bare, "God Loves Us (When We All Sing Together)" by Sami Jo, "How Great Thou Art" by the Statler Brothers, "Jesus Is the Same in California" by Lloyd Goodson, "See You On Sunday" by Glen Campbell, "Sunday School to Broadway" by Sammi Smith, and "Thank God I've Got You" by the Statler Brothers; in 1977 there was "Home Where I Belong" by B.J. Thomas, "Lean on Jesus Before He Leans on You" by Paul Craft, "Lord, If I Make It to Heaven Can I Bring My Own Angel Along" by Billy Parker, "Sunday School to Broadway" by Anne Murray, and "Thank God She's Mine" by Freddie Hart; in 1978 there was "God Knows" by Debby Boone, "God Made Love" by Mel McDaniel, "I Bow My Head (When They Say Grace)" by Daniel, "I Knew the Mason" by Chapin Hartford, and "I'd Like to See Jesus (On the Midnight Special)" by Tammy Wynette; in 1979 there was "My Prayer" by Glen Campbell, "On Business for the King" by Joe Sun, "Outlaw's Prayer" by Johnny Paycheck, "Preacher Berry" by Donna Fargo, and "Rhythm Guitar" by the Oak Ridge Boys.

In 1980 there was "Family Bible" by Willie Nelson, "Jesus on the Radio (Daddy on the Phone)" by Tom T. Hall, "My Special Prayer" by Freddy Fender, "One Day at a Time" by Cristy Lane, "Rock 'n' Roll to Rock of Ages" by Bill Anderson, "She's Made of Faith" by Marty Robbins, and a song that certainly was not a gospel song but taught a Christian lesson, "While the Choir Sang the Hymn (I Thought of Her)" by Johnny Russell. In 1981 there was "I'm Just an Old Chunk of Coal" by John Anderson, "Jesus Let Me Slide" by Dean Dillon, "Last Word in Jesus Is Us" by Roy Clark, and "Seven Days Come Sunday" by Rodney Lay; in 1982 there was "Lord I Hope This Day Is Good" by Don Williams, "Praise the Lord and

Send Me the Money" by Bobby Bare, and "Preaching Up a Storm" by Mel McDaniel; in 1983 there was "Everything from Jesus to Jack Daniels" by Tom T. Hall, and "Thank God for Kids" by the Oak Ridge Boys; in 1984 there was "God Must Be a Cowboy" by Dan Seals and "God Won't Get You" by Dolly Parton; in 1987 there was "God Will" by Lyle Lovett, "Good God, I Had It Good" by Pake McEntire, "He's Got the Whole World in His Hands" by Cristy Lane, and "Would Jesus Wear a Rolex" by Ray Stevens. The last year of the 1980s saw "Church on Cumberland Road" by Shenandoah, "Gospel According to Luke" by Skip Ewing, "Son of a Preacher Man" by Bobbi Lace, and "Sunday in the South" by Shenandoah on the country charts in *Billboard*.

The decade of the 1990s began with the contemporary Christian song "He's Alive" by Dolly Parton and "Praying for Rain" by Kevin Welch; in 1991 there was "Lord Have Mercy on a Country Boy" by Don Williams, "Unanswered Prayers" by Garth Brooks, and "Walk On Faith" by Mike Reid; in 1992 there was "Jesus and Mama" by Confederate Railroad, "Mama Don't Forget to Pray for Me" by Diamond Rio, and "Sacred Ground" by McBride & The Ride; in 1993 there was "God Blessed Texas" by Little Texas and "Thank God for You" by Sawyer Brown; in 1995 there was "Heaven Bound (I'm Ready)" by Shenandoah and "What if Jesus Comes Back Like That" by Collin Raye; in 1997 there was "God Bless the Child" by Shania Twain, "Thank God for Believers" by Mark Chesnutt, and "What if Jesus Comes Back Like That" by Collin Raye; in 1998 there was "Bless the Broken Road" by Melodie Crittenden, "Heaven Bound" by Shana Petrone, and "Holes in the Floor of Heaven" by Steve Wariner. The last year of the 90s saw "God Must Have Spent a Little More Time on You" by Alabama with N'SYNC and "Godspeed (Sweet Dreams)" by Radney Foster.

In the twenty-first century country music continued its trend of embedding Christianity in many of its songs. In 2000 there was "800 Pound Jesus" by Sawyer Brown, "God Gave Me You" by Bryan White, "Nothing Catches Jesus by Surprise" by John Michael Montgomery, and "Prayin' for Daylight" by Rascal Flatts; in 2001 there was "When God-Fearin' Women Get the Blues" by Martina McBride; in 2003 there was "Blessed" by Martina McBride and "Hello God" by Dolly Parton; in 2003 there was "Godspeed (Sweet Dreams)" by the Dixie Chicks, "Help Pour Out the Rain (Lacey's Song)" by Buddy Jewell, "Only God (Could Stop Me Loving You)" by Emerson Drive, "Pray for the Fish" and "Three Wooden Crosses" by Randy Travis, and "This Is God" by Phil Vassar; in 2004 there was "Long Black Train" by Josh Turner, "Face of God" by Billy Ray Cyrus, "Heaven" by Los Lonely Boys, "Jesus Was a Country Boy" by Clay Walker, "Lord Loves the Drinkin' Man," by Mark Chesnutt, "Son of a Preacher Man" by Sherrie Austin, "Sunday Morning and Saturday Night" by James Otto, "Thank God for Kids" by Kenny Chesney, and "Thank God I'm a Country Boy" by Billy Dean; in 2005 there was "Bless the Broken Road" by Rascal Flatts, "Drugs or Jesus" by Tim McGraw, "God's Will" by Martina McBride, and "That's What I Love About Sunday" by Craig Morgan.

"That's What I Love About Sunday" presents itself as a day in the life of the country music listener; they go to church but the folks ain't perfect. The guy at the service station covered with oil and grease now has on his Sunday best while in the pew behind him the singer hears "Sweet Miss Betty" singing off key. After church they go home, put on their old jeans and eat fried chicken and baked beans before playing football in the back yard. Another verse talks about reading the Sunday newspaper and finding a coupon for a sale on ground round. The song mentions naps, fishing, folks getting baptized, and Mama raising her hands in spiritual bliss.

In 2005 there was "Who You'd Be Today" by Kenny Chesney, "Jesus, Take the Wheel" by Carrie Underwood—an overtly Christian song—and "When I Get Where I'm Going" by Brad Paisley featuring Dolly Parton that talks about the afterlife. Also in 2005 was "Believe" by Brooks & Dunn, who sang another song with a religious message, "God Must Be Busy" in 2007.

THE DIXIE CHICKS

The issue of politics and country music came to the forefront in 2003 when the Dixie Chicks lead singer, Natalie Maine, told a London audience on March 10 that, "Just so you know, we're ashamed the president of the United States is from Texas." The event occurred at Shepherd's Bush Empire, a 2,000-seat venue, and the quote was printed in the *Guardian* newspaper two days later. This statement set off a fire storm that resulted in Dixie Chicks records being pulled off country radio stations.

Cumulus—the second largest chain (260 stations)—issued a directive not to play the Chicks on any of its stations while the Clear Channel chain claimed that they left it up to individual stations, telling them to "pay attention to their listeners." That message was code for "take the Chicks' records off the air," according to Chris Willmon.[17]

Although the major radio chains argued that pulling Dixie Chicks records from playlists was in response to listener demands and no politics was involved, there was a political connection between President Bush and the largest radio chain, Clear Channel, which owned over 1,200 stations that reached about 30 percent of the listening public. Tom Hicks, who was on the board of directors for Clear Channel, was a major contributor to Bush's campaigns for governor and president.

Hicks was chairman and cofounder of a private equity firm that merged with San Antonio-based Clear Channel in 1999. The previous year Hicks had purchased the Texas Rangers for $250 million. Bush had borrowed $605,000 for a 1.8 percent share in the baseball team; after the sale Bush received 12 percent or $14.9 million, which gave him a 2,400 percent profit from the sale. This paved the way for George W. Bush to run for governor of Texas in 1998, with heavy backing by Hicks and others.

POLITICAL AFFILIATIONS AND THE DIXIE CHICKS

A 2007 survey by Edison Media Research that profiled country radio listeners showed that in terms of political affiliation, 47 percent described themselves as "moderate" while 25 percent saw themselves as "somewhat conservative," and 13 percent described themselves as "very conservative." Only 4 percent described themselves as "very liberal" and 11 percent saw themselves as "somewhat liberal." Surprisingly, 37 percent said they "rarely or never" attended religious services. About a fourth said they attended at least once a week, 15 percent said at least once a month, and 32 percent of country radio listeners said they attended a religious service at least once a year.

When country radio listeners were asked about the Dixie Chicks in 2006, 21 percent thought country radio should never play any Chicks records again while 45 percent said they personally disagreed with what Natalie Maines said about President Bush but thought it was okay if country radio stations played their music. Only 15 percent said they agreed with what Natalie Maines said about President Bush; however, in 2007 19 percent said they agreed with her comments about the president, 32 percent said they thought country radio should never play a Chicks recording again, and 36 percent said they disagreed with Maines but thought it was okay for country radio to play their records.

In February 2007 the Dixie Chicks won Grammys for "Best Country Album" and "Best Country Performance by a Duo or Group with Vocal." Their album, released in May 2006, went platinumn in five weeks, but in October the Chicks were shut out of the Country Music Association Awards; they never even received a nomination.

CAMPAIGN CONTRIBUTIONS

The connection of country music with politics has come through individuals contributing to or campaigning for a candidate. Country artists who have contributed money to or campaigned for Republican candidates include the Oak Ridge Boys, Amy Grant, Larry Gatlin, Lee Greenwood, Hank Williams, Jr., Loretta Lynn, Toby Keith, Sara Evans, Trace Adkins, Kix Brooks, Ronnie Dunn, John Rich, Gretchen Wilson, Randy Owen (of Alabama), Eddy Arnold, and Charlie Daniels.

Country artists who have contributed money to or campaigned for Democratic candidates include Kris Kristofferson, Faith Hill, Tim McGraw, the Dixie Chicks, Willie Nelson, Charley Pride, Trisha Yearwood, "Big"

Kenny Alphin, Randy Travis, Emmylou Harris, Ashley Judd, Tom T. Hall, and Marty Stuart.

COUNTRY MUSIC AND PATRIOTISM

Country music has a long history of embedding patriotism in songs. In 1976 there was "America the Beautiful" by Charlie Rich, "Red, White and Blue" by Loretta Lynn, and "Sold Out of Flagpoles" by Johnny Cash; in 1978 there was "Back in the U.S.A." by Linda Ronstadt and "God Must Have Blessed America" by Glen Campbell; and in 1979 there was "What It Means to Be an American" by Billy Brown.

There were more country songs during the 1980s and 1990s that reflected a patriotic spirit or at least songs that had "America" or "American" in the title or lyrics. In 1980 there was "American Dream" by the Dirt Band, "America the Beautiful" by Mickey Newbury, "Dear Mr. President" by Max D. Barnes, "In America" by the Charlie Daniels Band, "Song of the Patriot" by Johnny Cash, and a song that addressed the issue of American hostages in the Iranian Embassy, "Message to Khomeini" by the Thrasher Brothers.

In 1982 there was "American Dream" by Hank Williams, Jr., and "Made in the U.S.A." by both the Four Guys and the Wright Brothers; in 1983 there was "Crazy Old Soldier" by David Allan Coe; in 1984 there was "America" by Waylon Jennings and "God Bless the USA" by Lee Greenwood; in 1985 there was "American Farmer" by the Charlie Daniels Band and "American Waltz" by Merle Haggard; in 1986 there was "America Is" by B. J. Thomas, "Bidding America Goodbye (The Auction)" by Bruce Hauser/Sawmill Creek Band, "Soldier of Love" by Billy Burnette, and "Somewhere in America" by Mac Davis; in 1987 there was "American Me" by Schuyler, Knoblock & Overstreet; in 1988 there was "American Man" by Frank Burgess, "American Trilogy" by Mickey Newbury, "Americana" by Moe Bandy, and "Tonight in America" by David Lynn Jones; in 1989 there was "American Family" by the Oak Ridge Boys and "More Than a Name On a Wall," a song about the Viet Nam monument by the Statler Brothers.

In August 1990 Saddam Hussein invaded Kuwait, which led to the Gulf War in early 1991. Those events inspired patriotic country songs in the very early 90s. In 1990 there was "American Boy" by Eddie Rabbitt and "Don't Give Us a Reason" by Hank Williams, Jr.; in 1991 there was "You've Got to Stand for Something" by Aaron Tippin, "Letter to Saddam Hussein" by Jerry Martin, "Point of Light" by Randy Travis, and "Soldier Boy" by Donna Fargo; in 1992 there was "We Must Take America Back" by Steve Vaus; in 1993 there was "America, I Believe in You" by the Charlie Daniels Band and "American Made" by the Oak Ridge Boys; in 1994 there was "Red, White and Blue Collar" by the Gibson/Miller Band; in 1996 there was "God's Country" by Marcus Hummon and "The Star Spangled

Banner" by Ricochet; in 1999 there was "What This Country Needs" by Aaron Tippin; and in 2000 there was "We the People" by Billy Ray Cyrus.

The events of 9/11 inspired a number of country artists to record patriotic songs. In 2001 there was a group of country singers doing "America the Beautiful," "America Will Always Stand" by Randy Travis, "America Will Survive" by Hank Williams, Jr., "God Bless America" by LeAnn Rimes, "God Bless the USA" by Lee Greenwood, "Only In America" by Brooks & Dunn, "Osama 'Yo Mama" by Ray Stevens, "Riding with Private Malone" by David Ball, "The Star Spangled Banner" by Faith Hill, "This Ain't No Rag, It's a Flag" by the Charlie Daniels Band, and perhaps the most touching song about the 9/11 tragedy, "Where Were You (When the World Stopped Turning)" by Alan Jackson.

In 2002 there was "American Child" by Phil Vassar, "Courtesy of the Red, White and Blue (The Angry American)" by Toby Keith, "Days of America" by BlackHawk, "God, Family and Country" by Craig Morgan, and "Where the Stars and Stripes and the Eagle Fly" by Aaron Tippin.

The Iraq War began in the spring of 2003; patriotically inspired songs that year were "Have You Forgotten?" and "I Will Hold My Ground" by Darryl Worley, "Hey Mr. President" by the Warren Brothers, "My Beautiful America" by the Charlie Daniels Band, "There Is No War" by Donovan Chapman, and "Travelin' Soldier" by the Dixie Chicks; in 2004 there was "American Soldier" by Toby Keith and "Letters From Home" by John Michael Montgomery; in 2005 there was "Arlington" by Trace Adkins, "Bumper of My S.U.V." by Chely Wright, "Soldier for the Lonely" by Jedd Hughes, and "Soldier's Wife" by Roxie Dean; in 2007 there was "If You're Reading This" by Tim McGraw.

SONGS OF THE SOUTH

Another major reason that country music has been linked to the Republican Party is that country music is linked to the South and southern ways as states have increasingly moved into the Republican column since the 1980s. Country singers certainly connect with the South, as evidenced by the number of songs with "South," "southern," "Dixie" (even if she's a girl), "redneck" and other southern oriented terms.

In 1976 there was "Sweet Southern Lovin'" by Mayf Nutter; in 1977 there was "I'm Coming Home to You, Dixie" by Shylo; "Southern Nights" by Glen Campbell, and "Sun in Dixie" by Kathy Barnes; in 1978 there was "I'm the South" by Eddy Arnold; in 1979 there was "You Ain't Just Whistlin' Dixie" by the Bellamy Brothers; in 1980 there was "Dixie Dirt" by Jim Rushing and "Theme from the Dukes of Hazzard" by Waylon Jennings; in 1981 there was "Dixie Man" by Randy Barlow, "Dixie on My Mind" by Hank Williams, Jr., "Dixie Road" by King Edward IV and The Knights, "Song of the South" by Johnny Russell, "Southern Rains" by Mel Tillis, "Sweet Home

Alabama" by the Charlie Daniels Band, and "Sweet Southern Love" by Phil Everly; in 1983 there was "If Heaven Ain't a Lot Like Dixie" by Hank Williams, Jr., "Redneck Girl" by the Bellamy Brothers, "Song of the South" by Tom T. Hall and Earl Scruggs, and "Sweet Southern Moonlight" by Narvel Felts; in 1983 there was "Dixie Dreaming" by Atlanta, "Dixieland Delight" by Alabama, "Heart of Dixie" by Tommy Overstreet, "Son of the South" and "Southern Fried" by Bill Anderson, and "Southern Women" by the Owen Brothers; in 1984 there was "Making Love to Dixie" by the Younger Brothers Band, "Southern Women" by the Wright Brothers, and "When We Get Back to the Farm" by David Frizzell; in 1985 there was "Dixie Road" by Lee Greenwood and "Dixie Train" by Carl Jackson; in 1986 there was "Dixie Moon" by Ray Charles and "Southern Air" by Ray Stevens; in 1987 there was "Deep Down (Everybody Wants to Be from Dixie)" by Danny Shirley; in 1988 there was "If the South Woulda Won" by Hank Williams, Jr., "Making Love to Dixie" by Heartland, "Southern Accent" by the Bama Band, and "Southern and Proud of It" by Jeff Golden; in 1989 there was "High Cotton" by Alabama, "I Sang Dixie" by Dwight Yoakam, "Song of the South" by Alabama, and "Southern Lady" by Arne Benoni.

In 1990 there was "(What This World Needs Is) A Few More Rednecks" by the Charlie Daniels Band, "Southern Star" by Alabama, and "Where Corn Don't Grow" by Waylon Jennings; in 1993 there was "Dixie Chicken" by Garth Brooks, "Dixie Fried" by the Kentucky Headhunters, and "Queen of My Double Wide Trailer" by Sammy Kershaw; in 1994 there was "High Tech Redneck" by George Jones and "Summer In Dixie" by Confederate Railroad; in 1995 there was "Southbound" by Sammy Kershaw, "Southern Grace" by Little Texas, and "Sweet Home Alabama" by Alabama; in 1997 there was "Southern Streamline" by John Fogerty and "Where Corn Don't Grow" by Travis Tritt; in 2000 there was "She Thinks My Tractor's Sexy" by Kenny Chesney; in 2001 there was "Southern Rain" by Billy Ray Cyrus and "Til Dale Earnhardt Wins Cup #8" by Kacey Jones; in 2003 there was "Southern Boy" by the Charlie Daniels Band with Travis Tritt; in 2004 there was "Redneck Woman" by Gretchen Wilson, "Sweet Southern Comfort" by Buddy Jewell, and "Suds in the Bucket" by Sara Evans.

Politics has become extremely partisan in the twenty-first century and there are certainly a number of partisans for each party in country music. But the music itself defies party affiliation. The cultural conservative who is a Republican can easily feel comfortable with country music and so can those Democrats who advocate an economic system that provides health care and a safety net for the lower middle class and the poor. Country music itself is too big and encompasses too many people with too many points of view to ever be limited to one political party. Still, the fact that the Republican Party has been able to link their vision of what America should be with country music has given them an appeal to the working middle class and enabled them to connect with the heartfelt emotions of those voters.

13

The Twenty-First Century

NAPSTER

Blame it on Shawn Fanning and Napster.

In the twenty-first century the music industry changed a great deal because of illegal downloads of music from the Internet, led by Napster which was created by Shawn Fanning in 1999. However, if it had not been Fanning and Napster then another young, tech-savvy person would have come along with another digital download system to take advantage of the Internet and its ability to carry music to individual computers.

What Napster did was provide a way for consumers to get music free through the Internet, which they downloaded onto their personal computers and made compact discs to play in their car, on their home systems, or share with friends. The music industry was taken aback; a loss in income followed because instead of buying CDs—which was income for the record labels—consumers got them free.

Country music was less directly affected than rock and pop music initially because the country consumer continued to purchase CDs; however, as time moved on and more country consumers became acclimated to the Internet, the illegal downloading issue did directly affect country sales. However, country music felt the effects of illegal downloading early because a number of retailers went out of business when downloads came in, which meant fewer places for country consumers to purchase CDs, and because downloading caused massive losses for major labels and the country divisions were not immune to what was happening with the parent company.

CHANGES IN THE 21ST CENTURY

Three aspects of the music business have changed in the twenty-first century: distribution, retailing, and consumer behavior. These changes have been brought about primarily because of computers and the Internet. The problems these changes have created for the music business are

(1) the industry no longer controls its product and (2) the business and legal infrastructure has not kept up with the technology.

Distribution used to consist of getting physical product from the manufacturer into stores; it was controlled primarily by the major labels and involved warehouses, trucks, and physical inventory. Today, consumers can download music via the Internet and a number of people have a large collection of songs on an iPod or iPod-like device but have no physical CDs. Because of the advent of music on the Internet and the fact that many consumers get their music for free, consumer behavior, especially among young people, caused labels to lose millions of dollars. This also caused a number of record stores to go out of business because many prefer shopping online either illegally—through "free" downloads—or legally, bypassing record stores.

Although losing control of its product is a problem for the music industry, many consumers view it as liberating the music and giving consumers more choice, putting them, instead of record companies, in the driver's seat. The problem of creating legislation that will help correct the issues that digital music has raised has taken a back seat to the Iraq war, international terrorism, and a host of other national and international issues that top the list for Congress to address before it gets to copyright and digital rights.

RECORD COMPANY CONSOLIDATION

The consolidation of the music industry has created a more complicated and complex life for executives in those companies that have consolidated. In 2004 the music divisions of BMG (formerly RCA) and Sony (formerly CBS) merged. Historically, this was an earth-shaking event because these are the two oldest record labels in the music business; their roots go back to the very beginnings of the recording business. What is now Sony Music began as the Columbia Phonograph Company in 1889; what is now BMG began as Victor Records in 1901. Now they are Sony/BMG, headed by Joe Galante, formerly the head of BMG/RCA in Nashville.

"When you're a parent and you have one child, you can focus all your attention on that one child," said Joe Galante.

> But when you get two and three and four and you have to go to all those games and school meetings it's harder to do. It gets more complicated because you keep multiplying the responsibilities that you have. With a record company, you not only have more artists, but you have more people you're responsible for. Instead of having 12 albums out a year you have 24 albums. That means 240 songs instead of 120 songs and in order to get those 240 songs you have to listen to 2,000 instead of 1,000 songs. How many concert dates are you going to for each artist? How many videos will you make? How many events will you attend for an artist? It just goes on and on. We've done well with what we've been able to hold on to over the years but it's hard and keeps getting harder. The major thing I've done over the years is to hire some really good people; some have stayed with me

and some have gone on to run other companies. The only way you can keep this train running on the tracks is to have really good people.

Galante and other Music Row executives have found many of these employees at local universities with music business programs. Belmont University, located at the head of Music Row, and Middle Tennessee State University, located about 40 miles away in Murfreesboro, have music business programs with internships where students work in the industry and then, after graduation, are first in line for jobs when openings occur.

One of the keys to the success of the Nashville music industry has been the music business programs at these two universities. Belmont alumni include country stars Brad Paisley, Trisha Yearwood, Josh Turner, Chris Young, and members of groups Restless Heart, BlackHawk, and Little Texas, as well as a roster of executives at every major record label, publishing company, booking agency, and management company in Nashville. This has helped both the music industry and the universities who offer these programs.

DIGITAL DOWNLOADS

The future of the music industry as it relates to digital downloads is the source of endless discussions in the music industry. The recording industry would like to see a subscription model where consumers pay a monthly fee and then listen to all they want. This is the model that works for cable television; pay your monthly cable bill and you can watch as much—or as little—as you wish. This model allows cable companies to try various shows to see if they attract an audience and allows audiences to explore programming they would normally not order. But cable consumers are increasingly pushing to be allowed to pick whatever channels they want and pay for those—ignoring all these other channels they never watch. The cable companies have been able to impose their model on consumers because consumers have not had a choice; it's all or nothing.

The music-buying consumer wants to pay for what they receive, not for a service where there's a lot of material available that they can't own. Even though the heavy music listener benefits from this model, the American consumer doesn't like paying for something that they cannot own and use as they wish.

When digital downloads first appeared some insisted that downloads would soon replace physical sales. That whatever profits the labels were reaping from selling physical CDs would be reaped by selling legal downloads. Well, it hasn't happened that way. First, a label receives roughly $10 wholesale when they sell a physical album to a retail account. A digital download only generates about 70 cents for a single. Traditionally, the single has inspired a consumer to purchase an album but with digital downloads, consumers only buy the single and put it on their iPod with other favorite singles, disregarding the album unless it is a favorite artist or a unique album. So major record labels have to reconcile themselves to a new paradigm: constructing a business model where they receive 70 cents instead of $10 for each sale.

The "long tail" theory has been applied to the music industry to mean that there are a vast number of songs that people want but, since not enough people want these songs—and retailers do not have shelf space to carry all these songs—they can be stored digitally for, essentially, no cost so when a consumer desires these songs they are able to purchase them. This vast number of songs that only a handful of people want is the "long tail." These don't generate enough revenue to make them profitable as a physical product but satisfy specific consumer demand for more obscure material and provide income to a label for material that would otherwise lay in a vault gathering dust. This is happening, but it is not happening in such a huge number as to offset the losses labels are feeling from the lack of physical CD sales.

The fact is that major labels are dependent on big sales numbers in order to survive as major corporations. Consumers can argue—and do—that labels should not have such a huge overhead that they cannot be profitable unless they sell millions of recordings by superstar artists. The labels themselves tend to agree. But consumers, for the most part, want the big superstar artists. There have always been small, boutique labels that specialize in music—jazz or folk or bluegrass or military music—that would not be profitable or worthwhile for a major label to pursue.

The situation at the end of 2007—eight years after Napster first appeared—is that physical CDs still outsell downloads. In terms of income, CDs account for 85 to 90 percent and the country consumer continues to purchase physical CDs.

BMG/Sony's country division has "about 15 or 20 acts who sell downloads in the 150,000 to 200,000 range," according to Joe Galante. "Everybody has downloads. Some have 5,000 and some have 10,000 but we're just not there where downloads can replace the income lost from consumers purchasing physical CDs."

"For the most part the record industry saw this coming," said Mike Curb. He continued,

> They saw the Internet downloading when it started with Napster, they saw this illegal activity coming and no one in the industry knew what to do, including me. The RIAA has tried suing and there have been successful court victories and other victories through law enforcement but no one has figured out how to stop illegal file sharing. We've lost control of that and I personally believe the industry has to continue doing the things that it's been doing to try to stop it but I think it is more important to make legal downloading easier. I believe that once the mobile telephone can download music in the simplest way possible then we'll have a chance to regain our position through legal downloads.
>
> For example, I should be able to download directly to my iPhone and not have to do it through my computer. I need to be able to play back the music easily.

On my iPhone I have to go through my computer to download or I have to find a Starbucks somewhere and when I try to listen my iPhone speaker is so low that I have to have an external speaker system. And the speaker system doesn't work through the Bluetooth in my car.

The future of downloading should also include videos. "I was talking to the head of one of the major publishing companies about how frustrating it is that we can't get our music or videos on the iPod," said Curb.

Well, that's not the fault of the iPod. The problem is that record companies and music publishers have not been able to get together to decide on a statutory fee that would allow this. Just imagine if every video that's ever been made was available on the video iPod now. The record companies will have to pay a little more than they want and maybe the publishers will get a little less than they want but to me it is such an embarrassment that the heads of these companies—and we've got really bright people in these publishing and record industry associations—haven't been able to get some kind of a rate to do this. The net effect is that for years now videos have not been available to be downloaded. Since I'm in the record business I have to take some of the blame. We haven't been able to strike a compromise so everybody gets hurt: the songwriters, artists, record companies, and the publishers. A lot of the loss of control is our own fault because if we don't offer something to the consumer legally and then make the experience easy and the price fair then we are contributing to our own demise.

RECORD LABELS

Record labels work much like a venture capitalist. First, they front the money for recording, tour support, and other needed expenses in order to get an artist into the marketplace. Much of this money invested is called "recoupables," which means the artist must recoup it from the sales of his/her albums. The artist earns royalties from the sale of recordings but this income is collected by the label which credits that royalty amount against the artist's account until all the recoupables are paid, at which time the artist receives the royalties they earn.

Many artists have long had a love/hate relationship with their record labels because, on one hand, the label pours a lot of money into an artist's career and provides necessary business support for the artist to gain national attention, but on the other hand, most artists never receive any royalties because all their earnings go to pay off the recoupables they owe the record company. Further, the record company owns the copyright to the master recordings, even if the recoupables have been repaid, so the artist has no control over his or her recordings.

The record companies argue that these recordings are assets that generate revenue from catalog (recordings they own going back years) which allows them to invest in new artists. Further, the record company notes that it takes the initial (and ongoing) risks of signing and promoting an act with no guarantee they will be profitable. So the labels feel they are justified in owning these masters.

The record companies also argue that, from a practical standpoint, it is best to have these masters in a central location so that someone wanting to license a recording (for example, in a movie or a "Greatest Love Songs" compilation) knows where to find it. Further, the record company is a business which seeks to maximize its assets so they will continue to market and promote these recordings long after an artist's career is over, guaranteeing that this product will be available in the marketplace.

These are all good, legitimate reasons for a record label to own the masters because most artists are not business people and are not geared to functioning in the role of a business executive. Further, even if the artist does have a business sense, there simply isn't enough time in the day to be an artist and business executive too. An artist needs to devote his or her time to being an artist, finding and recording the best songs available, touring and performing, and being available to the media.

The idea of the necessity of a record label has come into question since the spread of the Internet; young acts argue that they can produce their own CD—the technology is so good today that what used to be million dollar recording equipment is now affordable so "bedroom bands" can exist; these bands are often one person, or a group of friends, who gather in a basement or bedroom to record songs they have written. Computers have CD replicating abilities and stampers are available to make the CD look professional. The young act (or even old acts!) can set up a Web site, have a site on MySpace, Facebook, a video on YouTube (digital video equipment is also widely available and easily affordable), and have worldwide distribution.

When an artist is just beginning they only want to be heard. Those who are driven to create music don't do it because of the profit motive; they do it because they love it. And so having a song on the Internet available so people can hear it is its own reward in the early stages of a performer's career. However, when that person becomes a professional artist—and when that music becomes popular and in demand from consumers—then money becomes an issue. It particularly becomes an issue when there's a lot of it on the table. The young artist shuns the first few dollars that come in but when the money becomes a sizeable pile they suddenly become interested. The music business is a high risk/high payoff business; however, with the digital world it has become a high risk/no payoff business for many artists because their music is available free on line. The only way they can make money is through personal appearances and so we have a throwback to the previous era when record sales counted for little or no income and touring accounted for most of the money they made. It's always been that way in country music—touring is the financial backbone of an artist's career—but during the 1990s a number of artists were selling multi-platinum so record royalties became a major source of their income.

With the advent of the Internet came the idea that record labels are no longer necessary. Part of this was resistance to the idea of a gatekeeper; young people wanted to write and record the music that was important to them and release it to the world. The result has often been a cacophony of sounds on the Internet. Yes, an act on the Internet is available all over the world, but who is really watching and listening? There's a relative handful of videos or tracks that people tune into because they're goofy; it's mostly the abysmally bad performers who come up on computer screens when there's a room full of people for a good laugh. But for most acts on the Internet, they're either watching themselves or their friends are watching them but there's no great huge audience tuned in.

RECORD COMPANIES AND ARTIST MANAGERS

Jeff Walker points out there are two schools of thought as to which way major labels will evolve. One is that they will become more like motion picture distribution firms with labels shrinking their A&R operations and instead of finding and signing artists will become distribution hubs that pick up artists with master recordings. The second model has major labels centralizing their operations (finance, administration, marketing) with a global overview while maintaining regional A&R operations.

While both of these approaches are very different, both are being touted as prototypes of the new label model.

Whatever happens, the newly created "360 deal" is going to play a major role in the record label of the future. Under these 360 deals the record label participates in all the revenues generated by the artist—publishing, songwriting, touring, endorsements, and so on. Record company executives feel that under the old model where the label only made money from the sales of records that it was not equitable because the label absorbed all the costs of production, promotion, and marketing. In the new digital environment a label simply cannot afford to do this because of the reduced revenues from physical sales. Under these new arrangements the record labels will have an even closer synergy with management companies than they had in the past.

"Management gets a percentage of everything the artist does so why shouldn't the record labels?" asked Jeff Walker. "I think that's definitely the way it's going. Perhaps the management companies will be in partnership so you may see more joint logo situations where management has started up a production company and works in partnership with the record labels. I think that is going to be the new model."

The idea that record companies and management companies are somehow going to merge is an idea that's kicked around on Music Row. With the record labels losing money the consensus is that they're also losing power so there's a shift of power in country music with managers becoming more powerful as record labels decline. There have been examples of managers and artists starting their own label (T.K. Kimbrell and Toby Keith) and of artists forming their own label and dealing with major retail accounts. Garth Brooks and the Eagles have each formed their own label and made an exclusive agreement with Wal-Mart to sell their product. Some see this as the future of the music industry.

Mike Curb disagrees with this assessment; he believes these types of deals will be rare. "There are some artists who reach a point in their career where they prefer to make the music they want to make and they're successful enough to where they can command the attention of a major mass merchandiser and sell product," said Curb.

> They have the right to do that and the mass merchandiser has the right to buy the product. But in the long term, how long will it be before the mass merchandiser wants another artist? We have to remember that there's only a handful of artists who can do that at any given point. Many times it's an artist at the end of his or her career. In other cases, it's an artist who really enjoys doing the promotions and enjoys the marketing. A good example of an artist who really enjoys this type of thing and is really good at it is Garth Brooks. Garth Brooks is the kind of guy who has made a lot of things work that other artists haven't been able to do. The other thing to remember about Garth Brooks is that he's the biggest artist in our industry and maybe the biggest male artist of all time, in terms of his sales.

"There are a handful of artists who are big enough and successful enough to market their records directly through special accounts and that will always be the case," continued Curb.

> But through most of their careers those artists needed a record company. They may have reached a point now where they're so successful that they can sell directly to one or two accounts but those major accounts like Wal-Mart have historically not wanted to manage their own inventory; they've always wanted to have an effective distributor in between who will manage their inventories and choose the product. Not only are there just a handful of artists who are big enough to sell directly to a single account, I think you'll find that most of the individual accounts have a history of not wanting to buy their records from a thousand different recording artists. They may buy from one or two or five, and that's already taking place. But those are artists who are incredibly developed and have come through the record companies and have the ability to deal one on one with an account. But unless the artist is really big and sustains at a certain level, the major retailers, particularly the mass merchandisers, have not wanted to buy from numerous artists. Instead, they prefer to buy through a smaller group of distributors and have their product through a company where the inventory is managed by experts.

David Ross is the publisher and owner of *Music Row*, a music industry trade magazine in Nashville. Ross also serves as head of the "Future Task

Force" for the Country Music Association and pulls together "think tanks" to discuss the future of the music industry. In a report issued August 2007, "Embracing Change: The New Rules of Engagement," Ross interviewed Scott Borchetta, president of the startup independent label Big Machine. Borchetta noted, "Some of the emerging record and management companies are starting to look similar although there are things we can do as a record company that they aren't good at and vice versa. The point is we are both looking at artists as brands....What we can offer as a label that management companies can't, is real marketing power in the record business....We take you from 0 to 200 miles an hour. We are going to share because you probably can't get to 200 miles per hour without us."[1]

Mike Curb notes that,

> Record companies already perform a major part of the management function with many artists. When an artist succeeds, there are numerous people willing to provide the management services for that artist. But, during the many years prior to the artist succeeding, much of that responsibility falls on the record company and the personnel within the record company. When the artist goes through three or four records that don't hit, you have to try something new, you have to convince the artist to try something different or listen to the artist because maybe the artist has an idea that is better than the record company's idea. When the artist succeeds there are so many people willing to provide that function that they are almost tripping over one another. So, the question is should the record company participate in some of those other areas outside of just record sales? Well, everyone agrees that record sales have dropped substantially and it probably will be impossible for a record company to succeed in the future unless that record company also is involved in the merchandising, perhaps the concert revenues or some percentage of that, and music publishing revenues. The day will come where it won't make much sense to make the investment in a recording artist if you aren't in a position to participate in the merchandising and the concerts. So, there is a tremendous move at [the] present time within most of the record companies to utilize what is commonly referred to as the 360 contract that allows the record company that is investing in the artist to participate in all of the revenues, rather than just record sales.

ARTIST MANAGERS

An artist manager is someone who handles the business aspects of an artist's career. The artist and manager are a team who work together to further the artist's career. Although the artist manager is a behind-the-scenes person, almost every great artist has a manager.

Mike Curb believes that,

> A good manager is someone who works with the record company and helps the record company motivate their promotion staff and other employees. The worst managers are the ones who think they have all the answers and compete with the

record company. They usually end up damaging the relationship between the artist and the record company and then are usually unable to provide that service themselves so they end up losing the artist as a client. They participate more in the demise of the artist rather than helping the artist. The great manager is the person who can motivate the record company and the booking agencies and the media so that they help develop the artist without competing in such a way as to make the record company's job more difficult.

Erv Woolsey, who has managed George Strait—one of the most consistently successful artists in the history of country music—echoes Curb's comments. Woolsey states, "I really think the job as a manager is to represent that artist. I try to help them do what they want to do; they are all grown people. I think the term 'manager' is very old fashioned or maybe we're called that because there's nothing else to call us. I certainly don't 'manage' George Strait or LeAnn Womack. We talk about things, the goals that they each have and I try to make them understand a little bit from the music business perspective. It's like a pie; there are different pieces and I try to help them understand that if they do such and such, then this is what I think could happen."

Woolsey continued,

I think the manager can sit here and get the input from record companies, from radio, from the media—all those different things but to me it all starts with radio and then the record companies kick in what they do best, getting the product out there. It's a whole team working together. I know as a former promotion guy, I had people in the old days come into my office, get in my face, scream and yell and say terrible things and when that happens you go, "Okay, alright—I don't know if that was the thing to do." But, you know, they get caught up in it. Still, to me it's such a team effort and it always has been. No artist is bigger than the record company. It's all a machine and everybody working together is what makes it work.

Joe Galante believes a great manager is

somebody that is as invested in the artist as the artist is. They are not in this for the money. They really understand that they're going to have to scrimp and save for a period of time to make the right decisions and have the courage to tell an artist when they're wrong. Not pass the buck but instead give them constructive criticism or just criticism and encouragement. The manager is a coach and they need to be able to tell someone when they've done a good job performing or not done a good job performing. They have to be a communicator because it's very much a team. That's what a coach does; he communicates, teaches, mentors. All of those things are important for a manager to be great.

Then I believe the key to anything we do in this business is consistency. Anybody can have an act that breaks—has a hit record or two. The charts are full of them and some sell gold and platinum. Any manager can do that. The ability to do it over and over again is a consistency that only the great ones have. That's how they become great. Whether it's an executive in a record company, a publisher, an artist manager, a songwriter, or an artist, that consistency is the key to greatness. Anybody can be average, and that's not necessarily a bad thing. If you make the right call on somebody and that's your one shot and you saved your money, then good for you. But to be on top day in and day out, year after year, that's greatness. We're on a roller coaster here and there are ups and downs. But a manager has to be able to get their act to be consistent, to coach their performances along, to know their look, their image and all that. It's really on the job training and everybody working together. There's no handbook.

As for artist managers starting record companies, Curb observes that,

I could count on the fingers of one hand the number of managers that I have met who I believe could run a record company, but certainly under the right circumstances and with the right investment, some managers could run record companies. Some lawyers who are in the industry could run companies. Some agents and managers who are in the record industry could run record companies but they would all be exceptions. And I guess some of us who run record companies could also work as agents or work as managers, but the bottom line is if you look over the history of the music industry from the very beginning right up to today, you'll see that there is a need for some entity to provide the functions and responsibilities of the record company as we've seen for over a hundred years.

RADIO

Radio is perplexed today by a key fact: Young people don't listen to radio like they used to. In fact, the teenagers and young 20-somethings who used to be core consumers of radio have turned away from radio to iPods, CDs, the Internet, and other formats where they can pick what they want to hear when they want to hear it. They learn about new songs and new artists from their friends or the Internet; "buzz marketing," which means an artist creating a "buzz" is the key to reach them. The country consumer still listens to radio because "the country buyer is an adult and they still get into their car," said Joe Galante.

"The worrisome thing is we've lost a generation of radio listeners and the question is, Can we get the next generation?" said Lon Helton.

We've lost this one, especially with the Internet. The Internet is a pull medium: I take what I want, when I want it, and how much of it I want. Radio and network television by and large are push mediums. "I'm the program director, here's what I'm giving you. Here's what I think you want." Kids are pretty much, "No, I don't want to take what you want, I want to get what I want." That's why Internet radio and satellite radio have eight choices of country and eight choices of rock. That's appealing, because you can make it like a magazine rack. A magazine rack used to have one boating magazine. Now you have a magazine for small boating, small sail boating, small power boating, medium sized of all three, big boats, and on down the line on boating. As we get more and more audio delivery systems, people can take that little niche that they want. The question is, Can we get these young people back into radio? The radio station doesn't occupy an important piece of life the way it used to for young people. So, we've lost a generation, the same generation that thinks that music is free.

Helton paused, then added,

The one thing that has always saved radio and what it could do that no other medium could do was be local. It always went local, local, local. The bad news is that in consolidation, it was the perfect storm where all of these companies were vying to buy other companies back in 1996 to 1999. They paid a very high price for those stations and everything had to go perfect to make the numbers work. Then 9/11 happened and advertising dried up. What could they do? Well, they had to cut expenses to save money and they did that through technology. With technology you can take a disk jockey in Kansas City and put him on the air in five other markets through voice tracking. So all of a sudden you have a lot of local stations that are no longer local. They are taking a midday show from a guy in St. Louis or a guy in Baltimore and then they are running a syndicated show from seven to midnight or another show from midnight to six but it's not local. In the past, local always saved radio. Now, there's Internet radio and satellite radio but it's not local either and terrestrial radio is no longer set up to be local because of consolidation and voice tracking and all of this other stuff. So, if what's saved you in the past is not available to you now, what are you going to do? I don't think I know that answer.

COUNTRY RADIO LISTENERS

The aging of the country fan is also a problem that labels face, although country music has always managed to rejuvenate itself.

"Most people don't really start to become country fans until their mid-20s," said Lon Helton. "I always thought that life has to kick you around a little bit before you really understood a country song and if you're 19 years old, life really hasn't kicked you around so you don't understand what these guys are really writing and singing about."

Helton believes the reason that an "oldies" format has never been part of country music is because "oldies stations are really based about great memories from musically formative years. For most country listeners, there just really aren't that many memories. When you program a country station and it's built around the 25–54-year-old demographic or, if you're really hot the 18–54 age group, the upper end of your audience accepts the young artists but the young end of your audience doesn't accept hardly any of the older artists."

Helton is optimistic that country will continue to attract a young audience. He said,

It's funny. People in radio talk about how the country audience is aging and it seems like the audience gets older and older until one day some magical thing happens, the age of the audience drops and the whole thing begins again. For artists it means that all of a sudden a large group who have been on the charts are not there anymore. Every time there is a major change in the music only a handful of people transition because again, the older audience accepts the young people but the younger audience doesn't accept the older people. It's your father's Oldsmobile, it's your father's country music. The only way that older artists become relevant to young people is when a young artist talks about how they were influenced by, say George Jones or Merle Haggard. But the young people still don't want to hear them on the radio although they might buy one of their records.

14

The Road Ahead

COUNTRY RADIO IN THE FUTURE

Arbitron is a firm that measures radio listenership. In the past, it has done so through the use of diaries where people write down what radio station they listened to and how long they listened. During the ratings period the first day for the diaries was Thursday, which is why those big radio station contests always occurred on Thursdays. Now Arbitron has come up with a new measuring tool, the portable people meter (PPM), that could be as revolutionary as Soundscan was for album charts.

The PPM operates by picking up radio signals that people are tuned into. People carry the meter with them all day then put it into a "holder" where it downloads its collected information at night. Initial reports from PPM testing indicate that people listen to far more radio stations than they report in their diaries—it seems people tune into a lot of different stations, grazing on the radio dial—and that they listen for much shorter periods of time than they report in their diaries. But the most surprising discovery is that they listen to a lot more country music than previously reported. The reasons seem to be that, especially in northern and eastern cities, people don't like to admit they listen to country music, or at least don't like to admit it in their diaries. Second, the people who do listen to country radio are underreporting it. It is possible that in many major cities twice as many people are actually listening to country music than diaries report. This could have a tremendous effect on radio. To start, if so many more people are listening to country music than previously reported then there are bound to be non-country stations switching over to country music. Next, this could be a financial windfall for country radio because more listeners mean that the stations can charge more for advertisements.

TOURING

There is a tenuous link between touring and the sales of recordings, although touring is essential for the promotion and visibility of an artist.

"People spend a lot more money on tickets for shows and merchandise than they do for recordings," said Joe Galante. "If an artist tours, it helps the artist and in some ways helps the record, but I don't believe it is a one-for-one relationship. If an artist sells a million tickets on their tour that doesn't mean they're going to sell a million records. It's possible that an artist doesn't tour but will sell two million records. However, I believe touring perpetuates the brand and hopefully makes people want to go back and get more of the artist. Touring keeps an artist viable with the consumer."

It used to be that touring was needed to support a record; now a record is needed to support a tour. Previously, a single and an album were released and the artist started their tour to take advantage of that release date. However, since major superstars play big arenas today and those tickets go on sale 4–6 months ahead of time, an artist needs a hit record on the radio in order to drive ticket sales. A record label may want to release a single just before a tour so that the tour will help record sales but the artist insists on a single on the radio six months ahead of the tour. The label would like an album to be released as a single peaks—say 10–14 weeks after the release of the single—but that has to either be moved up to take advantage of a single on the radio or release it at the originally scheduled time—as the tour starts—and risk losing sales that might be generated from the hit radio single.

SINGLES VS. ALBUMS

The music business consists of the music, the business, and the technology all rolled together. It is easy to say that music is the most important of these because it is the music we remember; years later people will not remember the struggles with business or technology but they will remember songs and artists. But the technology and business are key because the technology captures the music in a form that allows us to listen and purchase it. The business provides an economic framework that allows music to be profitable and to be a profession.

The future of country music is tied to the future of technology, business, and music. There is no shortage of young people who want to sing country music, and there is no shortage of young people wanting to be part of the music industry. There is a shortage of answers to the questions of how music can be supported by a business structure that encompasses digital technology that, so far, has caused music to lose sales and profits. Twenty years from now the answers will seem obvious; however, the answers are difficult to see when facing those questions in this day and time.

For most of the twentieth century the record company has been the economic engine that drove the music industry. That is still true today, but in a more diminished role.

During the twentieth century an artist needed a record company in order to have a performing career in the mainstream music industry. The major asset that an artist manager brought to the table for a young artist was the ability to get him/her a record deal. The label financed the recording session, promoted the single to radio, marketed the album to consumers, and then obtained shelf space for the album through its distribution system.

The music business was a singles business until the 1960s. In the era of the 78 rpm record, only one song would fit on each side; in 1948 the long-playing record (LP) was introduced which allowed five to six songs on each side or a collection of 10 to 12 on a record. Broadway musicals and classical music took advantage of this new format first because their music demanded the LP. Consumers liked the fact that they did not have to get up after each song and turn that record over or put on another record. Rock, pop, and country music remained music for singles until the 1960s when the album became the preferred choice for young rock consumers. Led by the Beatles, the rock world discovered that fans liked the LP, and a number of artists became album artists who never had a hit single on radio; their medium was the album. Country music accepted the album a little later; it was not until the mid-to-late 1970s that albums were widely accepted in country music.

"When I started in the record business, I would say that clearly 90 percent of the hit records were singles," said Mike Curb. "Buying an album by those artists was just unheard of with the exception of Elvis Presley and a few others. Later in the 60s when the British Invasion occurred you had artists like Billy J. Kramer and the Dakotas, Freddie and the Dreamers, and the Dave Clark Five who were, for the most part, singles acts. The Beatles were different; people bought albums by the Beatles."

The recording industry has returned to that time when the hit single was key to a career. But just as artists had to experience a shift in thinking from singles to albums in the 1960s, young artists today have to shift their thinking from albums to singles. Young people—even young artists—have an iPod loaded with singles and actively search out single songs to add to their collection but yet want to record an album.

Record labels preferred albums to singles because there was a higher profit margin. As the years progressed, labels increasingly phased out singles until, in many cases, there was no single released to consumers—just an album.

Consumers were not always happy with the albums they purchased. Part of the reason was the fact that the single was the promotion for the album and the consumer, in essence, bought the single(s) when they bought the album but often found the other songs did not quite measure up to the hit single(s). A major reason for that was because many producers found ways to fill out an album with songs they wrote or published instead of hunting for the very best songs. There wasn't a lot of money in country album sales during the 1970s and early 1980s for most acts so there was an economic and financial reason to do that. Plus, songs that you write or publish always sound much better than songs from someone or somewhere else. There was also the time factor; it takes an incredible amount of time to listen and sort through hundreds or thousands of songs and the time for producers seemed to be spent more efficiently by writing and co-writing their own material or limiting their search to their own publishing company.

Later, artists were expected to write their own material because increasingly fans felt that an artist wasn't "authentic" unless they wrote their own material. This led to the practice where an artist who was not a songwriter would get signed to a label, would record a hit single (generally written by someone else), and then be set up with writing appointments with established songwriters. The artist may give a suggestion or two, maybe even a title or story line but, by and large, the songs were written by the established songwriter. These songs were usually not as strong as the hit single but, again, they made it on the album.

It made good financial sense to do this; it gave the artist another revenue stream, especially if the album sold well, and if the song made it to radio as a single then the artist as songwriter received money because artists do not receive money from radio airplay. The problem was that consumers were increasingly disappointed with the album, saying, essentially, "I bought the album for the single but the rest of it is crap."

Lon Helton pointed out that,

> The great growth in CD sales came, to some degree, because people saw them as a way to not wear out their old vinyl; you could buy all of the old vinyl you liked on CD and put your old vinyl away. There was a huge bubble in the python of people replacing that music and everybody kind of thought that was part of the normal business or normally the way things happened but now, in retrospect, it really wasn't. Even in the album days, what every CD cover or album showed was the hits. People might buy an album for those three songs but they really only wanted those three songs. Now with the technology such as it is, they can go back to getting just the songs they want. They're in control again. In the past they weren't in control. For awhile, the record companies made the decision to get rid of the single and forced people to buy albums that maybe they didn't really want. Maybe they really didn't want their three favorite hit songs and seven others. People in the music business love music, love the work of art that is the album: the beginning, the middle, and the end. They love what the artist is saying. To them, it's like a giant picture but the fans only want the piece of the picture that they want. The music business was in a position for awhile to force them to take that album but that's no longer the case.

COUNTRY MUSIC AS A BIG TENT

If you look at all the genres related to country music then country is a big tent. There's bluegrass, western, Americana, and southern gospel music all under that tent. But in reality, each of those genres has had to build their own tent and they have done so; each of those genres has their own trade organization, their own event(s) where that music is spotlighted and where those involved in the business of music gather together for the mutual benefit of all those involved in those genres.

Bluegrass is a thriving music in live venues; there are numerous bluegrass festivals throughout the year and the music attracts a loyal fan base. Bluegrass has elected to remain faithful to the music instead of the market; this genre has not altered its sound significantly during the past 60 years or so. And individual artists with few exceptions (Alison Krauss being the main one) do not sell large numbers of albums. The International Bluegrass Music Association (IBMA) each year sponsors a week-long series of concerts and business meetings in Nashville in October. The Society for the Preservation of Bluegrass Music in America (SPGMA) sponsors an event each Spring in Nashville.

Bluegrass has closer ties to mainstream country music than western, Americana, or southern gospel. Bill Monroe and Flatt and Scruggs are in the Hall of Fame while Del McCoury, Bobby Osborne, and Ricky Skaggs (who has returned to bluegrass) are all members of the *Grand Ole Opry*.

Western music is represented by the Western Music Association and holds its annual gathering in Albuquerque, New Mexico. This is a small organization whose member artists primarily make and sell their own CDs and perform at western festivals, which are abundant in the West. Nashville-based Riders In The Sky are members of the *Grand Ole Opry* and a ground breaking act in western music. Prior to the formation of the Riders In The Sky in 1977, western music was virtually dead; the Sons of the Pioneers still performed and there were a few Chuck Wagon groups (those who performed at a "chuck wagon" restaurant), but western music in general had ridden into the sunset. The Riders In The Sky played a major role in changing all of that. There are now over 200 western festivals each year and Riders In The Sky is probably the biggest star in that genre.

Southern gospel music holds its annual gathering in September in Louisville, Kentucky. This organization is an outgrowth of the Southern Gospel Quartet Convention, which was previously headquartered in Nashville and key to the founding of the Gospel Music Association, which is headquartered in Nashville but whose membership is dominated by contemporary Christian music or pop music with Christian lyrics. Southern gospel folks felt unwanted after they were pushed aside by CCM in the GMA and left town. Their sound is still based on the quartets of old and, musically, their recordings sound a lot like country music.

The Americana Music Association holds its annual convention and awards show in Nashville. Musically, it is harder to define Americana although in terms of country music it seems to be edgier, less polished, and not as commercial.

One can imagine a TV show—particularly the *Country Music Association Awards Show*—where these genres are featured in addition to mainstream country acts. It would make great television viewing if viewers could see a bluegrass act, a western music act, an Americana act, and a southern gospel act all perform. But that will never happen. The reason is that the Country

Music Association controls the CMA Awards and the major labels control the CMA TV committee. They fight to have their acts in a featured television spot because a strong performance on the *CMA Show* means a spike in record sales the following week. The jobs of the executives are on the line; they have to make sure their acts are seen on TV and have record sales in order to keep their jobs. Pleasing a TV viewer—who may or may not buy an album—by having a variety of acts on the show just ain't in the cards. Besides, the major acts sell the most recordings so, it stands to reason, they have the broadest appeal. And broad appeal is what TV network viewing is all about.

TODAY'S MUSIC BUSINESS

Joe Galante is widely acknowledged as the premier marketer of country music. He moved to Nashville two classes short of an MBA but brought a discipline to country music marketing that it had not had before as he moved through the ranks of the record label, from budget analyst to radio promotion to marketing and then to label president. His success "was more about a discipline than it was about anything else," said Galante. "First, it was a matter of trying to figure out cause and effect. If I do this, then what happens? Second was being staffed to pursue the areas you need to, to control your own destiny or else somebody else will. And then you have to make decisions but this business is a balance between art and commerce and you have to find people who get it. Picking the right artist and the right songs is not MBA stuff. It's more about knowing when to stop and when to continue. It involves getting knocked around a lot. I believe the music business is going through trial and error. I don't believe anyone has a lock on it."

Today's music industry is "a business but it is still an art form and people that run these companies are proud of the fact that we're a country music label," said Galante. "Still, it's the same bullshit we've had for the past 50 years; people in New York and L.A. don't really want to hear about it. You still get the jokes and the cowboy hats and the stereotypes. Then, every once in a while you have an album that sells over a million copies so somebody tips their hat to you."

A lot of people have tipped their hats to Mike Curb because he has managed to steer an independent label through the rough waters of the early twenty-first century in the music business. In 2003 for the first time in his life his label lost money; Curb made changes, restructured his label, and emerged as a profitable label again, although the profit margin has grown tighter. Since Curb owns his label, all of the expenses come from his pocket and he has to watch that pocket carefully. One of the biggest problems facing him is motivating people who have been in the music business a long time—and are used to doing business a certain way—to change.

"It's not unusual in our business to find a promotion person who says, 'My job is to promote records to terrestrial radio on the West Coast; here are the 50 stations that I cover; that's what I've done for 40 years and that's what I want to do until I retire,'" said Curb.

> Those people often have deep relationships there and are the right people for that job. But when you have to convince that person they should also visit with an Internet provider or should explore YouTube, MySpace, or Satellite radio then it becomes difficult. It isn't just the heads of the record companies that have to rethink all of this; the employees have to be open. It's not age related; some of the older employees are more excited about this phenomenon than some of the younger ones, but the younger employees tend to have a more natural way of moving through the new media because they've come up through it and they understand it, and it's been a part of their lives. It isn't something that they have to learn how to do because it's something that they have grown up doing and that they do with their friends so it comes naturally.

The advantage of an independent label like Curb Records is that it can adapt to the market and institute changes much quicker than a major label which is part of a multinational corporation with distant headquarters. Curb has taken advantage of that fact to keep his label competitive in a rapidly changing market.

THE FUTURE

Don't trust anyone who knows the future of country music.

The reason that history is important is because it teaches about human nature. History does not repeat itself but human nature does; the times change, situations change, and technology changes, but human nature does not change.

In the future there will be developments, inventions, events, and businesses that have not been anticipated and cannot even be imagined. On one hand the future is an extension of today and much of today will be carried into tomorrow. But, on the other hand, tomorrow will be entirely different from today. The problems the music industry faces today—illegal downloads, loss of revenue, consolidation of radio—will pass and the industry will be immersed in other problems.

The present music industry always feels difficult and unfathomable while the past seems simpler and easier. It has always been that way and always will be.

There will always be a set of people who thirst for stardom, a certain set of people who have the musical and singing talent to achieve stardom, but only a chosen few will attain it. It is more important that God believes in an artist than if the artist believes in God. By that I mean that only a few are chosen and most are not and there's really no logic to it if you try to look at it logically. It's not always the "best" singer or musician who ends up on top, but it is always the singer or musician who connects with an audience.

"We need to examine and respect yesterday for all its historical perspective and what it offers us because we can learn from that," said Jeff Walker. "In terms of tomorrow, there's a lot of uncertainty attached to it and I think that we need to go into it with our eyes wide open and be willing and adaptable to change because I think that people are always going to want to be entertained. I would not underestimate the consumer, because generally they know real talent or a real ability to entertain when they see it. So what we do and how we grow this industry is a balancing act from where we came from to where we're going and doing that with a real open mind."

Mike Curb observes,

We have to acknowledge the fact that when we sign an artist none of us knows if we will get a hit record and then, if we do get a radio hit, whether that will translate into huge record sales, average sales, or in some cases no sales at all. Sometimes a record goes into the top five or even all the way to the top of the singles chart and sells nothing. At other times a record comes along and barely hits the top 20 but it launches the career of an artist. For example, "Gentle On My Mind" by Glen Campbell barely reached the top 30—it was released twice—so it was never a big hit on the charts but it launched an album-selling career of an artist who sold millions of albums. On the other hand, I can name numerous records that went to number one but you never heard of the artist again. That's what's unique in the record industry so why should it be any different today? Why is artist *X* downloaded and artist *Y* is not? Why do people want to own a record by a certain artist like Garth Brooks but not own a record by another artist?

"I believe it has a lot to do with the ability of an artist to communicate," concludes Curb. "Communicating is not just how good or technically trained your voice is. It is how an artist expresses himself or herself on a recording and whether the audience connects to them live."

In the midst of an ever-changing world, some things never change.

Notes

CHAPTER 2

1. Wayne W. Daniel, *Pickin' on Peachtree: A History of Country Music in Atlanta, Georgia* (Urbana: University of Illinois Press, 1990), 41.

2. Ian Grimble, *Robert Burns: An Illustrated Biography* (New York: Peter Bedrick Books, 1986), 35.

3. Ken Emerson, *Doo-Dah! Stephen Foster and the Rise of American Popular Culture* (New York: Simon & Schuster, 1997), 301.

4. J.W. Williamson, *Hillbillyland: What the Movies Did to the Mountains & What the Mountains Did to the Movies* (Chapel Hill: University of North Carolina Press, 1995), 37.

5. Bill C. Malone, *Country Music U.S.A.: A Fifty-Year History* (Austin: University of Texas Press, 1968), 24.

6. Charles Wolfe and Ted Olson, eds., *The Bristol Sessions: Writings about the Big Bang of Country Music* (Jefferson, NC: McFarland, 2005), 24.

CHAPTER 3

1. Russell Sanjek, *American Popular Music and Its Business: The First Four Hundred Years: Volume III From 1900 to 1984* (New York: Oxford University Press, 1988), 120–22.

2. James Evans, *Prairie Farmer and W.L.S.: The Burridge D. Butler Years* (Urbana: University of Illinois Press, 1969), 229.

3. Charles Wolfe, *The Devil's Box: Masters of Southern Fiddling* (Nashville: Country Music Foundation and Vanderbilt University Press, 1997), 91.

4. Ibid., 93.

5. Charles R. Townsend, *San Antonio Rose: The Life and Music of Bob Wills* (Urbana: University of Illinois Press, 1986).

6. Daniel, *Pickin' on Peachtree*, 43.

7. Holly George-Warren, *Public Cowboy No. 1: The Life and Times of Gene Autry*, (New York: Oxford University Press, 2007), 168.

8. Ibid., 125.

9. Charles K. Wolfe, *Kentucky Country* (Lexington: University Press of Kentucky, 1982), 153.

10. Ivan Tribe, *Mountaineer Jamboree: Country Music in West Virginia* (Lexington: University Press of Kentucky, 1984), 109.

CHAPTER 4

1. Sanjek, *American Popular Music*, 222–25.

2. Dorothy Horstman, *Sing Your Heart Out, Country Boy: Classic Country Songs and Their Inside Stories by the People Who Wrote Them* (New York: Dutton, 1975), 174.

CHAPTER 6

1. Dan T. Carter, *The Politics of Rage: George Wallace, The Origins of the New Conservatism, and the Transformation of American Politics* (New York: Simon & Schuster, 1995).

2. Daniel McCabe, Paul Stekler, and Steve Fayer, *American Experience: George Wallace: Settin' the Woods on Fire* (PBS Home Video, 2000); and Maggie Riechers, "Racism to Redemption: The Path of George Wallace," *Humanities*, March/April 2000.

3. Paul Hemphill, *The Nashville Sound: Bright Lights and Country Music* (New York: Simon & Schuster, 1970), 153.

4. Ibid., 162.

5. Bill C. Malone, *Don't Get Above Your Raisin': Country Music and the Southern Working Class* (Urbana: University of Illinois Press, 2002), 238.

6. Information on country charts from Joel Whitburn, *Top Country Songs 1944–2005* (Menomonee Falls, WI: Record Research, Inc., 2005).

CHAPTER 7

1. "Songs from Texas," *Time* 37, no. 12 (March 24, 1941).

2. "Bull Market in Corn," *Time* 42, no. 14 (October 4, 1943).

3. "Pistol Packin' Mama," *Life* 15, no. 11 (October 11, 1943).

4. Maurice Zolotow, "Hillbilly Boom," *Saturday Evening Post*, February 12, 1944.

5. Doron K. Antrim, "Whoop-and-Holler Opera," *Collier's* 117, no. 4 (January 26, 1946): 18, 85.

6. "Strictly by Ear," *Time* 47, no. 6 (February 11, 1946).

7. Robert Scherman, "Hillbilly Phenomenon," *Christian Science Monitor*, March 13, 1948; and "Corn of Plenty," *Newsweek* 33, no. 24 (June 13, 1949).

8. "Corn of Plenty," 1949.

9. Allen Churchill, "Tin Pan Alley's Git-Tar Blues," *New York Times Magazine*, July 15, 1951.

10. Don Eddy, "Hillbilly Heaven," *American Magazine* 153, no. 3 (March 1952).

11. H.B. Teeter, "Nashville, Broadway of Country Music," *Coronet* 43, no. 4 (August 1952).

12. Rufus Jarman, "Country Music Goes to Town," *Nation's Business* 41, no. 2 (February 1953).

13. Nelson King, "Hillbilly Music Leaves the Hills," *Good Housekeeping* 138, no. 6 (June 1954).

14. Maurice Zolotow, "Hayride," *Theater Arts* 38, no. 11 (November 1954).

15. Roy Harris, "Folk Songs," *House & Garden* 106, no. 6 (December 1954).

16. Eli Waldron, "Country Music: The Squaya Dansu from Nashville," *The Reporter,* June 2, 1955.

17. "Country Musicians Fiddle Up Roaring Business," *Life* 41, no. 21 (November 19, 1956).

18. Goddard Lieberson, "Country Sweeps the Country," *New York Times Magazine,* July 28, 1957.

19. "Hoedown on a Harpsichord," *Time* 76, no. 20 (November 14, 1960).

20. Richard Marek, "Country Music, Nashville Style," *McCall's* 88, no. 7 (April 1961).

21. Morris Duff, "Make Way for the Country Sound," *Toronto Daily Star,* March 21, 1964.

22. "Country Music: The Nashville Sound," *Time* 84, no. 22 (November 17, 1964).

23. "Country Music Snaps Its Regional Bounds," *Business Week,* no. 1907 (March 19, 1966): 96–103.

24. "The Gold Guitars," *Newsweek* 67, no. 4 (April 4, 1966).

25. Charles Portis, "That New Sound from Nashville," *Saturday Evening Post,* February 12, 1966.

CHAPTER 8

1. Information about the number of country radio stations from the Country Music Association.

2. Joe Galante, in discussion with the author, September 10, 2007, Nashville, TN. All quotes from Joe Galante are from this interview.

CHAPTER 9

1. Lon Helton, in discussion with the author, December 12, 2007, Nashville, TN. All quotes from Lon Helton are from this interview.

2. Mike Curb, in discussion with the author, November 21, 2007, Nashville, TN. All quotes from Mike Curb are from this interview.

CHAPTER 10

1. Peter DiCola, *False Premises, False Promises: A Quantitative History of Ownership Consolidation in the Radio Industry* (Washington, DC: Future of Music

Coalition, December 2006), 8, http://www.futureofmusic.org/images/FMCradio study06.pdf.

2. Erv Woolsey, in discussion with the author, November 29, 2007, Nashville, TN. All quotes from Erv Woolsey are from this interview.

3. Jeff Walker, in discussion with the author, November 14, 2007, Nashville, TN. All quotes from Jeff Walker are from this interview.

CHAPTER 11

1. Mike McNally, in discussion with the author, July 14, 2005, London, England.
2. Craig Baguley, in discussion with the author, July 16, 2007, London, England.
3. Paul Fenn, in discussion with the author, July 17, 2007, London, England.
4. Mark Hagen, in discussion with the author, July 25, 2007, London, England.

CHAPTER 12

1. Chris Willman, *Rednecks & Bluenecks: The Politics of Country Music* (New York: The New Press, 2005), 7.

2. Malone, *Don't Get Above Your Raisin'*, 211.

3. Earl Black and Merle Black, *The Rise of Southern Republicans* (Cambridge, MA: The Belknap Press of Harvard University Press, 2002), 7.

4. Ibid., 246–47.

5. Ibid., 251, 257.

6. Thomas Frank, *What's the Matter with Kansas? How Conservatives Won the Heart of America* (New York: Metropolitan Books/Henry Holt, 2004), 8.

7. Ibid., 16.

8. Ibid., 20.

9. Ibid., 119.

10. Ibid., 136.

11. George Lakoff, *Moral Politics: How Liberals and Conservatives Think*, 2nd ed. (Chicago: University of Chicago Press, 1996, 2002), 114.

12. Ibid., 30.

13. Ibid., 35–36.

14. Drew Weston, *The Political Mind: The Role of Emotion in Deciding the Fate of the Nation* (New York: Public Affairs, 2007), ix.

15. Ibid., 15–16.

16. Ibid., 44, 35.

17. Willman, *Rednecks & Bluenecks,* 28.

CHAPTER 13

1. David Ross, "Embracing Change: The New Rules of Engagement," *Music Row,* Special Report, August 2007.

Bibliography

Adams, Frank. *Wurlitzer Jukeboxes and Other Nice Things II*. Seattle, WA: ARM, 1983.

Anderson, Bill. *Whisperin' Bill: An Autobiography*. Atlanta: Longstreet Press, 1989.

Atkins, Chet, with Bill Neely. *Country Gentleman*. Chicago: Henry Regenery, 1974.

Autry, Gene, with Mickey Herskowitz. *Back in the Saddle Again*. Garden City, NY: Doubleday, 1976.

Ayers, Edward L. *The Promise of the New South: Life After Reconstruction*. New York: Oxford University Press, 1993.

Baldwin, Neil. *Edison: Inventing the Century*. New York: Hyperion, 1995.

Barfield, Ray. *Listening to Radio 1920–1950*. Westport, CT: Praeger, 1996.

Barnouw, Erik. *A Tower of Babel: A History of Broadcasting in the United States: Volume I: to 1933*. New York: Oxford University Press, 1966.

———. *The Golden Web: A History of Broadcasting in the United States, Volume II: 1933–1953*. New York: Oxford University Press, 1968.

———. *The Image Empire: A History of Broadcasting in the United States: Volume III: from 1953*. New York: Oxford University Press, 1970.

Black, Earl, and Merle Black. *The Rise of Southern Republicans*. Cambridge, MA: The Belknap Press of Harvard University Press, 2002.

Brooks, Tim, and Earle Marsh. *The Complete Directory to Prime Time Network TV Shows 1946–Present*. (8th edition.) New York: Ballantine Books, 2003.

Brylawski, Samuel. "Armed Forces Radio Service: The Invisible Highway Abroad." *The Quarterly Journal: The Library of Congress*, Summer, 1979.

Bufwack, Mary A., and Robert K. Oermann. *Finding Her Voice: The Saga of Women in Country Music*. New York: Crown, 1993.

Burton, Thomas G. *Folksongs*. New York: Holt, Rinehart and Winston, 1984.

Business Week. "Country Music Snaps Its Regional Bounds," March 19, 1966.

———. "Country Music: The Nashville Sound," March 19, 1956.

Byworth, Tony. *The History of Country & Western Music*. New York: Exeter Books, 1984.

Carr, Patrick, ed. *The Illustrated History of Country Music.* Garden City, NY: Doubleday, 1979.

Carter, Dan T. *The Politics of Rage: George Wallace, The Origins of the New Conservatism, and the Transformation of American Politics.* New York: Simon and Schuster, 1995.

Cash, Johnny. *Man in Black.* Grand Rapids, MI: Zondervan, 1975.

Cash, Johnny, with Patrick Carr. *Cash: The Autobiography.* New York: HarperCollins, 1997.

Chanan, Michael. *Repeated Takes: A Short History of Recording and Its Effects on Music.* London: Verso, 1995.

Coffey, Frank. *Always Home: 50 Years of the USO.* Washington: Brassey's, a division of Maxwell Macmillan, 1991.

Coontz, Stephanie. *The Way We Never Were: American Families and the Nostalgia Trap.* New York: Basic, 1992.

———. *The Way We Really Are.* New York: Basic, 1997.

Cooper, Daniel. *Lefty Frizzell: The Honky-tonk Life of Country Music's Greatest Singer.* Boston: Little, Brown, 1995.

Country Music Association. "Country Connects." Simmons Country Listener Analysis, 1993.

———. "The Country Radio Listener: A New Profile." A Special Arbitron Ratings Study, 1988.

———. National Survey by Edison Media Research, November 1997.

Cusic, Don. *Eddy Arnold: I'll Hold You in My Heart.* Nashville: Rutledge Hill, 1997.

———. *Gene Autry: His Life and Career.* Jefferson, NC: McFarland, 2007.

———. *The Cowboy Way: The Amazing True Adventures of Riders in the Sky.* Lexington: University Press of Kentucky, 2003.

Daniel, Wayne W. *Pickin' on Peachtree: A History of Country Music in Atlanta, Georgia.* Urbana: University of Illinois Press, 1990.

Davis, John T. *Austin City Limits: 25 Years of American Music.* New York: Watson-Guptill, 1999.

Dawidoff, Nicholas. *In the Country of Country: People and Places in American Music.* New York: Pantheon, 1997.

Dellar, Fred, and Roy Thompson. *The Illustrated Encyclopedia of Country Music.* New York: Harmony 1977.

DiCola, Peter. *False Premises, False Promises: A Quantitative History of Ownership Consolidation in the Radio Industry.* Washington, DC: Future of Music Coalition, December 2006.

Doyle, Don H. *Nashville Since the 1920s.* Knoxville: University of Tennessee Press, 1985.

Dumenil, Lynn. *Modern Temper: American Culture and Society in the 1920s.* New York: Hill and Wang, 1995.

Dunning, John. *On the Air: The Encyclopedia of Old-Time Radio.* New York: Oxford University Press, 1998.

Emerson, Ken. *Doo-Dah! Stephen Foster and the Rise of American Popular Culture.* New York: Simon & Schuster, 1997.

Emery, Ralph, with Patsy Bale Cos. *The View from Nashville: On the Record with Country Music's Greatest Stars.* New York: William Morrow, 1998.

Eng, Steve. *Satisfied Mind: Porter Wagoner.* Nashville: Rutledge Hill, 1992.

Escott, Colin, with George Merritt and William MacEwen. *Hank Williams: The Biography*. Boston: Little, Brown, 1994.

Evans, James. *Prairie Farmer and W.L.S.: The Burridge D. Butler Years*. Urbana: University of Illinois Press, 1969.

Feiler, Bruce. *Dreaming Out Loud: Garth Brooks, Wynonna Judd, Wade Hayes and the Changing Face of Nashville*. New York: Avon, 1998.

Frank, Thomas. *What's the Matter With Kansas? How Conservatives Won the Heart of America*. New York: Metropolitan Books/Henry Holt, 2004.

Freidel, Frank. *Franklin D. Roosevelt: A Rendezvous with Destiny*. Boston: Little, Brown, 1990.

Gelatt, Roland. *The Fabulous Phonograph: From Tin Foil to High Fidelity*. New York: Appleton Century, 1965.

George-Warren, Holly. *Cowboy: How Hollywood Invented the Wild West*. Pleasantville, NY: Reader's Digest Books, 2002.

———. *Public Cowboy No. 1: The Life and Times of Gene Autry*. New York: Oxford University Press, 2007.

Giddens, Gary. *Bing Crosby: A Pocketful of Dreams: The Early Years 1903–1940*. Boston: Little, Brown, 2001.

Goldstein, Norm. *The History of Television*. New York: Portland House, 1991.

Goodwin, Doris Kearns. *No Ordinary Time: Franklin and Eleanor Roosevelt: The Home Front in World War II*. New York: Touchstone, 1994.

Graebner, William S. *The Age of Doubt: American Thought and Culture in the 1940s*. Boston: Twayne, 1991.

Green, Douglas B. *Country Roots: The Origins of Country Music*. New York: Hawthorne, 1976.

———. *Singing in the Saddle: The History of the Singing Cowboy*. Nashville: The Country Music Foundation Press and Vanderbilt University Press, 2002.

Griffis, Ken. *Hear My Song: The Story of the Celebrated Sons of the Pioneers*. Northglenn, CO: Norken, 2000.

Grimble, Ian. *Robert Burns: An Illustrated Biography*. New York: Peter Bedrick Books, 1986.

Gubernick, Lisa Rebecca. *Get Hot or Go Home: Trisha Yearwood: The Making of a Nashville Star*. New York: William Morrow, 1993.

Guralnick, Peter. *Careless Love: The Unmaking of Elvis Presley*. Boston: Little, Brown, 1999.

———. *Last Train to Memphis: The Rise of Elvis Presley*. Boston: Little, Brown, 1994.

Haden, Walter Darrell. "Early Pioneers." In *Stars of Country Music,* edited by Bill C. Malone and Judith McCulloh. Urbana: University of Illinois Press, 1975.

Halberstam, David. *The Fifties*. New York: Villard, 1993.

Hall, Wade. *Hell-Bent for Music: The Life of Pee Wee King*. Lexington: The University Press of Kentucky, 1996.

Hardy, Phil, and Dave Laing, eds. *The Faber Companion to 20th Century Popular Music*. London: Faber and Faber, 1990.

Harrison, Nigel. *Songwriters: A Biographical Dictionary with Discographies*. Jefferson, NC: McFarland, 1998.

Harvith, John, and Susan Edwards Harvith. *Edison, Musicians, and the Phonograph*. New York: Greenwood Press, 1987.

Haslam, Gerald W. *Workin' Man Blues: Country Music in California.* Berkeley and Los Angeles: University of California Press, 1999.

Hemphill, Paul. *The Nashville Sound: Bright Lights and Country Music.* New York: Simon & Schuster, 1970.

Hopper, Lawrence. *Bob Nolan: A Biographical Guide and Annotations to the Lyric Archive at the University of North Carolina, Chapel Hill.* Limited publication by Paul Lawrence Hopper, 2000.

Horstman, Dorothy. *Sing Your Heart Out, Country Boy: Classic Country Songs and Their Inside Stories by the People Who Wrote Them.* New York: Dutton, 1975.

Ivey, Bill. "The Bottom Line: Business Practices That Shaped Country Music." In *Country: The Music and the Musicians.* New York: Abbeville Press, 1988.

Jensen, Joli. *The Nashville Sound: Authenticity, Commercialization, and Country Music.* Nashville: Vanderbilt/Country Music Foundation Press, 1998.

Kenney, William H. *Recorded Music in American Life.* New York: Oxford University Press, 1999.

Kingsbury, Paul, ed. *The Country Music Reader.* Nashville: Vanderbilt University Press, 1996.

———, ed. *The Encyclopedia of Country Music: Compiled by the Staff of the Country Music Hall of Fame and Museum.* New York: Oxford University Press, 1998.

———. *The Grand Ole Opry History of Country Music: 70 Years of the Songs, the Stars, and the Stories.* New York: Villard Books, 1995.

Kingsbury, Paul, and Alan Axelrod, eds. *Country: The Music and the Musicians.* New York: Abbeville Press, 1988.

Kosser, Michael. *How Nashville Became Music City U.S.A.* New York: Hal Leonard, 2006.

Lackmann, Ron. *Same Time . . . Same Station: An A–Z Guide to Radio from Jack Benny to Howard Stern.* New York: Facts on File, 1996.

Lakoff, George. *Moral Politics: How Liberals and Conservatives Think.* (2nd edition.) Chicago: University of Chicago Press, 1996, 2002.

Leamer, Laurence. *Three Chords and the Truth: Hope, Heartbreak, and Changing Fortunes in Nashville.* New York: HarperCollins, 1997.

Lemann, Nicholas. *The Promised Land: The Great Black Migration and How It Changed America.* New York: Vintage, 1992.

Lewis, Tom. *Empire of the Air: The Men Who Made Radio.* New York: Edward Burlingame Books, An Imprint of HarperCollins, 1991.

Lieberson, Goddard. "Country Sweeps the Country." *New York Times Magazine,* July 28, 1957.

Life. "Country Music Fiddles Up Roaring Business," November 19, 1956.

Logan, Horace, with Bill Sloan. *Louisiana Hayride Years: Making Musical History in Country's Golden Age.* New York: St. Martin's Press, 1998.

Lynch, Vincent, and Bill Hankin. *Jukebox: The Golden Age.* New York: Perigee Books, 1981.

MacDonald, J. Fred. *Don't Touch That Dial! Radio Programming in American Life, 1920–1960.* Chicago: Nelson-Hall, 1979.

Mademoiselle. "Country Music Goes to Town," April 1948.

Malone, Bill C. *Country Music U.S.A.: A Fifty-Year History.* Austin: University of Texas Press, 1968.

————. *Don't Get Above Your Raisin': Country Music and the Southern Working Class.* Urbana: University of Illinois Press, 2002.

————. *Singing Cowboys and Musical Mountaineers: Southern Culture and the Roots of Country Music.* Athens, GA: The University of Georgia Press, 1993.

Malone, Bill C., and Judith McCullough, eds. *Stars of Country Music.* Urbana: University of Illinois Press, 1975.

Maltin, Leonard. *The Great American Broadcast: A Celebration of Radio's Golden Age.* New York: Dutton, 1997.

McCloud, Barry, ed. *Definitive Country: The Ultimate Encyclopedia of Country Music and Its Performers.* New York: Perigree, 1995.

McElvaine, Robert S. *The Great Depression: America 1929–1941.* New York: Times Books, 1984.

Millard, Andre J. *America on Record: A History of Recorded Sound.* Cambridge: Cambridge University Press, 1995.

Montana, Patsy, with Jane Frost. *Patsy Montana: The Cowboy's Sweetheart.* Jefferson, NC: McFarland, 2002.

Morris, Edward. "New, Improved, Homogenized: Country Radio Since 1950." In *Country: The Music and the Musicians.* New York: Abbeville Press, 1988.

Nachman, Gerald. *Raised on Radio.* New York: Pantheon, 1998.

Newsweek. "Country Music Is Big Business, and Nashville Is Its Detroit," August 11, 1952.

Nye, David E. *Electrifying America: Social Meanings of a New Technology, 1880–1940.* Cambridge, MA, and London, England: The MIT Press, 1991.

Oermann, Robert K. *America's Music: The Roots of Country.* Atlanta: Turner, 1996.

Pearce, Christopher. *Vintage Jukeboxes: The Hall of Fame.* Secaucus, NJ: Chartwell, 1988.

Pearl, Minnie, with Joan Dew. *Minnie Pearl: An Autobiography.* New York: Simon & Schuster, 1980.

Peterson, Richard A. *Creating Country Music: Fabricating Authenticity.* Chicago: University of Chicago Press, 1997.

Phillips, Robert W. *Roy Rogers.* Jefferson, NC: McFarland, 1995.

————. *Singing Cowboy Stars.* Salt Lake City: Gibbs Smith, 1994.

Porterfield, Nolan. *Jimmie Rodgers: The Life and Times of America's Blue Yodeler.* Urbana: University of Illinois Press, 1979.

————. *Last Cavalier: The Life and Times of John A. Lomax.* Urbana: University of Illinois Press, 1996.

Pugh, Ronnie. *Ernest Tubb: Texas Troubadour.* Durham, NC: Duke University Press, 1996.

Read, Oliver, and Walter L. Welch. *From Tin Foil to Stereo: The Evolution of the Phonograph.* Indianapolis: Howard Sams, 1977.

Rosenberg, Neil V. *Bluegrass: A History.* Urbana: University of Illinois Press, 1985.

Ross, David. "Embracing Change: The New Rules of Engagement." *Music Row,* Special Report. August, 2007.

Russell, Tony. *Country Music Records: A Discography, 1921–1942.* New York: Oxford University Press, 2004.

Samuelson, Robert J. *The Good Life and Its Discontents: The American Dream in the Age of Entitlement: 1945–1995.* New York: Times Books, 1995.

Sanjek, Russell. *American Popular Music and Its Business: The First Four Hundred Years: Volume II From 1790 to 1909.* New York: Oxford, 1988.

————. *American Popular Music and Its Business: Volume III From 1900 to 1984*. New York: Oxford University Press, 1988.

Savage, William W., Jr. *Singing Cowboys and All That Jazz: A Short History of Popular Music in Oklahoma*. Norman: University of Oklahoma Press, 1983.

Sears, Richard S. *V Discs: A History and Discography*. Westport, CT: Greenwood Press, 1980.

Shaw, Arnold. *The Jazz Age: Popular Music in the 1920s*. New York: Oxford, 1987.

Shelton, Robert, and Burt Goldblatt. *The Country Music Story: A Picture History of Country & Western Music*. New York: Bobbs-Merrill, 1966.

Shepherd, John. Tin Pan Alley. London: Routledge & Kegan Paul, 1982.

Sokol, Jason. *There Goes My Everything: White Southerners in the Age of Civil Rights, 1945–1975*. New York: Alfred A. Knopf, 2006.

Stambler, Irwin, and Grelun Landon. *Country Music: The Encyclopedia*. New York: St. Martin's Press, 1997.

Stamper, Pete. *It All Happened in Renfro Valley*. Lexington: University Press of Kentucky, 1999.

Swenson, John. *Bill Haley: The Daddy of Rock and Roll*. New York: Stein and Day, 1982.

Terrace, Vincent. *Radio's Golden Years: The Encyclopedia of Radio Programs, 1930–1960*. San Diego: A.S. Barnes, 1981.

Tichi, Cecelia. *High Lonesome: The American Culture of Country Music*. Chapel Hill: University of North Carolina Press, 1994.

Tinsley, Jim Bob. *For a Cowboy Has to Sing*. Orlando, FL: University of Central Florida Press, 1991.

————. *He Was Singin' This Song*. Orlando, FL: University of Central Florida Press, 1981.

Tosches, Nick. *Country: The Biggest Music in America*. New York: Delta, 1977.

Townsend, Charles R. *San Antonio Rose: The Life and Music of Bob Wills*. Urbana: University of Illinois Press, 1986.

Tribe, Ivan. *The Stonemans: An Appalachian Family and the Music that Shaped Their Lives*. Urbana: University of Illinois Press, 1993.

————. *Mountaineer Jamboree: Country Music in West Virginia*. Lexington: University Press of Kentucky, 1984.

Wakely, Linda Lee. *See Ya Up There, Baby: The Jimmy Wakely Story*. Canoga Park, CA: Shasta Records, 1992.

Walton, Sam, with John Huey. *Made in America*. New York: Doubleday, 1992.

Weston, Drew. *The Political Mind: The Role of Emotion in Deciding the Fate of the Nation*. New York: Public Affairs, 2007.

Whitburn, Joel. *Top 40 Country Hits: 1944–Present*. New York: Billboard Books, 1996.

————. *Top Country Albums 1964–1997*. Menomonee Falls, WI: Record Research, 1997.

————. *Top Country Singles 1944–2005*. Menomonee Falls, WI: Record Research, 2005.

White, Raymond E. *King of the Cowboys, Queen of the West: Roy Rogers and Dale Evans*. Madison: University of Wisconsin Press, 2005.

Whiteside, Jonny. *Ramblin' Rose: The Life and Career of Rose Maddox*. Nashville: Vanderbilt/Country Music Foundation, 1997.

Wiggins, Gene. *Fiddlin Georgia Crazy: Fiddlin' John Carson, His Real World, and the World of His Songs*. Urbana: University of Illinois Press, 1987.

Wilder, Alec. *American Popular Song: The Great Innovators, 1900–1950*. New York: Oxford University Press, 1972.

Williamson, J.W. *Hillbillyland: What the Movies Did to the Mountains & What the Mountains Did to the Movies*. Chapel Hill: University of North Carolina Press, 1995.

Willman, Chris. *Rednecks and Bluenecks: The Politics of Country Music*. New York: The New Press, 2005.

Wolfe, Charles K. "The Triumph of the Hills: Country Radio, 1920–1950." In *Country: The Music and the Musicians*. New York: Abbeville Press, 1988.

———. *Kentucky Country*. Lexington: University Press of Kentucky, 1982.

———. *Classic Country: Legends of Country Music*. New York: Routledge, 2001.

———. *Tennessee Strings: The Story of Country Music in Tennessee*. Knoxville: University of Tennessee Press, 1977.

———. *A Good Natured Riot: The Birth of The Grand Ole Opry*. Nashville: Country Music Foundation and Vanderbilt University Press, 1999.

———. *The Devil's Box: Masters of Southern Fiddling*. Nashville: Country Music Foundation and Vanderbilt University Press, 1997.

Wolfe, Charles K., and Ted Olson, eds. *The Bristol Sessions: Writings About the Big Bang of Country Music*. Jefferson, NC: McFarland, 2005.

Woodward, C. Vann. *Origins of the New South, 1877–1913*. Baton Rouge: Louisiana State University Press, 1951.

Zwonitzer, Mark, with Charles Hirshberg. *Will You Miss Me When I'm Gone? The Carter Family & Their Legacy in American Music*. New York: Simon & Schuster, 2002.

Index

About the Author

DON CUSIC is an internationally known scholar and writer, one of the premier historians of country music, and a pioneer in the field of music business education—developing courses, curriculum, and material for the music business programs at Belmont University and Middle Tennessee State University (MTSU). As an author, teacher, historian, songwriter, and executive, Cusic has been actively involved in the music business since 1973. He is also the author of 16 published books, including the biography *Eddy Arnold: I'll Hold You In My Heart* and an encyclopedia, *Cowboys and the Wild West: An A–Z Guide from the Chisholm Trail to the Silver Screen*. Other books include *Johnny Cash: The Songs; The Sound of Light: A History of Gospel and Christian Music; Music in the Market; Baseball and Country Music; Poet of the Common Man: Merle Haggard Lyrics; Willie Nelson: Lyrics 1959–1994;* and *Hank Williams: The Complete Lyrics.*